the Rise

the Rise

Saunière's magical workings and the penitential movement in Europe

© 2009 Isaac Ben Jacob and Sarah Fishberg

Cover design: Corjan de Raaf www.rlcresearch.com
Layout: Buro kunst en drukwerk, Sylvia Carrilho

ISBN : 978-1-931882-87-3

 FRONTIER PUBLISHING
P.O. Box 10681
1001 ER AMSTERDAM
Netherlands
Tel. +31-(0)20-3309151
Fax: +31-(0)20-3309150
E-mail: info@fsf.nl
www.frontierpublishing.nl

Adventures Unlimited Press
303 Main St., P.O. Box 74
Kempton, IL 60946, USA
Tel: 815-253-6390
Fax: 815-253-6300
E-mail: auphq@frontiernet.net
www.adventuresunlimitedpress.com

the Rise

Saunière's magical workings and the penitential movement in Europe

Isaac Ben Jacob and Sarah Fishberg

FRONTIER PUBLISHING

Contents

Introduction

On first sight, the small village of Rennes-le-Château exudes an atmosphere of peace. High above the surrounding valley, the village could have been a hermit's retreat, or a fortified structure… or the hideaway of a treasure or a secret?

Its old church, dating back to at least the 11th century, is worked into the fabric of the village, surrounded by the customary cemetery, a presbytery built for the local priest, and village houses. Little has changed since the start of the 20th century, when this side of the town was "reworked" by the local village priest, Bérenger Saunière. It is he, and his constructions, that have transformed this formerly quiet village into a hub of intrigue and conspiracy; some go as far as to claim that the village holds "a secret" that could rock the world – or at least the foundations of the Catholic faith.

Rennes-le-Château has become a concentrate of the history of France. Each episode of this country's history, whether Celtic tribal leaders or Merovingian kings that ruled 1500 years ago, whether the Albigensian Crusade against the Cathars or the treasure of the Knights Templar after their demise of 1307, whether the royal intrigues of Louis XIV's court in the 17th century or the magical encounters of Parisian esoteric lodges in the late 19th century, seems to have a connection with this miniscule village. It is believed to be the trump card in the games of politics, and whoever holds this card, will rule the game.

Today, visitors come to Rennes-le-Château as pilgrims venture to sacred religious sites. Pilgrims try to touch the sacred relics of a saint; in Rennes-le-Château, the tourist wants to experience the "puzzle" that they believe Saunière encoded into his buildings, especially the village church. Each tourist is thus equally suited to decode "The Saunière Code", and it is indeed no coincidence that Dan Brown, in *The Da Vinci Code*[1], used the name Saunière for the curator of the Louvre – the man who left the puzzles for the novel's protagonists to decode.

Some visitors come for more: some have come to dig, some to explode (indeed), some to penetrate, each of those often only succeeding in causing consternation within the local community; some of these treasure hunters have left the village without running water for months, some have frightened visitors to the graveyard… by crawling out of the ground, from holes dug in the graveyard, often from a grave itself.

Why? Because "somewhere" underneath the feet of these visitors, it is

---

1   Dan Brown, "The Da Vinci Code", published by Doubleday Books, 2003.

believed that "it" – the secret, the treasure – still remains. It was either left behind, or secreted away, by the Visigoths, the Cathars, the Knights Templar, the Merovingians, etc. Though it is often claimed that this "treasure" is guarded – by the enigmatic Priory of Sion – it seems that no-one is able to stop, slow down or regulate treasure hunters. If the Priory guards this treasure, it is not as powerful as some people seem to claim – or perhaps it indeed does not exist, as others claim.

Just like Rennes-le-Château rises from the landscape, so Saunière rises as the only certainty amidst oceans of speculation. Though the subject of intense speculation himself, there are certain incontestable facts: he existed, he had a lot of money, it was unclear where he got that money from, and in his lifetime he never explained how he acquired his wealth – not even when his superior, the Bishop of Carcassonne, ordered him to do so.

François-Bérenger Saunière was born on April 11, 1852, in Montazels – just at the foot of the hill on top of which sits Rennes-le-Château. He was one of seven children, the eldest. Unfortunately, the Saunière family were not wealthy, and hence being the oldest did not amount to certain privileged birthrights. Still, it was customary for the family to make a special effort for the eldest. In this case, he had a priest's calling, and so his family made sure he could fulfil his ambition. If he had chosen any other profession, perhaps the mystery of Rennes-le-Château might never have occurred.

Saunière was ordained in 1879, became vicar in Alet, then the priest of the small village of Le Clat. Three years later, he was promoted to professor at the Seminary at Narbonne. A bright future seemed to be ahead of him, yet it seems Saunière had plans of his own. He only remained in Narbonne for one month; on June 1, 1885, he was nominated priest at Rennes-le-Château. Why he opted for this posting is unclear, as it was definitely a step down.

When he arrived, the church was in near ruin and the presbytery where he was supposedly to live, was even worse. Fortunately, the Dénarnaud family offered him lodgings. Their daughter, Marie, would become his "bonne", his maid – though some have argued she was even his lover, if not partner-in-crime.

Whether it was an alchemical wedding, fate, or a plan in which he was either the master or the executor, eleven years later, Saunière had transformed the tiny village into a small version of Disneyland: there was a large estate, with verandas, greenhouses, a newly decorated church, and – the Disney effect par excellence – the Tour Magdala and the zoo. The priest had bought up almost half of the village – but with what money?

Antoine Captier, whose forefather knew Saunière (and according to some accounts was there when the priest discovered the key to his fortune) explains that "the Villa Bethania (dedicated [like the Church] to Mary Magdalene), was very luxuriously furnished. My father has told me what he was told by his grandfather. He had descended from the bell tower, one evening when the labourers had been at work in the church. He saw an old wooden pillar, on the ground, completely deconstructed, with one part that had broken. Something shining was inside. It was, in fact, a small glass vial, which had been illuminated by a ray of light, and which contained a piece of paper. He carried the document to Father Saunière." He decided to stop all further work in the church and apparently began to carry out some work of his own. It seems that from here onwards, Saunière became a different man – a very wealthy man.

But apart from a wealthy man, Saunière was, or at least hoped to be seen as, an important, influential figure. When the local authorities were displeased with him for carrying out certain unauthorised work in the cemetery, he was ill-disposed to accept their opinion. When the bishop wanted to see his accounts and called him to account for his expenses, he showed the bishop utter disdain, and did everything to fight the man.

He was, it appears, often absent from the village, having provided Marie with a set of instructions of what to do if he – for one reason or another – would not be back for the Sunday service. Some have hence speculated that he had a relationship with the famous opera singer Emma Calvé in Paris, others have said he spent time in Lyon, and others that he "knew" an important person working for the Ministry of Culture. Recently, some have claimed he even went to Budapest, where he had a bank account, and to the Spanish city of Gerona, where he may have had a mistress and where he may have fathered a child.

Saunière was therefore in his time, at least within the village, a man of mystery. No doubt, all villagers worked together in trying to piece together the life and times of Saunière. Chief amongst their concerns was, however, what Saunière did at night, in their cemetery. "No-one knew what Saunière went in search of in the cemetery at night. A clue? A message? A treasure hidden in a tomb? What we know is that his parishioners often caught him, at night, while he was profaning the tombs in the cemetery. He didn't leave any whole", is what Jean-Luc Robin tells the visitors to his restaurant today.

When the priest stated he started a new project, a replica of the grotto of Lourdes, in which the Virgin Mary had appeared a few decades before, we see primary evidence of how Saunière manoeuvred. The replica – itself now restored and in the garden in front of the church – was an excellent excuse for Saunière to explain away why he needed to go on long walks in the countryside: he had to collect appropriate rocks for the grotto. When the local villagers saw – if not followed – him, they saw him painstakingly choosing some, and rejecting some other stones that he found on his way. Yet, when we look at the final product, it is clear that Saunière could have sourced the stones locally – or just asked others to bring some stones for this "oeuvre". But did Saunière know he was being observed? And did he search his stones in certain locations that were perhaps of interest for other things than their quality of stone?

The construction of the grotto does show that Saunière had an eye for detail. And hence, this eye for detail, coupled with his intellect, are seen as the prime ingredients that would allow Saunière to code his estate. Researchers thus point out various anomalies in his church – such as his colouring in of the Stations of the Cross – or wonder whether it is a coincidence that the paving slabs in his Tour Magdala (Magdala Tower) add up to 64 – and that some of these stones reveal certain anomalies too.

Soon, an observation of an anomaly would lead to the construction of a theory, like Saunière having hidden something underneath the tower. Half a century of illegal and authorised excavations have nevertheless revealed nothing under the tower – or anywhere else in the village.

The absence of evidence for some is merely fuelling a continued search for the truth or the treasure. For others, those of a sceptical disposition, it is seen as further confirmation that there is no secret and that the enigma is based on a lie – or rather, a denial of the known truth. For these sceptics, the "truth" is that Saunière trafficked in masses and that this is the known and only means as to how he acquired his wealth. Though it is shown that Saunière trafficked in masses and received money for masses, Jean-Luc Chaumeil has pointed out that if "traffic in masses" was the total of the mystery, Saunière would have had to receive just under 400,000 demands – begging the question why so many French people wanted Saunière, an obscure village priest in the South of France, to say masses for them. Rennes-le-Château was not, after all, a pilgrimage site – not yet.

Indeed, it was the anomalous nature of his income that caught the attention of bishop de Beauséjour and which would lead, on December 5, 1911, to a formal condemnation: a "suspensio a divinis": Saunière was no longer allowed to administer the sacraments, which included saying mass. The suspension lasted until 1913, when Saunière won his appeal with the Vatican[2].

---

2 *With the help of Canon Huguet as his attorney. The services of Canon Huguet were rec-*

Apparently, the bishopric nevertheless "forgot" to fully reinstate Saunière – though he, it must be said, did not really care about such details; that he had won his battle with the bishop seemed more important.

Saunière died relatively shortly afterwards, on January 22, 1917. It would, nevertheless, take half a century before he would become the subject of first national and than global interest. As his fame rose, so rose the calibre of his alleged discovery. In 1996, authors Andrews and Schellenberger[3] argued that Saunière had discovered no less than the Tomb of Jesus Christ. Such a discovery would indeed shake if not destroy the very foundations of the Christian faith, for their central dogma is that Christ rose – body and soul – to Heaven. However, a more popular theory is that Saunière found the body of Mary Magdalene, and that he had evidence that she was married to Jesus. Such a relation might shake, but definitely not destroy, the foundations of Christian faith. It is this theory that inspired Dan Brown[4]. The main problem for these imaginative authors is that neither theory is supported by much – if any – factual evidence, other than conjecture.

Hence, when we set out our search, in our approach, we wanted to return to factual evidence – of which there is remarkably much, but which is nevertheless put to one side by most authors – and see where that evidence would lead to. It soon became apparent that Saunière, at least when it comes to attaining his wealth, had stumbled upon a local dimension of a larger movement, which dated back to – at least – the Cathar crusades, i.e. the 13th century. But rather than being a thing of the past, there continued to exist a network of "priests" that seemed to perform certain specific – and heretical – rites and for which certain adherents of this heresy were willing to pay dearly for, as it was believed that the administration of these rites was instrumental for the salvation of their soul. It seems that Saunière became a member of this underground network and that it was masses of an altogether different kind that brought about his wealth. In short, hidden in the pool of available evidence about the mystery of Saunière, lay an unknown dimension, there for the taking, but which everyone – it seems – had missed. Hence, the mystery of the Rise rose from the largely unused pieces of evidence – and the truth would set us all free?

---

ommended to Saunière by Father Grassaud, priest of Amélie-les-Bains, a mysterious (and, as we will see, influential) character.

3   Richard Andrews & Paul Schellenberger, "The Tomb of God – the Body of Jesus and the Solution to a 2,000-year-old Mystery", published by Little Brown & Company, 1996.

4   Dan Brown, "The Da Vinci Code", published by Doubleday Books, 2003.

Chapter 1

A priest for which saints?

Bérenger Saunière. For more than a century, the village priest of Rennes-le-Château has intrigued so many people, because of his sudden and unexplained wealth – money which he invested in various building projects that continue to dominate Rennes-le-Château. Almost every possible and impossible suggestion has been proposed as to how he acquired his wealth. But reading all the various books on the subject, we still feel like spectators, watching his life – and yet another theory – unfold on the screen in front of us. As each book progresses, reality disintegrates and the authors' pet theories slowly take over.

Projected onto this screen, it is clear that the real Saunière has become distorted; he has became an excuse, an allegory, a pretext which merely serves as a point of focus so that the author – or director – can project onto this man anything he desires. The true history of this village priest has therefore become nothing but a distant echo of his true self; and it has become difficult to separate the legend from the man... in which both the popular and the sceptical author often mistake fact for fiction, and vice versa.

Let us leave the comfort of our cinema seat and enter into the reality that lies beneath the projected fiction. So many have rewritten the life of Saunière, that in order to return it to its true origins, it feels as if we also have to rewrite his life – to remove layer upon layer of imagination or conjecture.

Basic accounting practices

In 1898, Pope Leo XIII ruled the Christian world from the Vatican. While the pope was known throughout the world, Saunière found himself at the other extreme of the popularity scale. This meant that he could largely do as he pleased; the only people interested in his comings and goings were his small village flock – and being a village, they they were steeped in a country mentality in which they wanted to know everything about everyone else in the village. The lives of the local priest, mayor and school teacher were the prime subjects of debate, for they represented the three basic pillars of society: religious, political and educational.

If anyone, back in 1898, had stated that the fame of abbé Saunière would one day eclipse that of Pope Leo XIII, he would now be taken for a prophet – but in his own time, he would have been seen as a deluded individual. At the turn of the 20th century, for a man like Saunière, a priest of no importance, who did not preach about fire and brimstone, who did not prophesy an impending cataclysm or the end of times, achieving any sort of notoriety was most improbable. A man in his position, regardless of his intelligence and passion, was destined to roam the countryside in total obscurity. Which is unfortunate, for it means that there is no contemporary evidence showing how he was seen at that time – except to note that he never rose above the level of obscurity to which he had been assigned by his position. But it is precisely those shadows that have provided the priest with a smokescreen, both in his times and ours. In his time, it allowed him to operate in the manner of a secret agent; in our time, it impedes us in an easy understanding of who he was and what he did.

The only tangible clues we have from that period and which shed some light on the darkness that surrounded him, are his diaries and his booklets in which he listed his accounts. The account ledgers survived in three batches: one set is owned by Antoine Captier, a researcher native to Rennes-le-Château; a second lot is in the possession of Laurent Buchholtzer, another researcher; the remainder has disappeared, although it still existed in the late 1960s, for one researcher, René Descadeillas, spoke of these documents, stating that there were donations from Belgium, Switzerland and the north of Italy listed inside these ledgers.

For a man whose financial activities are shady, these accounts may shed some light on the problem. Although accounts can be used to hide information, Saunière kept his purely for his own means and ends; they were private accounts, not to be shared with anyone, and thus of primary importance – and more than likely a correct statement of what went on. Nevertheless, it is clear that they do not encompass everything and researchers have noted that Saunière did not show every item of expenditure in these books. This is but normal: he kept the accounts for purely personal purposes and so petty cash for grocery shopping, a train ticket, etc., were not entered into his ledgers. But a large order placed for wine, or large sums of money received from a benefactor, were. In fact, the accounts are quite revealing, as they show that the priest received major donations from more than a dozen of his parishioners, as well as from certain convents, specifically that of Castelnaudary, a town geographically not too distant, but for which there is no clear reason to date as to why Saunière should be receiving their money.

To the list of donors we need to add priests from neighbouring towns and villages, equally begging the question of what Saunière was doing, or able to do, that they could not – or were unwilling to – do themselves.

Certain names appear repeatedly – regularly even – including Guillaume and Barthélemy Denarnaud. These two people seem to open their wallets easily and readily. It seems that they are providing the priest with financial support. It is Marie Denarnaud, who is the priest's maid and who remains at his side until the bitter end, who will eventually be his heir; the title deeds of the Villa Bethania were placed in her name, to the horror of the bishop of Carcassonne when he found out during an inquiry into the origins of Saunière's wealth that started in 1906 and lasted until 1915. Marie Denarnaud is considered to be his confidante, his love, his soul mate and wouldn't it be normal for her to ask her parents, Guillaume and Barthélemy, to help out not only herself but also her partner? Perhaps…

The sums received by Saunière are not small amounts of money. Normally, they are 50 or 60 francs, which at the time were considerable sums. To put this into context: Saunière's starting salary was 60 francs per month, roughly today's equivalent of 900 dollars. So, already, 50 or 60 francs would double his and many of his fellow priests' basic monthly income.

The identities of these purveyors of funding remained secret; Saunière never revealed who was sponsoring him. But they do not pass unnoticed in his accounts. One of them is the chaplain of Rennes-les-Bains, abbé Justin Sarda.

When we look into his contributions, we see that:
- in 1899, he makes Saunière a payment of 50 francs three times in March;
- May 1899: two payments of 50 francs;
- July 1899: a similar payment;
- August 1899: the same
- November 1899: three payments of 50 francs;
- April 1900: two payments of 50 francs;
- September 1990: three payments of one hundred francs and one of 50 francs, i.e. a total of 350 francs in one month!
- January 1901: 34 francs.
- February 1901: 110 francs.
- April 1901: two payments of 20 francs, one of 75 francs;
- June 1901: two payments of 75 francs, one payment of 10 francs.
- February 1902: 211 francs.

In total, over a period of three years, Sarda paid Saunière 1485 francs, or about 22,275 dollars!

This is a gigantic amount of money. Why would a chaplain of Rennes-les-Bains pay such an extraordinary amount of money to the neighbouring village priest?

The man himself definitely does not have the funds he gives to Saunière, for like Saunière, he is a salaried priest. Nevertheless, he is one of Saunière's biggest donors. Looking further into the accounts, it seems that he acts on behalf of others, each one apparently having a family connection to him. The ledgers list Sarda Cuxac, Sarda Pons, Sarda Raynaud, Sarda Maupome, Sarda Cazaux; they are just some of several names that we can associate with him, as gleaned from the accounting books.

These donations through Sarda drew our attention, for it was clear that not only was there an association between him and the donors – an apparent family connection – but there was also one with Saunière. In the published history of the enigma of Bérenger Saunière, there is little or no attention given to this chaplain of Rennes-les-Bains. Who was he? And more importantly, why did he not keep all of this money for himself? Why did he channel it to Saunière?

What is known about him is that he was a comrade, if not a good friend, of our village priest, and that he officiated at masses in the neighbouring spa town of Rennes-les-Bains. This in itself is not unimportant. The chaplain of Rennes-les-Bains obviously knew and worked with the priest of that village: that man was Henri Boudet and he is a known ingredient of the mystery – and also a name we find in the accounts. For some authors, abbé Boudet was the real man of mystery, the one whose hand directed Saunière; for others, he was a co-conspirator with Saunière. In truth, no-one knows what type of relationship the two men had; just that there was one.

From the late 1970s onwards, people specifically looked towards the publication of his book, *La Vraie Langue Celtique*[5], as a possible "clue" in the mystery. But what we want to underline is the question of the money that Boudet got to publish this book privately; where did that money come from?

Let us look further into the accounts that Saunière kept. When we trace all the donations from the Soeurs de St Joseph de Cluny in Limoux, we find a somewhat similar scenario.
- In October 1895, they gave 1.85 gold francs for the "souls in Purgatory". That same month, there is a second donation of 3.10 francs.

---

5 Henri Boudet, « La Vraie Langue Celtique et le Cromleck de Rennes-les-Bains » ("The True Celtic language and the Cromleck of Rennes-les-Bains"), Carcassonne, 1886. Recently republished as a facsimile by Editions L'Œil du Sphinx, collection « Le Serpent Rouge » (The Red Serpent), volume 7, Paris, May 2006, [foreword by Gérard de Sède].

- November 1895: another "Purgatory donation" of 4.50 francs;
- February 1896, a donation for a sepulchre of "Moulins" of 15 francs and a Purgatory gift of 6 francs.
- April 1896: another Purgatory donation of 5.35 francs. The same month, a donation for the sepulchre of one Rivière, for 36 francs.
- October 1896, a donation for a sepulchre of "S", worth 35 francs.
- November 1896: a donation from an institution known as "St Joseph", for 15 francs.
- December 1896: a donation of St Joseph de Cluny worth 35 francs.
- February 1897: donation from the hospice in Limoux, whereby Saunière adds "mass", worth 16 francs. There is a second such entry that same month, for 10 francs.
- March 1897: anothere donation, now worth 50 francs.
- May 1897: Saunière notes "masses, offerings to Purgatory", worth 13.15 francs.
- June 1897, a large donation, of 100 francs, plus a donation for "Purgatory" of 27.30 francs.
- September 1897: 50 francs, and one for 34.40 francs for a sepulchre.
- October 1897, a donation of 100 francs and a "charitable donation" (we could ask what the difference between both forms of donations are) of 50 francs.
- November 1897: one donation of 27 francs, another worth 100 francs, plus a donation for the sepulchre of Fontecave of 38 francs.
- May 1898: 20 francs, plus a donation for a sepulchre in September 1898, worth 38 francs.
- That same month, another donation worth 50 francs.
- November, another 50 francs.

In 1899, donations continue to arrive from Limoux, roughly in the order of 50 francs. The donations become larger and larger, and our priest no longer writes "purgatory", "masses" or "sepulchres" in his notebooks.

Limoux is still roughly within the bailiwick of Rennes-le-Château, but what is to be made of the donations Saunière received from Northern France? The following overview is not exhaustive.

- In the area of Soissons/Lille, in July 1899, the hospital of Soissons makes three payments of 50 francs.
- September 1899: four payments of 50 francs.
- October: the sisters of Bodin de Soissons pay 50 francs.
- January 1900: the hospital pays four payments of 50 francs and one of 100 francs – a total sum of 300 francs in one month!

- July 1900: the town of Stenay pays Saunière 50 francs.
- August 1900: from Soissons comes payment for a sum of 50 francs and the towns of Douai and Calais give two payments, totalling 150 francs.
- November 1900: Soissons and the town of Calais make three payments of 100 francs each.
- January 1901: Calais pays 100 francs.
- February 1901: establishments in Soissons and Calais each pay 50 francs twice;
- March 1901: donations from Lille, Calais, Tourcooing, Douai, Soissons, Amiens, worth 44, 75, 50, 10, 15, 50 and 11 francs respectively.
- April 1901: Soisons 10.35 francs; Tourcoing 10 francs; Lille 15 francs.
- May 1901 : Calais and Tourcoing pay 50 and 10 francs respectively.
- June/July 1901 : Soissons 10, Tourcoing 10 and 20 francs.
- August 1901: Calais 50 and Douai no less than 225 francs!
- October 1901: Soissons 100 and Tourcoing 20 francs;
- November 1901 sees Soissons paying 100 and Calais making three payments of 50 francs, as well as payments from Lille, Tourcoing and Douai, each worth 20 francs,
- December 1901: Soissons and Amiens pay 41 and 20 francs.
- February 1902: Amiens pays 100.50 francs;
- April 1902: Soissons and Calais make two payments totalling 90 francs;
- May 1902: Calais and Tourcoing: 71 francs.
- July 1902: Soissons, Calais, Tourcoing, pay 100, 100 and 24 francs.
- August 1902: Calais pays 50 francs.
- September 1902: Calais, Douai and Soissons send a total of 123 francs.
- And let us finish in December 1902, with Soissons donating 100 francs.

A grand total of 3240.6 francs, or the equivalent of about 48,609 dollars. Fifty grand!

When we look at his accounting books as a whole, we note that 1899 is an important fiscal year for Saunière: his ambitions rise and thus, so does his income. But his additional income is now no longer local to the region; donations are coming in from all over France. Indeed, this small country priest is not just receiving money from his parishioners, or the surrounding countryside; somehow, from all corners of France, people want to send him… are sending him money.

Principal donors are the hospitals of Soissons and those of Carmel de

Caen (the institute "Bon Sauveur"). Why these and other institutions in Normandy and the Pas-de-Calais, are eager to provide an unknown priest in the opposite end of the country with money, is a question never before posed – and hence never answered. But first, let us be clear that it is impossible to argue that these sums originate from trafficking in masses or generosity, as some sceptics of the mystery have argued. The rate for having a normal mass said was 1 franc – far removed from the sums Saunière was cashing in, sometimes on a monthly basis.

What is most remarkable is the fact that it comes from people he has never seen; they are strangers to him, but they give money as if they are helping out their best friend or a long lost family member in desperate need of money. They send him the cash of their convents and hospitals and provide a small fortune for this obscure village priest who is of no obvious importance. Why?

The following year, 1900, we see another increase of funds arriving into the Saunière household: Chartres, Lourdes, La Rochelle, Calais and Valence are added to the list of places from which Saunière is receiving donations. Some of the names are now illegible, but in 1900, these towns provide a minimum of 2,200 and a maximum of 3,500 francs. La Rochelle gave between 150 and 250 francs; Calais, Valence, Soissons and other towns in the north offer 1,500 francs. From that year onwards, the network of donations coming in from outside the department of the Aude and Pyrénées-Orientales can be divided into two distinct groups: one is found in Normandy and surrounding areas, namely Caen (Bon Sauveur), Rouen (les Soeurs de Ste Thérèse), Chartres (making up about 10% of his donations); the other area being the North, Pas-de-Calais, the Champagne region, namely Lille, Soissons (at least 30% of the priest's income), Troyes, Tourcoing, Douai, Calais, Amiens, and even further afield, abroad, from Brussels and Flanders.

Although the accounts explain how much and where his money was coming from, they do not explain why. Why should a village priest of a god-forsaken hill village receive money that we should only expect to see given to a person on the way to sainthood or an illustrious hermit? Indeed, why was Lourdes giving money to him? Surely we would expect to see Saunière give money to Lourdes, as Lourdes was and remains one of the most illustrious pilgrimage sites in the Christian world. You would expect to see a local parishioner in Rennes-le-Château wanting to ask the Virgin Mary of Lourdes to intervene on his or her behalf and giving some money to the local priest, so he can send it onwards to Lourdes. But instead, we see people in Lourdes giving money to Saunière. Why?

Even if he was trafficking in masses, as the sceptics argue, why would anyone in Lourdes want an obscure village priest in Rennes-le-Château to say a mass for them, rather than the local priest who could do it at a site blessed by the very presence of the Virgin Mary? The same applies to Chartres, with its splendid cathedral. In fact, there is nothing to indicate why these religious institutions would be so liberal as to part with their money to support a priest on the other side of the country who appears to be – is – a total nobody. If Saunière were then to pass on the money to other individuals, we could suspect him of being an agent or middleman – if not a type of mafioso – and some sense of logic would be present. But the money he receives is for him and him alone.

The proposed solution that these donations were because he would say masses does not stand up to scrutiny, confronted as we are with not only the regularity but specifically the extent of the donations. Furthermore, who would entrust a priest that is unknown to you, of whom you know neither his intent, his eloquence, his renown, nor even his honesty, to say masses for your most dearly departed? Although masses for the dead are a vital component of the Catholic faith and add an extra source of income, such masses are either said by the local priest, or the priest of a highly respected or renowned sanctuary, such as Lourdes or another saintly or miraculous site. Rennes-le-Château does not feature on that list and even today, we would surmise that the local priest does not receive too many requests for masses, despite the renown of the village. So it is clear that, based on his accounts, these institutions trusted Saunière with their money and felt he was worthy of receiving it. But why remains a mystery.

It is not a new mystery. In 1906, the new bishop of Carcassonne, Monseigneur de Beauséjour visited Saunière in Rennes-le-Château and became highly suspicious of the man and his wealth. He asked for details and thus began the infamous investigation that would last several years. In fact, what de Beauséjour was actually after, was to get a look at Saunière's accounts, the very accounts we are studying. But Saunière never put these at the disposal of his bishop. In fact, he did everything he could to make sure he did not have to surrender these accounts to the bishop. It is therefore clear that they contained vital information, which he was unwilling to share with anyone and specifically not the bishop, who could obviously have used the power of the Catholic network in France to find out why these institutions were sponsoring our priest – and that discovery is, in my opinion, why

Saunière never surrendered the accounts to his bishop: the bishop would have been able to piece together the truth from them. The question, worth much more than 64,000 dollars, is: what truth?

The North of France may seem to be very distant from Rennes-le-Château. Geographically it is, but in history, they are not so far apart. The Languedoc, the region where Saunière was born and decided to live, saw the emergence of a heresy, Catharism, which many authors have integrated into the story of Rennes-le-Château – though no-one has been able to show any evidence of a connection between a heresy of the 13th century and the wealth of our parish priest at the end of the 19th century. For the moment, let us note that this religion remains ill-understood and that, although it is often seen as "typically" present in Southern France, it is known that it was also implanted in Amiens and – coincidentally – at Soissons, two sources of income for Saunière. These towns were described by Guibert de Nogent[6] as the seat of a heresy that was on all points comparable with that of the Razès.

Evervin, the provost of Steinfeld, in a letter addressed to Bernard de Clairvaux, remarked that Catharism was in fact not confined to these cantons, but had "infected" Tourcoing, Brussels, Lille, Douai, Calais, Troyes and Flanders[7] (as well as the whole of the Champagne).

Though nothing can be proved at this moment, we should at least note that there is a remarkable coincidence in the geographical overlap: Saunière receives money from monasteries with which he has personally no single link, but they were all involved in the Cathar heresy, seven hundred years earlier. Is it possible that these monasteries, or some of the people living in them, retained some "memories" of these heresies? What we are trying to say: is it possible that Catharism was still alive and still had some followers, inside some of the convents that had played a role in the heresy several centuries before?

We will leave it as a question for now, but the correlation is there. And

---

6 « *De Vita Sua* », *Book III, chapter XVII.*
7 *Regarding the presence of Cathars in Flanders, see « Continuat. Proesmonstrat., loc. cit. ep. Traject. Eccles. Ad Tridentinum Episcopum » (extract from a letter of the church of Maastricht to the Bishop of Trent). For their presence in Champagne, Liège and the North of France : « Ep. Eccles. Leodiens. Ad Lucium Papa » (Letter of the church of Liege to Pope Lucius II). Regarding the heretics of Cologne, see: « Evervini Epist. » (Letter of Evervin), in: la Patrologie Latine de l'abbé J.P. Migne (the Latin Patrology of abbé J. P. Migne) Tome CLXXXII, pp. 676-680.*

even though the living tradition of Catharism may have died out, perhaps the monasteries were in the possession of certain knowledge about a historic secret? Is it possible that Saunière somehow became associated with a network of heretics – or heretical knowledge – in the North of France, in Normandy, that tied them in with the Razès? It is a question, but one thing is certain: the priest of Rennes-le-Château used a religious network to get funds. And if it was not Catharism, then it was something else that tied a bond between him and these monasteries in the North of France. Was it a brotherhood? A sect? A religious order? Whatever it was, it is clear that the majority of the funds came from monks and nuns – religious institutions. The money seems therefore to have been donated to our priest as part of a type of religious service, which for the moment remains impossible to identify.

The Cathar possibility

With this evidence on the table, let us follow a double route: that of the Cathars, and that of a confraternity. The key question in this enquiry is who would have an interest in financing Saunière, and for what purpose.

Saunière knew Boudet and Sarda, both pillars of the parish of Rennes-les-Bains, the village that neighbours to and shares its name with Rennes-le-Château. Although Boudet is part and parcel of the mystery, what is less-known, is that there was a peculiar presence in this town, namely an old weavers' community in Verzeille. The story is written in *Origine du nom 'Verzeille'*, according to research by S. Raynaud[8]. The community of Verzeille was an important centre of the local fabric-weaving industry; it was a place where there were "Lollards": heretics that often grouped themselves into brotherhoods. In the chronicles of St Andrew of Cambrai[9], as well as in letters from Evervin, provost of Steinfeld, addressed to St. Bernard de Clairvaux, we are told that the Cathars could often be identified with the weavers. As such, Cathars were often not called by that name, but instead were referred to as weavers, or, in French, "Tisserands", or "Textores", as it was a common profession practiced by these particular heretics. So, was the weaving community of Verzeille in origin a Cathar community? If they were, were Sarda and Boudet aware of the possibility that Cathars – or descendants of Cathars – were living in their religious hunting grounds?

8 *S. Raynaud is a local historian who lives in Verzeille. His research entitled "Origins of the name Verzeille" is published on the official website of the village. Refer to http://verzeille.lwd. fr/historique.php for further detail (text in French).*

9 *St. Andreae Cameracens (St. Andrew of Cambrai), III, ap. Mon. Germ. VII, 540.*

The question may seem to be farfetched, but we need to add some additional detail, which will make our case more convincing. First, we note that Rennes-les-Bains was a spa town. In the Pyrénées-Orientales, there are several such sites, some of which continue to attract visitors and tourists today, specifically in the Tech valley, with towns such as Amélie-les-Bains. The town has numerous sulphur springs, which were used as baths by sufferers from rheumatism and maladies of the lungs. One of the baths in the town already existed in Roman times, suggesting the antiquity and popularity of these installations.

In this valley, to the west of Perpignan, the capital of the Pyrénées-Orientales, there is a remarkable presence of what is popularly known as "La Sanch" (pronounced, in Catalan, as "La Sank"), meaning "the blood". The organisation is best known for its various local processions on Good Friday, the biggest and most impressive being held in Perpignan, the seat of the "Arch-confraternity of La Sanch". Today, they are perhaps most memorable for wearing a piece of clothing that is identical to that worn by the Klu Klux Klan, although the colours of La Sanch are normally black and red. The Klu Klux Klan copied their dress from La Sanch, whose robe was a typical dress for the penitent throughout several centuries.

La Sanch was not present in Rennes-les-Bains – at least, they did not hold processions there – and the town itself sits somewhat outside their core area – but not by much. The link between La Sanch and Saunière has never been analysed, and this should be seen as a major omission, for it is clear that Saunière knew about the existence of these organisations – and was associatd with them.

Researcher Jean-Patrick Pourtal interviewed Sonia Moreu, who ran a bookshop in Rennes-le-Château for many years[10]. Moreu knew many of the people who were actually alive at the time of Saunière. Amongst these was one Madame Olive, who also knew abbé Boudet. She remembered that Saunière had taken the education of a small child upon himself. The name of the child was Abdon and he was the son of a foster sister of Marie Denarnaud[11]. It meant that the small child was very close to the maid, her master (i.e. Saunière), as well as the Denarnaud family, who we know went

---

10   Sonia Moreu settled in Rennes-le-Château as a bookseller in 1986. She and researcher Alain Féral are the founders of "Atelier Empreinte", the first bookshop dedicated to the Rennes-le-Château mystery. It was initially located in the Tour Magdala, i.e. Saunière's library, before moving to the main street of the village. Sonia Moreu's interview was given in July 2000, and its full transcript can be found at the "Rennes-le-Château : le Dossier" website: http://www.rennes-le-chateau.org/rlctoday/int-soniamoreu.asp (text in French)
11   The mother of Abdon was called Julie Fons.

beyond the normal call of duty to provide financially for the priest. In fact, Abdon was raised under the guardianship of Saunière, no doubt with motherly love provided by Marie.

According to author Gérard de Sède and Sonia Moreu, the child was given this rather bizarre name (Abdon) as recognition for a miraculous healing that had occurred due to the holy relic in Arles-sur-Tech, a neighbouring village to Amélie-les-Bains (which was, in fact, originally called Arles-les-Bains). Arles-sur-Tech's holy relic is the tomb of St Abdon and Sennen, located just outside the main church of the town. The famous "Sainte Tombe" is in the abbey of the town and is an old and heavy marble sarcophagus, dating to at least the 4th century. The "miracle" is this: every day, the tomb fills up with a quantity of water (a litre per day on average). The water is very pure and many ascribe curative powers to it. Although one litre is the average, there are times when the tomb has so much water that it spills over. It has, on occasion, produced as much as 800 litres per year. And it should be noted that despite the quite intense public and scientific scrutiny, there seems to be no trickery or other easily available explanation. It is a genuine scientific enigma.

The child's family had entrusted him to the care of the local La Sanch brotherhood, in the conviction that he was about to die. But the brotherhood, who was and remains to this day in control of the sanctuary, decided to use the sacred waters on the child. It seems that the end result was indeed a miracle, for he recovered from his illness. In recognition of this miracle, he was baptised "Abdon". What is highly significant is that Marie Denarnaud, his foster aunt, and/or her family had a very important and close relationship with the organisation, as it was La Sanch who gave the child into their care. It is equally clear that Saunière cannot have been ignorant of this connection[12], for he took personal care of the child. In fact,

---

12   *With regard to how Saunière's knowledge of this miracle underscores his relation with the La Sanch penitent brotherhood, Laurent Buchholtzer, a French researcher and specialist of Saunière's letters and account books, confirmed in writing that Bérenger Saunière did "ascribe the miraculous healing to St. Abdon. He actually filled out the forms necessary to have this 'miracle' officially recognised by the Catholic Church, and attributed to the saint." It is therefore obvious that abbé Saunière harboured in his heart a very special devotion to the "Sainte Tombe", i.e. the water-oozing sarcophagus of Arles-sur-Tech, as well as, by extension, to the two Manichaean Babylonian saints Abdon and Sennen, who have found their final resting place in it and to whom it is dedicated. Saunière's actions are quite remarkable in this case, in that they show a definite intent of officially enshrining before the Vatican a "miracle" linked to St. Abdon, in other words, an attempt at promoting a very peculiar, non-Christian cult rendered to a "healing sepulchre" and to Babylonian heretical "saints". It is simply unavoidable that Saunière had to know the very un-Christian nature of this cult while he was attempting to further it, in effect, by expanding the worship of Abdon, Sennen and their "Sa-*

perhaps it was not the Dénarnaud family, but Saunière himself who was responsible for the adoption of this child, but had to use the cover of the Denarnaud family to achieve this desire; after all, priests are not encouraged to raise children, adopted or not.

Furthermore, let us note that Saunière had a close personal friendship with the priest of Amélie-les-Bains. In 1886, Saunière offered a vermeil chalice to the priest of Amélie-les-Bains, abbé Grassaud[13]. Why he gave this, has never been explained. The chalice still exists and is known to date from the 18th century. Was it evidence of a mutual friendship, or a sign of recognition? It is an intriguing gift and we became convinced that some important bond united the two. Were they perhaps members of the same fraternity? If so, la Sanch was a logical option. Such a "fraternal bond" could also explain the mutual assistance they provided for each another throughout their lifetime.

Guardians of the spas

La Sanch is one of several penitent movements. In the Pyrenees-Orientales, there are three famous organisations: one in Perpignan, the "Arch confraternity", another in Collioure and a third in Arles-sur-Tech. In the Aude, there are the "Pénitents blancs de Narbonne", in Narbonne. These towns and cities are where these penitent organisations still exist today – although since Saunière's time, some have disappeared. La Sanch in Perpignan was originally founded on 11th October 1416, by Saint Vincent Ferrer, but in Saunière's lifetime, it was revitalised. Today, they are well-known for their annual procession, which occurs at 3pm on Good Friday through the streets of Perpignan.

As well as being resident in these towns, their members live in neighbouring or even distant places. The fraternity of Arles-sur-Tech watched over the religious life and community of this thermal spot. Thermal spas seem to be a particular ingredient of the organisation as a whole and they seem to suggest a link with the penitents' establishment in some locations and not in others – but that is not a rule, more an indication. Let us also

---

cred Tomb" with the approval of the La Sanch penitent brotherhood. As to Saunière's other possible motives, we can speculate that he might have envisioned the personal fame and fortune that he would have reaped from being the "discoverer" whose action may ultimately have led to a pilgrimage to the sepulchre of Arles-sur-Tech being established. In any case, such reasoning would fit especially well into Saunière's personality as a power-hungry individual, as evidenced by his ambitious character and seemingly insatiable thirst for money.
13   Refer to Jacques Rivière, « Le fabuleux trésor de Rennes-le-Château » ("The Fabulous Treasure of Rennes-le-Château"), Bélisane, 1983, p.73, where this episode was first mentioned.

remind ourselves that Sarda was not just any priest, but was the chaplain of the spa of Rennes-les-Bains.

As to Arles-sur-Tech, the thermal springs were given miraculous properties and placed under the patronage of the archangel Raphael. Today, we see visits to such spa towns as a "holiday", to which the sick and infirm were taken, to be looked after in a hotel and/or hospital, during which time they enjoyed "hydrotherapy" from the waters. That is a very mundane approach. Although it was a holiday for some, for several others, these visitors – pilgrims – were "displaced" and often desired the help of a local priest. It thus fell upon Sarda and his colleagues in other spas to take care of the religious health of the patients that came to the springs.

But it seems that for some priests, if not the confraternity, the springs of the town had another religious connotation. Just as baptism washed away sin, water also seemed to heal. This interest in the curative properties of certain springs is also noted in the writings of Henri Boudet, the colleague of Sarda in Rennes-les-Bains and a man integral to the story of Rennes-le-Château. But what made the fraternity of La Sanch special, was that it ascribed the cures to the intervention of the archangel Raphael.

Let us look more closely into the history of Arles-sur-Tech and Amélie-les-Bains. Mankind's presence in the area goes back far into history. Amélie-les-Bains was first of all the seat of a Benedictine abbey, founded by the monk Castellan. Originating from Spain, in 778, this monk had built a cell close to the spring of the hot waters. In 881, the abbey was transferred by Sunifred to Arles-sur-Tech, where he also placed the famous tomb of white marble, which would later heal the small child Abdon. As the abbey of Arles-sur-Tech was originally located in Amélie-les-Bains (the two towns are separated by a distance of only three kilometres), it is most likely that Grassaud officiated in the ceremonies of La Sanch in Arles-sur-Tech. It was this confraternity that ruled over the cult of Saints Abdon and Sennen, and organised all ceremonies that involved these saints, the Sacred Tomb, as well as the various village festivals, including those of Amélies-les-Bains. As Grassaud and Saunière were very close friends, perhaps it was even he, not the Denarnaud family, that engineered the adoption of Abdon by the Denarnaud family.

Amélie-les-Bains always maintained its link with Arles-sur-Tech and, as the name suggests, was more of a spa town than Arles. But many of the numerous sick that came to seek the cures of its spas asked the religious leader(s) of Amélie to take them to the Sacred Tomb in Arles, as well as to the spectacles that were organised by La Sanch.

The sick were not the only ones who came: Bérenger Saunière was also very familiar with these two towns and during his visits to his friend Grassaud, he did not miss the opportunity to visit the Sacred Tomb. To quote French researcher Pierre Jarnac: "The priest did in fact visit Amélie. Arles-sur-Tech was therefore on his path. He took it to go and see his friend Father Grassaud, priest of Amélie. It is certain that Father Grassaud showed his colleague around the site of Arles-sur-Tech, as a postcard was sent from Arles by Saunière to his maid Marie, in October 1904. Saunière also took with him a container of the famous 'miraculous' water." This is conclusive proof that there is a connection between Saunière, Arles-sur-Tech, and the Sacred Tomb. It could be seen as "just" evidence of a tourist visit, but we need to remember that the connection must have been more profound, as is shown in his guardianship over little Abdon, a miracle child whom he and Marie received from this confraternity, to raise him.

La Sanch frequented Amélie-les-Bains and it is impossible that the priest of that town was not a member of this fraternity; logic suggests that every priest officiating in the town must have been a member; and that would thus include Grassaud on its membership list. As mentioned, Grassaud is an important man in Saunière's life; like Sarda, he is a source of income, but also a friend, a very trusted friend. When Saunière began to have major problems with Bishop de Beauséjour (from roughly 1906 onwards), Grassaud takes up the defence of his friend. This is an intriguing "coincidence". At a time when Saunière is told to reveal his source of income, Grassaud is there to help him. It is in fact Grassaud who suggests that Saunière uses the canon Huguet as his defence attorney.

This could indeed be nothing more than a friend helping out a friend, but it could also be that Grassaud "needed" to help his friend out, for several reasons. Perhaps Saunière was not just a friend in the ordinary sense of the word, but a "friend", both being members of the same fraternity and bound by an oath to help out a "friend" when he is in need. Perhaps Grassaud wanted to make sure that the investigation by the bishop did not bring him or his fraternity into it – which it would have done if they had given him money. So, in this scenario, Grassaud would not be truly "just" helping Saunière out, he would be helping himself out, and La Sanch too. For any doubters, we refer to Pierre Jarnac, who confirms that it was Grassaud who arranged Saunière's defence. But we also learn that it was Grassaud who, when Saunière died, *"gave money to Marie Denarnaud, under the pretext of a fictitious loan, to help her survive.*"[14] It is unlikely that Grassaud was able to support Denarnaud by himself or loan her money. Isn't it more likely that he, like Saunière, was able to take from the same donating hand from which Saunière received money? Did Grassaud go to the same source, asking now for money for Saunière's comrade in arms, his maid? Was La Sanch this helping hand? So far this is the most logical scenario, and hence the one we will continue to explore.

So far, we note that we have three priests, all residents of a spa town, who are connected with Saunière and who seem to know the origins of his fortune: Sarda, Boudet and Grassaud.[15] We also know, from studying Saunière's accounts, that large sums of money were transferred to him. This money did not only originate from the religious community in his area, but also as far away as Normandy and the North of France. A network of monasteries and religious hospitals intervened in his favour, sending him money. We also note that Sarda, Boudet and Grassaud are more than likely members of this network themselves, and we have so far argued that this network is, or is related to La Sanch. So, what is La Sanch?

La Sanch, the Penitents, Boudet and Father Lasserre
La Sanch is best described as a mysterious secret society, which even in the 21st century has not surrendered all of its mystique or its secrets. To under-

---

14 *According to the same researcher.*

15 *According to Saunière's correspondence, it turns out that at least two other priests (by "other", we mean "from non-spa towns") also knew the source of Saunière's fortune: Father Gazel, from the parish of Floure and Barthélémy Rouanet, priest of Bagès-les-Flots. Abbé Rouanet, who died in 1911, remained in constant contact with Saunière throughout his trial. But nowhere is his intimate knowledge of Saunière's secret better in evidence than in one letter sent in July 1910, in which he urged him to stand fast and not to reveal the source of his money, as it was given in confidence and there was nothing illegal about it: "And now, as a friend, let me tell you that you would do well not to come. Why? Here are the reasons: The charges levelled against you [in the original text, "the things some people want to blame you for"] do not fall under the jurisdiction of the ecclesiastical court, considering that no civil action for fraud or theft has been taken against you. If somebody gave you money under the seal of natural secrecy, you must keep it, and nothing can release you from maintaining this secrecy, except the very person who confided in you, and even in such an event, you have to ponder whether the disclosure you would be allowed to make would result in moral damage, and in this case, you should stay silent. You should not show your account books, the money you spent was neither stolen nor extorted; you have spent it in accordance with your wishes, and nobody has any say whatsoever in that. Something you could do, would be to write a summary along the lines of what I said, and to send it to them. Write it with the utmost serenity, with much dignity and respect. And then, come what may." Another English translation of this document can be found in The Rennes Observer No. 1.2.*

stand it, to study it, is not an easy task and even joining the organisation would only lift a part of its veil. Although the organisation may appear to be very public because of its processions, in truth they remain very private. While they are not present in every town from the Pyrénées-Orientales, where their main seat is at Perpignan, to Saunière's region, everyone in this area is familiar with the movement and all speak of it as if it was a holy institution. They are part of the local religious fabric, ranging from old people who follow their devotions, nuns and priests that are in liaison with them – to the local villagers whose lives are brightened by their festivals. But when we want to discuss the organisation, its memberships, its grades, any type of detail, invariably, the conversation turns into a strange silence and no questions are ever answered. For those who do not know how to contact them, they remain invisible. Outside of the towns in which they have a residence, their presence is only revealed by the existence of certain typical crosses or engravings, but to whom anyone should go to contact them is unknown. Even today, in the age of the Internet, they have donned on a cloak of visibility which is actually throwing more shade on their activities than illumination. Of course, the identity of its members cannot be found out during the procession either, as all are cloaked.

We were most interested to learn about its origins and felt that there was a direct relationship between the organisation and the object they were extremely interested in: the Sacred Tomb of Abdon and Sennen.

From records, we know that the location of the tomb and the neighbouring church and abbey is the site where Castellan founded Arles-les-Bains, as it was originally known. The hermit's cell was placed next to a sulphurous spring and contained an empty tomb, the one we see a few years later in Arles-sur-Tech, our Sacred Tomb. The archives of the abbey state that when the monks transferred from Amélie to Arles in 881, they brought with them a marble tomb, and set it before the principal door of the building.

A key episode occurs when Arnulf was abbot in 957. He went to Rome in an effort to get Pope John XII (955-63) to grant him certain relics. It was in Lent of 960 that he received a vision and during his audience with the Pope, the latter explained to him that the visions he had during the night can be explained: they indicated that the saints Abdon and Sennen needed to be present in Arles-sur-Tech. The pontiff then declared that these relics needed to become the focus of a procession. The two men then apparently entered the Pontian cemetery on the road to Porto, near the gates of Rome, where their bones had apparently been deposited a long time before, although some parts had already been given to certain churches. A fresco found on the sarcophagus that was supposed to contain their remains represented them receiving crowns from Christ. According to Martigny, this fresco dates from the 7th century. Several cities, notably Florence, claim possession of their bodies, although Rome remained their most accepted place of burial – and it was where the Pope and Arnulf got the relics from.

After their gravedigging, Arnulf hastened back to Arles-sur-Tech with the relics. He decided to keep only half of the bones and donated the other half to the abbey of Saint-Médard de Soissons, a town north-east of Paris and thus in the North of France. We note that Saunière's accounts clearly show that he had close and amicable contacts with various religious organisations in Soissons - and this is unlikely to be a coincidence.

After a perilous voyage, Arnulf arrived back in Arles[16] on 24th October 960, just in time for the feast of the Archangel Raphael – to whom all miracles of the Sacred Tomb were ascribed. The congregation decided that on that day, some bones of the saints needed to be thrown into the Sacred Tomb. From then onwards, the tomb was transformed into the tomb, with water gushing out continuously. It cannot be a coincidence that it is the archangel Raphael who is known as the angel who stirs the healing waters and who blesses the thermal springs!

So we see that the miracle of the tomb goes hand in hand with the bones of these two saints. But who were they and why had they been canonised? Abdon and Sennen were of Persian origin, living in the 3rd century AD, officers in the Imperial army of Shapur, the Persian king, and contributed to the fall of the Roman Empire. Shapur had set his sight on Rome, moved on to Antioch and took it by siege. The Roman Emperor Gordian III (238-244) was furious about this act of aggression and directed the Imperial army to march, driving the Persian legions back. High on the success of this relatively minor victory, the army continued its march to Babylonia, where our two princes, Abdon and Sennen, were captured. Both were good friends of Shapur and were therefore treated in a manner befitting their

---

16   One version of this story can be found in Prosper Mérimée, « Notes d'un voyage dans le Midi de la France » ("Notes about a Journey to Southern France"), 1835. For the other one, refer to the regional historical website "Histoire du Roussillon", in the article entitled "Les simiots du Vallespir – Des êtres malfaisants chassés par St Abdon et St Sennen" ("The "Simiots" of the Vallespir Region – Evil Creatures Repelled by Sts. Abdon and Sennen"), which traces the very first written version of the legend back to an unspecified chronicle from the 17th century. (http://histoireduroussillon.free.fr/Decouvrir/Legendes/Simiots.php)

status. They were even allowed to walk about freely and they settled in Cordula, a town in Persia. But just after they had become established, they were accused of heresy: there was suspicion that they performed certain rites upon the bodies of the dead. As a consequence, they were deported to Rome.

Early in 244, the Roman and Sassanian armies met near the city of Misiche (modern Fallujah in Iraq, 40 miles west of Baghdad). Shapur's forces were triumphant and Shapur commemorated his victory with a sculpture and trilingual inscription that claimed that Gordian III was killed in the battle. Roman sources do not mention this battle, indicating instead that Gordian III died near Circesium, along the Euphrates some 250 miles upstream from Peroz-Shapur, and that a cenotaph was built at a location named Zaitha. Philip the Arab, Gordian's successor as Emperor, was universally blamed in these sources for causing Gordian III's death, either directly or by fomenting discontent against the emperor by cutting off the troops' supplies. Philip seems to have reported that the 19-year-old emperor died of an illness.

Philip the Arab decided to keep Abdon and Sennen for a few more years, before setting them free. Succeeded by Decius (249-251), the new ruler became more and more intrigued by the two princes, who now claimed to be Christian. Apparently unwilling to believe their claims, he had them judged and then condemned on charges of Manicheism by the Senate. On 29th July 250, both Persian princes were taken to the Colisseum, where they died at the hands of the gladiators, their bodies dragged around the arena before being thrown at the feet of a statue of God.

Why were such accusations levelled against these princes? Why did such a fate befall these men? Furthermore, what is the discrepancy between these men seen as saints by the Church of Rome, but in their time, considered to be not Christians, but Manicheists?

The answer is simple: as mentioned, Abdon and Sennen were Persian princes, intimate friends of Shapur, the Persian Emperor. In 242, Shapur had met Manes, the leader of the Manichean movement. He had known the princes and the Emperor since 240, when he gave his first public lecture. Shapur became interested in his cult and realised that the ancient doctrine of the Magi needed to be transformed, adapted to the new times, specifically to become more "Christian-like" in appearance. Manes was thus given the opportunity to carry out this religious reform and enlarge his community, all under the auspices of the Emperor. After a few years of preaching, Manicheism became the primary religion of Persia. That Abdon and Sennen were Manicheans upon their arrest and may have continued their faith in Rome thus seems logical.

Abdon and Sennen are "bizarre" saints, to say the least. The veneration paid to them dates from as early as the 3rd century. Their Acts were written for the most part prior to the 9th century, though they contain several fictitious statements about the cause and occasion of their coming to Rome and the nature of their torments. The Acts state that their bodies were buried by a subdeacon, Quirinus, and transferred during the reign of Constantine to the Pontian cemetery on the road to Porto, near the gates of Rome – from whence Arnulf and Pope John XII apparently collected them. Still, how did they come to be seen as Christian martyrs… and what is the link with Arles-sur-Tech?

Chapter 2

Abdon & Sennen, the Manichean saints of La Sanch… and of Bérenger Saunière?

Where does this leave us? In Arles-sur-Tech we have a cult of Abdon and Sennen, who are Christian martyrs, who in their time were considered to be Manicheans. Their local cult became organised by a confraternity of La Sanch, with whom Saunière had an interesting and apparently close relationship. We also find that the cult of Abdon and Sennen was installed in Soissons[17], and we find that Saunière had a link with that town too. In a larger framework, we have observed a connection between La Sanch and other spa towns in the region, including Rennes-les-Bains, which is another source of income for Saunière and a point of interest in his enigma.

To provide the answer as to where all of this will lead us: La Sanch. La Sanch is a Manichean society, which requested – required – a Manichean relic for their worship. That is why the bones of these two saints were transferred to Arles-sur-Tech. But the bones of the saints are not the only Manichean relic or symbol that is of interest to La Sanch; there are a multitude of Manichean and Babylonian symbols and objects present in their "Christian" sanctuaries. What is more: this Babylonian cult still survives today in the Pyrénées-Orientales, at the heart of an organisation that was close to Saunière.

Origins

It may seem strange that the origins of La Sanch are to be found in Persia – Iraq – but that is where Abdon and Sennen came from. And it is an uncontested fact that their relics are linked with the enigma of the Sacred Tomb and are central to the cult of La Sanch. For any doubting Thomas, we invite him to visit the churches in the region; wherever he stumbles upon symbols of La Sanch, he will stumble upon statues of Saint Abdon and Sennen, whether at Arles-sur-Tech, Prats-de-Mollo, Serralongue, Peyrestortes, Perpignan, etc.

    Indeed, La Sanch claims to be Catholic, but in our opinion, La Sanch **is two-faced**: to the outside world, it is piously Catholic, but this hides

---

17   *Soissons is a town located in Northern France, in the Aisne department, Picardy region, just above Paris.*

an inner, darker, medieval organisation that has guarded its Zoroastrian origins. They are a Babylonian island floating in the French district of the Pyrénées-Orientales.

Let us explain. There are two stories about the origins of La Sanch. One is that it originates from the Franciscan order; this is a Roman Catholic order which follows the monastic rule of St. Francis of Assisi (1182 – 4 October 1226). The other story is that it comes from the Dominicans; a contemporary of Francis of Assisi, St. Dominic founded his order in the early 13th century and was given the Augustinian rule by him. It is one of the great orders of mendicant friars that revolutionised religious life in Europe during the High Middle Ages. The Order is famed for its intellectual tradition, having produced many leading theologians and philosophers, but was in its time most famous for combating heresy. As such, in 1542, when Pope Paul III established a permanent congregation staffed with cardinals and other officials, whose task was to maintain and defend the integrity of the faith and to examine and proscribe errors and false doctrines, the Congregation of the Holy Office, now called the Congregation for the Doctrine of the Faith, part of the Roman Curia, became the supervisory body of local Inquisitions.

The Pope appoints one of the cardinals to preside over the meetings. There are usually ten other cardinals on the Congregation, as well as a prelate and two assistants, all chosen from the Dominican Order. If La Sanch is a heresy and if it were to reside within the Dominicans, this would truly be an astonishing revelation – and at the same time almostimpossible to believe.

So, as its origins are unlikely to be Dominican, perhaps they are Franciscan? Francesc Rozalén Igual,[18] in an article published in the official account of the *Fiestas en Honor de la Purísima Concepción de Llíria*[19] stated that there is a confraternity in Llíria, Spain, known as "Blood of Jesus Christ", which, in Catalan is "Sanch". The house in which these Franciscans lived is

---

18   Now a history scholar, author Francesc Rozalén Igual (in Spanish, Francisco Rosalen Igual) graduated in history and geography at the Polytechnic University of Valencia in 1981.
19   This article, which is entitled "Los Franciscanos del convento de Llíria – ¿Impulsores de la Cofradía de la Sangre?" ("The Franciscans of the Convent of Llíria – Instigators of the Confraternity of La Sanch?") was published in the 1997 volume of the "Feasts in Honor of the Immaculate Conception of Llíria" and afterwards its copyright was ceded by Mr. Igual to the La Sanch confraternity of Lliria, and to this day it is still on display on the official website of the brotherhood. (http://www.galeon.com/lasanglliria/colab01.htm).

now called "la Font de San Vicent Ferrer", or "The Fountain of St. Vincent Ferrer" – the saint who founded the Arch-Confraternity of La Sanch in Perpignan. The organisation was founded in 1401 and the confraternity wore hoods and lived in secret, in an ordinary house in the village. Several times a year, they walked around the streets of the town, flagellating themselves. It was a public mortification ritual that covered the streets of the town with their blood.

Igual discovered a document dating from 1574 and deposited in the archives of the kingdom of Valencia[20], which detailed the history of this fraternity and proved that it originated from the Franciscan order. When the order arrived from the Italian town of Assisi, it was said that amongst the community were members of a Manichean weaver sect. The community itself came via Lombardy, from Bulgaria and apparently even from Armenia.

So, all of a sudden, we know that the Franciscans had, amongst their members, a Manichean community. This appears to have been customary practice in Italy, and by 1401, the community was present in Catalonia, where it was known as "La Sanch". We note that France sits between Italy and Spain and to find "La Sanch" in the 15th century in Arles-sur-Tech and Perpignan suddenly fits into a context, but equally begins to take on a heretical connotation. Furthermore, their specific interest in Arles-sur-Tech becomes clear too: the town possessed the bones of two Manicheans (Abdon and Sennen) and the Manichean community would thus have desired to establish themselves in that city - which, as we know, is exactly what they did.

If Manichean worship was – and still is – occurring in the streets and behind closed doors of towns such as Arles-sur-Tech and Perpignan, it is clear why the organisation had and continues to indulge in its extreme devotion to secrecy. In the past, it was key to their survival. Today... who knows?

What remains perplexing, is the attitude of the Franciscan Order. It seems that the Franciscan order grouped these various people together, and gave them statutes. From that period onwards, these confraternities seem to do as they please – which includes practicing their rites in the strictest secrecy.

---

20 This document was first published in 1973 in the book written by Luis Martí Ferrando, another local historian, on the La Sanch confraternity of Llíria. Ferrando also wrote another book on the same subject: "Las fuentes de Liria o font de Sant Vicent" ("The Fountains of Liria, or the Fountain of St. Vincent (Ferrer)", which was published in Valencia in 1981.

Though of Franciscan origins, we also do know why the Dominican Order became "suspect". This was largely due to a Dominican, Vincent Ferrer, who founded La Sanch in Perpignan on 11th October 1416. As elsewhere, Ferrer integrated several heretics within this fraternity, including Cathars and Flagellants. We need to remember that this whole area was a hotbed of Catharism.

In the 13th century, Catharism had driven the pope to despair, forcing him to organise the first and only crusade against a Christian nation. The Papal Army descended on towns like Béziers and Narbonne, demanding the surrender of the Cathars. Béziers was the first city to see the army arrive, demanding the surrender of 222 suspects. When the request was denied, the city was sacked on 22nd July 1209, burning the cathedral of Saint Nazaire, which collapsed on the terrified inhabitants who had taken refuge inside. Béziers was then destroyed and its surviving inhabitants slaughtered. When the first commander of the crusade, the Papal Legate Arnaud Amaury (or Arnald Amalaricus), Abbot of Citeaux, was asked by a Crusader how they should treat the inhabitants of the city (because most of them were Catholics, not Cathars), the abbot famously replied, "Kill them all, God will recognize His own". All were killed – more than 10,000. No surprise therefore that when the army moved on, Narbonne quickly surrendered and most other towns followed. In the end, only some strongholds remained, which became the subject of a second wave of fighting, resulting with the siege of Montségur in 1244. At Montségur, the Cathars were given the option to surrender and embrace Christianity; they preferred to die by fire instead.

Many consider 1244 to be the end of Catharism. In truth, it was the end of the power of Catharism in the region. But the heresy was simply too widespread to wipe out completely; merely its head could be cut down. Thus, various people remained practicing Cathars well into the 14th century, though it seems that in the 15th century, the few remaining clusters of Catharism had died out. Or were they instead incorporated into the Franciscan and Dominican Order?

Bernard Duhourceau[21] has done a detailed study on the history of the Archconfraternity of La Sanch in Perpignan and tells us that *"the origins*

---

21 Bernard Duhourceau, « Guide des Pyrénées Mystérieuses » ("A Guide to the Mysterious Pyrenees"), collection « Les Guides Noirs » ("The Black Guides") Editions Claude Tchou, Paris, 1976. The following quotations can be found in chapter 7 "Mystères et processions" ("Mysteries and Processions"), part 2: "Donner son sang pour celui qu'on aime" ("Giving your blood for the one you love"), paragraphs 4 and 5 of this book.

of La Sanch need to be searched for in the 15ᵗʰ century, when the Schism infested the soul of the people with moral doubts and anxieties. [...] And then a man arrives [in Perpignan] who has a reputation of preaching to the masses, a Dominican from Valencia, Vincent Ferrer." One day, as Vincent was preaching to the masses with his usual vigour. *"an immense procession formed itself, led by his disciples, dressed in the long clothes of penitence and humility."* Soon afterwards, *"on 11ᵗʰ October 1416, in the church of St James, Vincent Ferrer founded the Confraternity of the Precious Blood [...]"* (La Sanch).

It should be underlined that Ferrer's organisation was not "new". What he had specifically accomplished was to unite the two largest confraternities of the region: La Sanch was therefore the union of the "weavers", a profession "infested" by Cathars, and that of the "gardeners", i.e. people who were specialists in vegetation and specifically herbalism.

Heretics

It may seem strange that a pious Christian decided to incorporate heretics in his organisation. From our modern historical perspective, we tend to think that heretics were always burnt at the stake – as they were during the Cathar crusade. But Vincent Ferrer and other preachers had an apostolic mission to convert people to Christianity. They considered themselves to be like the early Christian missionaries, whereby souls were swayed not by the power of the sword, but the power of the word. Of course, conversion to Christianity by default is directed towards people who are not yet Christians and Ferrer directed his efforts primarily towards the Saracens (Spain had been in Arab hands until the 12ᵗʰ century), the Manicheans and the Cathars.

Still, when we say "pious Christian" to describe Ferrer, let us note that he himself was not exempt from accusations of heresy. He was "a penitent flagellant" himself, a man who was half monk and half layman, living with his disciples, and whose mysticism was focused by long periods of mortification. He may have been Christian, but in practice, he was exactly like the Manicheans, flagellating himself in the streets. When the weavers and garderners joined him in the street procession in Perpignan, it was largely because they saw in him one of them.

Pope Clement VI, in his bull "Inter Sollicitudines", dated 19ᵗʰ November 1350, had already spoken out against this flagellant movement as it apparently distressed the clerics. The penitents seemed to be a "reincarnation" of the Cathars, originating as they did from the Cathar regions in Flanders and Central Italy, where they had not been subjected to a crusade, but must have realised that reform was necessary in order to survive. Fifty years later, we find them in the South of France, the former heartland of the Cathar religion, near and in Perpignan, with Ferrer at the helm. Under the direction of Ferrer, large processions were organised, and soon, the streets were full of people dressed in the now infamous "cagoules" (hoods with eye holes), flagellating themselves, sometimes to the brink of death (hence the term mortification)… if not actually into that realm.

The issue of flagellation occurred within a larger framework: a Schism within the Church. The Council of Constance (1414-1418) was organised to end the Papal schism which had resulted from the Avignon Papacy, or as it is sometimes known, the "Babylonian Captivity of the Church". In the history of the Roman Catholic Church, the Avignon Papacy was the period from 1309 to 1377 during which seven popes, all French, resided in the French city of Avignon. In 1378, Gregory XI moved the papal residence back to Rome. But due to a dispute over the election of his successor, a faction of cardinals set up an anti-pope back in Avignon.

Although the Council of Constance dismantled the last vestiges of the Avignon papacy, we cannot treat the episode as a one-liner. For one, we note that the foundation of La Sanch occurred in 1416, in the middle of the Council's existence. In 1415, at about the same time as the Council was in operation, a popular book on how to die, *Ars Moriendi* (The Art of Dying), was published. It offered advice on the protocols and procedures of a good death and on how to "die well", according to Christian precepts of the late Middle Ages. It was written within the historical context of the effects of the macabre horrors of the Black Death sixty years earlier and the consequent social upheavals of the 15th century. But we should also note that the Cathars were renowned for a specific methodology of dying, with a rite known as the consolamentum, and that the mortifications of the penitent movement were gaining popularity and fame and thus required an admonition from the Pope.

In theory, the Council of Constance was there to mediate, but in practice, to end the Avignon line. Vincent Ferrer was in the Avignon camp, first supporting Clement VII and then Benedict XIII, or Pedro de Luna, a fellow Catalan, who had to flee Avignon and lived in Perpignan at the time. In 1417, the Council, advised by the theologian Jean Gerson, deposed John XXII and the Avignon Pope Benedict XIII, secured the formal resignation of the Roman Pope Gregory XII (who had abdicated in 1415), and elected Pope Martin V, thereby ending the Schism and recognising the line of Roman popes as the legitimate line.

But before this outcome, the Council had also observed that despite such agreements at the top of the church, the heretics might ruin the Church as an entity, preaching, as they were, for a society that had neither a clergy nor priests. Hence, the Council condemned Vincent Ferrer, a condemnation that was no doubt the result of his religious doctrine and his political alliance. On cue, several erudite scholars spoke out against what they called "Maniacal" movements, reusing the terms that previous centuries had used against the Manicheans, thus seeding public antipathy against Ferrer and the heretics.

Again it was Jean Gerson[22] who was one of the severest critics of Vincent Ferrer and La Sanch. He was the great theologian of the University of Paris and scandalised by the sect "which infects the Languedoc". He wrote a discourse to Ferrer[23], in which he accused him of practicing "cruel rites" as well as "not respecting God's Law" and also of keeping bad company – which must have implied Pope Benedict XIII, but may have implied others.

Fast forward five centuries, to the time of Saunière (i.e. the end of the 19th century) and the confraternity had hardly changed. It clung jealously to its dogma and its rites, and had not abandoned anything of its ancient doctrine. Although it may seem to have abandoned its obedience to Manicheism, they appear to have merely added an Oriental Christian veneer, but at its core, nothing had changed – merely the packaging. The processions were also going to rediscover their initial zeal and slide into morbidity. To once again quote from Bernard Duhourceau[24]: *"the exhibition of symbols of death multiplied, creating ambiguous sentiments: the penitents walked around with skulls, with panels bearing 'Memento Moris'[25], with plates filled with ashes... But the most attended spectacle, the most troubling and most violent, was the sight of the Flagellants, their faces hidden by their hoods, the naked torso, whipping themselves with cords laced with iron. [...] blood ran over their skin. The cries of the masses mixed with liturgical*

---

22 Jean Charlier de Gerson, "Epistola ad Vincentium. Tractatus contra sectam flagel-lantium" ("Letter to Vincent. Treatise against the sect of the Flagellants"), se. Opera, Dupin editions, vol. 2, p. 658, 660.

23 Ibid.

24 Bernard Duhourceau, « Guide des Pyrénées Mystérieuses » ("A Guide to the Mysterious Pyrenees"), collection « Les Guides Noirs » ("The Black Guides") Editions Claude Tchou, Paris, 1976. The following quotation is an excerpt of chapter 7 "Mystères et processions" ("Mysteries and Processions"), part 4 "Le goût du sang" ("The taste of blood"), paragraph 1.

25 Traditional text as admonishing you to "remember that you are going to die".

chants, accompanied by the "coblas" of the famous "goigs"[26]. *The lights of the torches and candles illuminated the poignant images of the "misteris"*[27] *[...]. The procession, which only stopped at daybreak, revealed the atmosphere of the old oriental cults and their erotic cruelty. The penitents, dressed in red, evoked the adepts of Mithras emerging from their pits, covered in the red boiling blood of the divine bulls sacrificed over their head."*

This description is far from what we see in the streets today. Today, there are no more flagellations, just men walking in a procession, carrying their relics, while totally unidentifiable. It is the Church that forbade the public flagellations and what today seems to be nothing more than an expression of good Catholics walking through the streets of town with their Christian relics, in previous century had an entirely different atmosphere... and a not so Christian message.

Duhourceau also suggests that the origin of these flagellants is Oriental, linking it with the cult of Mithras. Mithras was the central god of Mithraism, a syncretic Hellenistic mystery religion of male initiates that developed in the Eastern Mediterranean in the 2nd and 1st centuries BC and which was practiced in the Roman Empire from the 1st century BC to the 5th century AD.

The name Mithras is the Greek masculine form of Mithra, the Persian god, who was the mediator between Ahura Mazda and the earth: he was the guarantor of human contracts. Like Manicheism, Mithraism was therefore of Persian origin and four centuries older than Manicheism. When Manicheism was born in Persia, the cult of Mithras was very popular in the West, with temples of Mithras found throughout the Empire. Today, ruined temples exist in Rome, London and along Hadrian's Wall, east of the English city of Newcastle.

Duhourceau was not alone in observing a "heretical" component in these processions. This non-Christian element did not escape the attention of the bishop of Perpignan, Monseigneur Gouy, who forbade the procession and the activities of La Sanch in 1777. Both procession and organisation would not be allowed again until they were sanctioned by Monseigneur

---

26   *"Coblas" is the Catalan word referring to the groups of singers who chant the "goigs", i.e the traditional Catalan songs featured in these processions.*
27   *'Mysteries': such is the name of the large and heavy wood carvings and scenes carried by the penitents, depicting moments from the life of Christ.*

Leuillieux[28], who was Saunière's first bishop[29]. Leuillieux did not hide his sympathy for the fraternity and became an Honorary Canon of the church of St. James in Perpignan, the headquarters of La Sanch[30]. In the rear sacristy there remains a commemorative stone showing his link with their cause[31].

Blue Penitents

"La Sanch" is part of the penitent movement, which is pan-European. The name "penitent" has come to cover several different ideas. Penance or penitence comes from the Old French "penance", from the Latin "poenitentia". It means repentance, the desire to be forgiven of sins, and the willingness to suffer whatever is necessary to obtain such forgiveness. In medieval times, a penitent was repentant for the life he led before he found the Christian god, doing penitence for his previous errors. Heretics who repented by default fell into this category: they had turned away from their sinful life, towards a religious life, which normally meant a life inside a religious community.

Penitent people – those who have seen the error of their previous life – are unlikely to be found in only one place and hence why their presence is pan-European. At one point, a town like Narbonne would have had several penitent movements. One of these was the "Blue Penitents", who guarded the tombs of the dead and the cemeteries. When Saunière entered the Seminary in Narbonne in 1870, it is more than likely that he came across members of this organisation. We have no way of knowing whether he became a member, but we do know that several of his closest friends were very close to this movement... abbé Boudet, for example.

---

28   François-de-Sales Albert Leuillieux was archbishop of Chambéry before he was appointed bishop of Carcassonne by decree of 16th December 1872. Rennes-le-Château was under his jurisdiction.

29   During his career as priest of Rennes-le-Château, Saunière had to report into three different bishops. Monseigneur Leuillieux, bishop of Carcassonne, was his first superior, followed by Monseigneur Billard, then Monseigneur de Beauséjour.

30   Since Mgr. Leuillieux became an honorary member of La Sanch shortly after his nomination as bishop, we can assume that his reauthorization of the full outdoor processions of La Sanch should date back to the very beginning of his episcopate, possibly even the first months. Furthermore, the penitential tradition was far from dead in Mgr. Leuillieux's time, since a small version of the La Sanch procession had already been re-established in Perpignan a long time before, as early as December 1790. However, it used to take place strictly behind the closed doors of the Eglise St. Jacques (Church of St. James), since the flagellants were forbidden to go out.

31   Vapereau, « Dictionnaire des Contemporains » ("A Dictionary of the Contemporaries"), 1893.

Boudet was very interested in Narbonne, specifically its history and its religious past. But it is his good friend, the priest of Alet-les-Bains, Joseph-Théodore Lasserre, who was a frequent and long-time visitor to the penitent confraternities. Most of his family were members. François Lasserre, one of his direct ancestors, was in fact Prior of the Blue Penitents of Narbonne and was involved in a bizarre incident. As French researcher André Douzet has noted, this group seems to have been involved in a strange episode that occurred in Notre-Dame de Marceille, just outside of Limoux, at the time of the French Revolution. At that time, an inventory of the basilica of Notre-Dame de Marceille was taken, so that the new authorities could sell off its contents. The most prized possession of the church was the Black Madonna, a precious relic that continues to be the centre of intense devotion.

It was during this tumultuous time that a "penitent", dressed in his normal habit, stole the Black Madonna. He – or she; how could one tell? – was seen running with the statue, before disappearing into the middle of a field into what must have been a tunnel, known only to this person. A search afterwards did not, however, reveal the entrance. But what is more interesting to us here is that shortly afterwards, the Black Madonna made a sudden reappearance… she was found in the personal coffer of François Lasserre. It suggests that Lasserre was involved with the theft of this incredibly important artefact. Why did he steal it? Did he try to save it from being sold off? Did the statue play an important role in the religious life of the Blue Penitents? These are questions that need to be answered.

But the most interesting part is yet to come, for the vicar of Notre-Dame de Marceille, César Brudinou, who himself was leader of a confraternity of Blue Penitents (of Saint Bertrand de Comminges), insinuates, in a short report, that the site itself – Notre Dame de Marceille – was apparently a sanctuary of the sect. He speaks about how in the underground tunnels and rooms that sit beneath the basilica "strange things" went on. He also notes that during a period of 21 days, three people had worked continuously inside the church.

Douzet has picked up this trail. He found out that the work that needed to be carried out was to the crypts and various other subterranean "aspects" of the church. It turns out that the people who were performing this work did so voluntarily, as part of a "penance". But what is intriguing, is that they came from Italy and asked if they could work without any interruption. It meant that they did not speak the local language, and that they had no contact with the local community. It means that the secret of the layout and the extent of the underground network were not divulged to the local people; no "leaks" of information occurred. It means that a basilica like Notre-Dame de Marceille was better known by a penitent movement than by the local villagers!

Henri Boudet himself was very interested in this site. In his work, *History of the Pilgrimage of Notre-Dame de Marceille*,[32] Lasserre often quotes his friend Boudet and his work. In fact, it seems that Boudet had done a vast amount of research on the site and that Lasserre's work could not have been accomplished without his friend's involvement. Some authors have even queried whether Boudet himself might have written large sections of Lasserre's book.

If Lasserre and Boudet frequented the penitent groups, they must have possessed specific information about these groups' activities. And if Boudet knew, it is possible that he spoke about it to his friend Saunière. It would form the second inroad, after Grassaud and Arles-sur-Tech, of Saunière's exposure, either knowing or unknowing, to the penitent movement.

"Penitence, Penitense"

There are other clues which lead us to the conclusion that Saunière knew about the penitent movement – and was if not a member, then at least sympathetic to them. At the base of the altar in his church, he added the following inscription: "JESU MEDELA VULNERUM + SPES UNA PO-ENITENTIUM + PER MAGDALENAE LACRYMAS + PECCATA NOS-TRA DILUAS", which means: "Jesus, cure for the injuries + sole hope of the penitents + through the tears of the Magdalene + erase our sins". Above, we see a depiction of Mary Magdalene praying inside a cave, in front of a cross, with a human skull at her feet. The altar piece has become one of the key ingredients in the mystery of Saunière... but few have noted that it may be the inscription underneath that holds the answer.

It is not the only reference to penitence and a "unique hope" that Saunière used in his work. Elsewhere, just outside of his church, there is a statue of the Virgin Mary, sitting on what is said to be a pillar of Visigothic origins. On top of the pillar, we can read "PENITENCE, PENITENSE!" Indeed, Saunière is "screaming it out": Penitence, penitence!

These are key indications that Saunière and penitence were no strangers to

---

32   *Joseph-Théodore Lasserre, « Histoire du Pèlerinage de Notre-Dame de Marceille »*
("History of the Pilgrimage of Notre-Dame de Marceille"), 1891. Duplicated in fac-sim: Impr. C. Lacour, published by RediViva, Nîmes, 1998.

one another. But we do not know whether he was a member of a penitent fraternity, or a member of the Archconfraternity of La Sanch. If – IF – he was, is it possible that he stumbled upon a secret? Was it their secret? Is this perhaps the true origin of his fortune? If so, what type of secret was it? Was it a secret linked with the Cathars?

In whatever scenario we follow, we know what the next step of the story is: after visiting Saunière in 1906, his bishop, Mgr. de Beauséjour, ordered him to open up his accounts. De Beauséjour was trying to follow the money, to see where it was coming from. And for Saunière, it was therefore vital to make sure that de Beauséjour would never lay his hands on his true accounts, for that would mean that the bishop could consequently piece everything together – which is actually what we are doing here. And we know that in his efforts to block this investigation, Saunière was helped by the penitent organisations… as always. Still, this does not give us the answer as to what was truly going on. In our search for answers, let us delve deeper into La Sanch and their customs.

Bernard Duhourceau[33] states that La Sanch practises particular if not peculiar rituals. In Perpignan, those that were condemned to die were placed inside the church of St. James, where they passed the night before their execution in the company of these penitents. La Sanch was there to comfort those who were on death row, preparing them for their demise. On the morning of the execution, the penitents dressed themselves in a "red cape" and hid their faces with the customary "cagoule" (a hood, originally made out of hemp cloth, and pierced with two holes for the eyes). They then accompanied the condemned person to his execution, while asking money from the crowds. It appears that this money was used to pay for a tomb for the condemned soul, as well as to fill the coffers of the fraternity. That money was used for other services, which in essence involved organising the burials of people who would otherwise not be buried.

Is there something in these practices that Saunière could have used – or abused – to make money, in one form or another? From the sort of relationships that the priest had with hospitals and monasteries, could it be that Saunière recouped the money to perform such burial rites? Religious hospitals, at that time, attracted the very ill and the dying. Saunière was

---

33   Bernard Duhourceau, « Guide des Pyrénées Mystérieuses » ("A Guide to the Mysterious Pyrenees"), Tchou editions. Refer to chapter 7 "Mystères et processions" (Mysteries and Processions), part 3 "Le vêtement d'infamie" ("The garment of infamy"), paragraphs 1 to 5.

in regular contact with such institutions, as we can see from his accounts. And whenever he wrote to one, he seemed to get money in return. Could it be that Saunière assured those that were dying a death in conformity with their desires? And did he receive fees for burial rites from them?

Let us summarise what we are implying: certain people had set money aside for their funerals. Some of these people entrusted this to a religious hospital: they would take care of the ill person, until he died, and then bury him. La Sanch had originally practiced this service for those that were condemned to death: they stayed with the condemned in the period before their death, accompanied them to their execution, at which time they were "paid" by the watching crowds. They then used the money to bury the corpse afterwards. Did Saunière write to these various institutions, asking whether anyone in their hospitals had requested a special type of preparation for their death? If so, did he inform the hospital that he would take care of these "details", which may have involved guidance for the deceased, as well as taking care of the burial? Or saying masses after a person's death? If he did, then the hospitals would indeed transfer money to Saunière, for it was he, and no longer the hospital, that was in charge of the funds that had been set aside by the ill or dying for this service.

Let us add that this type of "service" was also practiced by the Cathars. They had priests – known as "perfects" – who travelled the breadth and width of the country, performing this function. One of their main tasks was to perform a rite for the dying, the consolamentum, which was the immediate preparation for death – and thus similar to the "services" La Sanch offered.

Chapter 3

The Sanch and the Tau

Saunière may be part of a mystery that is now synonymous with Southern France, Rennes-le-Château having become a new pilgrimage site, but a century ago, there was only one truly major enigma in the region: the mystery of the sacred tomb of Arles-sur-Tech. This was, as mentioned, the alleged tomb of Abdon and Sennen, a sarcophagus, sitting just outside the main entrance to the church of the town. It has a capacity of 331 litres and could indeed have contained a body at one time.

The sarcophagus is dated to 260 AD. On one side, it has an emblem made up of two Greek letters: the khi (X) cut across by the iota (I). This emblem is also known as a "Rho". Specialists have therefore concluded that this symbol indicates that the tomb belonged to a Christian person; the Rho emblem, they argue, signifies "Christos" or "Ichtus". But let us note that there is no cross on the tomb and that apart from the inscription, there is nothing that could lead one to conclude that it is a Christian tomb. To find such a sepulchre in this region dating from 260 AD would mean that this was a very early Christian artefact – Constantine had not yet made Christianity the official religion of the Roman Empire. In short: if the symbol on its side turned out not to be Christian, neither could the sarcophagus be classified any longer as a Christian tomb.

It should therefore not come as a surprise that we strongly disagree with the consensus view that the symbol shown on the side is the combination of the letters Khi and Iota; we argue that the sign is actually another symbol, namely "Tau". The Tau is a special type of cross shaped like the letter T[34]. It is commonly believed to have originated in Egypt, but experts such as Félix Lajard[35] argue that the symbol comes in fact from Mesopotamia. Regardless of the location of its origins, everyone agrees that it is a very ancient symbol, predating Christianity. Because it is so old, it is found within

---

34   *Another very common form of the Tau cross is the ansate cross (ankh). The T-shaped Tau cross is also called "Cross of St. Francis", a reference to its extensive use by St. Francis of Assisi and the Franciscan monks during the Middle Ages.*

35   *The opinions of Félix Lajard and M. Letronne (both erudite scholars from the 19th century, members of the French "Académie Royale des Inscriptions et Belles-Lettres" – Royal Academy of Inscriptions and Letters) were taken from Daniel Castille's « La Croix Ansée et le Livre de l'Invisible Divin » ("The Ansate Cross and the Book of the Divine Invisible"), published in 2002 by Ediru. The work tackles the Persian and Babylonian origins of the ansate cross, i.e. the Tau, which is improperly believed to be solely Egyptian in nature (the "ankh" hieroglyph).*

various cultures and religions, including a Christian context.

In short, we have one symbol, the Tau, but depending on an Egyptian, Babylonian or Christian context, it has a different meaning. To make the matter even more complex: it is easy to confuse the Tau symbol with the monogram of Christ, IX – as we believe has occurred in Arles-sur-Tech.

The Persian triad

Within a Babylonian context, the Tau is the symbol of the Persian triad, known as Mihir, which is made up from the deities Ormazd, Ahriman and Mithra. It is one of the most ancient symbols archaeologists have discovered and can be found on several Babylonian depictions. Like the Christian Holy Ghost, the Mihir was also represented as a white dove, with its wings spread, on top of which sat a human being, identified as the god Baal. Over time, this complex symbol was simplified, specifically for inclusion within the cuneiform script, to a simple sign, i.e. Tau.

To quote Félix Lajard and M. Letronne (both members of the Académie Royale des Inscriptions)[36]: *"When we see, on the Assyrian cylinders, an ansate cross in front of two Magi, and in the hand of the initiate, the novice, we observe the intermediary symbol between the ansate cross (ankh) and the cuneiform tetragram, are we not tempted to conclude that this transformation from the [ansate cross] to the emblem of the divine triad was the subject of an education that the initiate received from the Magi?"* Thus the authors link the sign, Mihir, or the Tau cross, with the Babylonian Magi, i.e. the Babylonian priesthood. As the quotation suggests, the Babylonian religion allowed for an initiation, at the hands of the Magi, in which the initiate is believed to have acquired the skills to transform himself into a "divine person", learning the secrets of the Magi – and the Babylonian gods, in which the Holy Triad were of course the most important deities.

The symbol for this triad, the Mihir, took the form of four cuneiform characters, which was later modified into a single sign, the Tau... or the symbol that is represented on the side of the sarcophagus of Abdon and Sennen in Arles-sur-Tech.

Can it be a coincidence that a Babylonian representation of the Tau cross is found on the sarcophagus of Persian princes? It seems highly unlikely. But it also implies that the person(s) responsible for depositing the relics of these "Christian" martyrs in this sarcophagus was familiar with Persian iconography. Finally, we note that this is a "miraculous" tomb, because

---

36   *Ibid.*

of the water that gushes out from it. In ancient times, miracles were the bailiwick of the magicians, such as the Babylonian Magi, from whom the name "magician" actually originates. Is this yet another coincidence or is it evidence that a Babylonian magical tradition existed – or exists – in Arles-sur-Tech and that the arrival of the bones of our two Persian princes may have been in response to a specific desire of the local pagan magicians?

It is also important to underline that the Tau was associated with the dove, which was the symbol of the Persian triad – centuries before it became associated with the Holy Ghost. The dove was a Persian symbol of initiation. It was therefore linked with the Chaldaean Magi, which links it in turn with Manicheism, the followers of Mani. As the dove is also a well-known Christian symbol, it is understandable that confusion has arisen over the centuries as to what is and what is not Christian. It is also easy to understand how a Babylonian cult in Southern France could easily hide behind and within Christianity, using symbols that on the surface appear to be purely Christian, but which turn out to be in fact Babylonian – magical.

The Tau was seen as the symbol of a baptismal ceremony. This was the case in Egypt and in Babylon, but equally within a Christian context; there are numerous examples in Christian iconography in which we see the white dove flying above the head of Jesus when he is baptised by John the Baptist in the waters of the river Jordan. To quote Félix Lajard again on the Babylonian tradition: *"As such, we have proof that with the Chaldaeans, Assyrians and Persians, the act of baptism carried with it the idea of a purification, made efficient through the intervention of the Persian Triad and the Tau."*[37]

Where does this leave La Sanch? Why did La Sanch decide to use this symbol, the Tau? To answer this question, we need to add that in certain parts of ancient Egypt, the Tau was seen as the symbol of purification. Purification is specifically linked with water – baptism. We note that one form of the Egyptian ansate cross is the Ankh, which resembles the Tau. The Ankh is often seen as a visual representation of the Nile – the divine river. Elsewhere, we have traditions that it represents the river Ganges, in India. This connection with water – and the miracle of water – is present in Arles-sur-Tech with the miraculous – watery – tomb of Abdon and Sennen. But such a connection is equally present in all thermal towns, where the "miracle of the water" cured the sick – a magical act if ever there was one. That follow-

---

37   Daniel Castille, « La Croix Ansée et le Livre de l'Invisible Divin » ("The Ansate Cross and the Book of the Divine Invisible"), Editions Ediru, 2002.

ers of an ancient, magical tradition would thus want to be present in spa towns, suddenly takes on a "pagan logic".

In conclusion, the central message is that there is a close relationship between the Tau, the dove and water, specifically "curative water". Let us not forget that of all spa towns in Southern France, it is the tomb of Abdon and Sennen in Arles-sur-Tech that stood out for its magical curative powers: they were held to be responsible for healing the young Abdon, the sick child who was raised by Marie Dénarnaud and Bérenger Saunière. And if there was any remaining doubt as to whether the sign on the side of the sarcophagus is the Ichtus or the Tau, it is clear that this is more than likely to be a Tau. It was, after all, that symbol – and not the Ichtus – that was primarily linked with the power of healing through miraculous waters.

During the procession of La Sanch through the streets of Arles-sur-Tech, the participants held up a cross in the form of a Tau, in memory of Sts. Abdon and Sennen. Photographs of this cross exist and it shows a peculiar circle, into which a spiral is fashioned – the symbol of the labyrinth. Another photograph shows another cross, with the same spiral circle on top, but having a small Tau cross on its side. The labyrinth is therefore another key ingredient in the symbolism of La Sanch.

In our opinion, there is even a connection between the name of the town and the Tau: Arles-sur-Tech, or Arles-sur-Tau? The comparison may seem to test the frontiers of logic, but let us try to explain. There are three main rivers in the Pyrénées-Orientales: the Agly, the Têt and the Tech. The Tech runs through what is now known as Vallespir, the "Wild Valley" (Valles Espirium in Latin) and is born from various small streams at the foot of the Eoque-Colomb, near the Spanish-French border. "Eoque-Colomb" is ancient Catalan and means "The Waters of the Dove". It is quite a coincidence that of all possible names, the source of La Tech is linked with the dove... and hence with the Tau.

Is it possible that Arles-sur-Tech was a town where a pagan cult of Babylonian origin was present before the arrival of Christianity? Did the pagan cult continue to exist after the arrival of Christianity, and continue to live on through La Sanch? It is a distinct possibility, seeing that the enigmatic tomb dates from 260 AD and thus predates the arrival of Christianity in the region. Before the coming of Christian missionaries, did missionaries from other religions arrive in the region from the East?

By this sign – Tau – you will conquer

Let us return to Saunière. In his desire to decorate his church, he placed a hideous devil just at the church entrance. A stoup was placed on top of the devil, which itself is surmounted by four angels, who together make the sign of the cross; below is an inscription: *"By this sign you will conquer him."*

Gérard de Sède, in his book *The Accursed Treasure of Rennes-le-Château*[38], observed that *"we can feel that this strange, artificial assembly of pieces that fit together uneasily, is a sort of hieroglyph."* The use of the word "hieroglyph" is intriguing, for this group of statues is indeed a "hieroglyph" – made up from various parts that together form a whole.

The devil in question is Asmodeus, who is a character that we find in the apocryphal and Chaldean book of Tobit; he is a demon, sometimes linked with treasure, but more often linked with King Solomon. The stoup holds the "holy water", surmounted by the four angels symbolising the cross. On a basic level, the composition thus suggests that by making the cross, by placing our hand in the holy water of the stoup, we will conquer evil – the demon.

"By this sign you will conquer" is a very famous quote, addressed by an angel to the Roman Emperor Constantine. With Galerius' death in 311 AD, a power vacuum was left amongst the Roman emperors, leaving them to struggle for dominance. In the East, Licinius and Maximinus Daia fought for supremacy, while in the West, Constantine began a war with Maxentius. In 312 AD, Constantine invaded Italy. Maxentius is believed to have had up to four times as many troops, although they were largely inexperienced and undisciplined. Brushing aside the opposition in battles at Augusta Taurinorum (Turin) and Verona, Constantine marched on Rome. After the campaign, he claimed to have had a vision on the way to Rome, during the night before battle. In this dream, he supposedly saw the "Chi-Ro" shining above the sun. Seeing this as a divine sign, it is said that Constantine had his soldiers paint the symbol on their shields. He went on to defeat the numerically stronger army of Maxentius at the Battle at the Milvian Bridge; Maxentius, together with thousands of his soldiers, drowned when the bridge of boats that his force used when he was retreating collapsed.

Constantine saw this victory as directly related to the vision he had had the night before and thus saw himself as the Emperor of the "Christian people". Christians have seen Constantine as a Christian, although historians

---

38   Gérard de Sède, « Le Trésor Maudit de Rennes-le-Château », "J'ai Lu" editions (1972). *For the English translation, refer to "The Accursed Treasure of Rennes-le-Chateau", DEK Publishing, 2001, translated by Bill Kersey.*

argue that he was only baptised on his deathbed. Instead, it seems that Constantine was the first Roman Emperor who did not persecute Christians, but allowed them to live and practice their religion. But it is dangerous to swing too much the other way, for he definitely did not abolish the other religions. In particular, the worship of the sun god remained closely related with him for some time to come, as can be seen on the carvings of his triumphal Arch in Rome and on several coins minted during his reign.

The story of the sign by which Constantine conquered was reported by Eusebius of Caesarea[39] in *The life of Constantine*[40] and the well-known Lactantius[41], who provide further detail: the night before Constantine's victory, when the future emperor is lying in his tent, a powerful light exploded in the sky. An angel hung high over the Sovereign and slowly descended towards him, surrounded by a reddish light. It was the heavenly creature that gave him a message: *"With this sign you will conquer."* The symbol, declared Lactantius, was a very ancient pagan symbol, an X intertwined with an I, shaped like a P on top.[42] So is this the "Chi-ro"? No. It is exactly the same symbol as the inscription that is carved on the grave of Saints Abdon and Sennen in Arles-sur-Tech. It is the XI, the old Mihir, the sign from which the Tau evolved.

Christians can interpret it any way they want to, but Constantine was a "pagan" emperor, a follower of a solar cult, the cult of Sol Invictus, a monotheistic form of sun worship that originated in Syria. The cult of Sol Invictus (the Undefeated Sun) was a comparatively late (3rd century BC) arrival from the East (Syria) and became the chief Imperial cult of the Roman Empire, until it was replaced by Christianity. In the interests of unity, Constantine deliberately chose to blur the distinction between Christianity, Mithraism and Sol Invictus. This is the reason why Constantine decreed that Sunday, "the venerable day of the sun", would be the official day of rest. Early Christians had celebrated their holy day on the Jewish Sabbath, Saturday. The celebration of Jesus' birthday was moved from January 6 (Epiphany today) to December 25, which was celebrated by the cult of Sol Invictus as Natilis Invictus, the rebirth of the sun. In the old calendar, the winter solstice fell on December 25, so this was the day on which the

---

39   *Eusebius (c.260-340 AD), Bishop of Caesarea, is considered to be the greatest early Church historian. His illustrious work "Ecclesiastical History and Chronicle" is one of the main sources of early Church history.*
40   *Eusebius of Caesarea, "Vita Constantini" ("Life of Constantine").*
41   *Lucius Caecilius Firmianus Lactantius, "Of the Manner in which the Persecutors Died".*
42   *Ibid.*

sun proved itself to be yet undefeated

We need to underline furthermore that the cult of angels is not typically Christian, however much angels have become part of the fabric of this doctrine; rather, it is pagan in origin, and specifically, it is Babylonian, where they were seen as messengers of the gods. Constantine's religious allegiance was thus a mixture of various religions. And what applied to him, also applied to his family, who had largely become Manichean. So it is absolutely normal to find the Chaldaean X intertwined with an I, shaped like a P on top, as being seen by Constantine in a dream. Finally, at the end of his life, Constantine was baptized by the Manichean Eusebius of Nicomedia. We emphasise that everything connected to this monogram can be explained through the Manichean doctrine, and thus fits with the worship of the Chaldaean Magi.

So where does this leave us in Rennes-le-Château? It is clear that Saunière was familiar with the legend of Constantine. He used the expression "By this sign you will conquer" and linked it with the sign of the cross, which is made by four angels; it corresponds with the vision of Constantine seeing an angel make a sign and stating that it is by that sign that he will conquer. But Constantine's sign was not the cross; at best, it was the Chi-Ro. The sign is made by four angels and the presence of four angels is exclusive to the Book of Enoch.

The Book of Enoch is a title given to several works that attribute themselves to Enoch, the great-grandfather of Noah.[43] Most commonly, the Book of Enoch refers to 1 Enoch, which only exists as a whole in the Ethiopian language, though a copy of the Book was retrieved amongst the Dead Sea Scrolls. It is known that the Book was once very impotant, but it does not form part of the Canon of Scripture for the larger Christian Churches.

There is a tradition that Enoch hid the texts of his prophecies inside one or more pillars. Is it just a coincidence that the "official legend" states that Saunière found his coded parchments inside a pillar and that their decypherment guided him to his wealth? The identity of one of these angels is Raphael. And does this therefore mean that "the sign" they make is perhaps not the Christian cross, but the Tau? We need to underline that the Penitent movement used – and uses – "I.H.S.", "In Hoc Signo (Vinces)", which is Latin for "By this sign (you will conquer)" as its motto[44]. Is this

---

43   There are also three other characters named Enoch in the Bible: the son of Cain (Gen. 4:17), the son of Midian (Gen. 25:4), and the son of Reuben (Gen. 46:9; Ex. 6:14). The last two are transcribed "Hanoch" in the modern translations.

44   Refer to the chapter "A Concise Guide to the Penitent Symbolism" for further details

just a coincidence?

The Tau, i.e. "X, I interlaced with P", is a prominent sign on other monuments in Rennes-le-Château: on the grave of Marie de Negri d'Ables, the wife of François D'Hautpoul, Marchioness of Blanchefort, Lord of Rennes. It is this tomb, together with coded parchments recovered from a pillar, which is said to have been a key indicator for Saunière in his efforts to "find the treasure". Intriguingly, in the inscription on the tombstone, her name was carved as "Noble Lady of Arles" and not the expected "Noble Lady of Ables" – an intriguing reference to Arles-sur-Tech perhaps? We must also note that the first name of this noble lady was Marie, and this we could read "Marie of Arles", which is the name of the Sainte-Marie abbey of Arles-sur-Tech.

According to de Sède, the other stone on her tomb had the inscription "ET IN ARCADIA EGO", which is the inscription which we also find on the tomb in Nicolas Poussin's painting *The Arcadian Shepherds* (1638). This inscription is only found in four places: this Poussin painting, on the tomb of Marie d'Ables, on a monument in Shughborough Hall (England), and on a painting by Guercino, dating from 1618.

Intriguingly, Poussin made two versions of *The Arcadian Shepherds*. In the first version, done in 1627, there is no such inscription. Instead, there is a group of shepherds that find a tomb, whilst a third shepherd sits at the foot of the sarcophagus, pouring water! Is it possible that the artist was inspired by the tomb of Abdon and Sennen in Arles-sur-Tech, out of which miraculous waters gush as well.

But back to Marie's tomb. Three letters on her grave's inscription stand out from the rest: PAX – peace in Latin. But PAX is also the name given to the composition of the symbol "X,I", present in Arles-sur-Tech and seen by Constantine in his vision. When we re-read Lactantius' description[45]: "*The angel gave this sign, a composition of an X and an I, slightly curved in the shape of a P in its extremity.*" We get XP or XI, which is the sign we usually call PAX, as PX was the abbreviation.

The archangel Raphael

It is essential to recall that around 960 AD, in the abbey of Arles-sur-Tech, after a long and difficult journey, the abbot Arnulf placed the relics of our

---

about the I.H.S. acronym.

45   *Lucius Caecilius Firmianus Lactantius, "Of the Manner in Which the Persecutors Died".*

two Saints, Abdon and Sennen, in the sacred tomb[46]. It was October 24, the feastday of the Archangel Raphael, and it is on this day that we see the water gushing out of this sepulchre. The stoup, similar to a baptismal font, is a typical symbol of Raphael, the angel of the healing springs, and of Arles-sur-Tech's "sweating" tomb.

On the feastday of the Archangel, October 24, the Roman breviary says: *"Saint Raphael, Archangel - When praying in tears, he declared to Tobit* (Apocryphal book of Tobit, Vulgate) *'you hid the deceased during the day in your house and during the night buried them; it is I who has submitted your prayer to the Lord.' Tobit became blind because of this pratice, and the loss of his sight, according to Saint Augustine, resulted for this old man in the blessing of receiving the visit of an angelic doctor: St. Raphael was indeed sent, like the angel who comes to stir the waters at the Probatic pool, to cure Tobit. The reading of the day is from the book of Tobit: Tob. XII, 7-15."*

This text cleverly shows a link between Tobit and Abdon and Sennen: Tobit became blind because he buried the dead, apparently performing a forbidden rite. Was this rite similar to the rites performed by Abdon and Sennen, who were sentenced to death by the Roman Emperor for performing rituals upon the dead? The reason for the court's rage regarding Abdon and Sennen's actions is well known: they performed a ritual that was inspired by a Manichean procedure, having "secretly buried corpses under the walls of their native city, Babylon, making use of a horrible burial rite."

So, Tobit and Abdon and Sennen share much in common, including the Archangel Raphael. The name Tobit may well come from the expression "Tau Obitus", which in Latin means "Dead Tau", "Deceased Tau", "Tau in Decomposition", "Putrefying Tau" and thus explains perfectly the nature of the rites that Tobit performed. Tobit hid and buried the deceased in his home, but he was protected by the Archangel Raphael. Abdon and Sennen and Tobit performed a specific ritual upon the dead. In the case of Abdon and Sennen, the miracles that were performed in the presence of their mortal remains in Arles-sur-Tech were attributed to Raphael. But in their lifetime, they merely "copied" the rituals practiced by Tobit, and referred to in the Book of Tobit.

The final component in the "hieroglyph" of Rennes-le-Château is the demon. The inscription reads "By this sign you will conquer him" – and it is implied that the "he" that needs to be conquered is the devil, falling on his

---

46   See note 16 for the reference of the legend.

knees as if he is surrendering, conquered by the weight of the stoup – and specifically its holy water – and the sign of the cross made by the angels. It is Gérard de Sède who identified him with Asmodeus. And, wonders of wonders, it is Asmodeus that features prominently in the Book of Tobit.

To summarise book: it is the story of a righteous Jew of the Tribe of Naphtali, named Tobit, living in Nineveh after the deportation of the northern tribes of Israel to Assyria in 721 BC under Shalmaneser V. He was noted for his diligence in attempting to provide proper burials for fallen Jews who had been slain by Sennacherib[47], for which act the king seized all his property and exiled him.

After Sennacherib's death, he was allowed to return to Nineveh, but again buried a dead man who had been murdered on the street. That night, he slept in the open and was blinded by bird droppings that fell into his eyes. This put a strain on his marriage, and ultimately, he prayed for death. Meanwhile, in faraway Media, a young woman named Sarah prayed for death in despair. She had lost seven husbands to the demon of lust, Asmodeus, who abducted and killed every man she married, on their wedding night, before the marriage could be consummated. God then sent the angel Raphael, disguised as a human, to heal Tobit and to free Sarah from the demon.

Before we return to Saunière, we need to finish the Book of Tobit. Tobias, Tobit's son, is sent by his father to collect a sum of money that the latter had deposited some time previously in Media, where Sarah lived. On this journey, Raphael introduces himself as Tobit's kinsman Azariah, and offers to aid and protect Tobias. Under the guidance of Raphael, Tobias successfully makes the journey to Media, though the voyage is not without tribulations: along the way, he is attacked by a giant fish, whose heart, liver and gall bladder are removed to make medicines.

Upon arriving in Media, Raphael tells Tobias of the beautiful Sarah, whom Tobias has the right to marry, because she is related to his tribe. He instructs the young man to burn the fish's liver and heart to drive away the demon when he attacks on the wedding night.

Sarah and Tobias are married, but rather than fall victim to the evil Asmodeus, the fumes of the burning organs drive the demon away to Upper Egypt, where Raphael follows him and binds him. Meanwhile, Sarah's father, unaware of the magical rituals that had been performed, has been

---

47   The name "Sennacherib" is only present in the modern (heavily modified) translations of the Book of Tobit, which mostly rely upon the Greek translation made by Theodotion. However, the translation closest to the Chaldaean original is the Latin version made by St. Jerome, which uses the name "Schennab" and not "Sennacherib".

digging a grave to bury Tobias secretly, assuming he will soon be dead. Surprised to find his new son-in-law alive and well, he orders a double-length wedding feast and has the grave secretly filled in. Since he cannot leave because of the feast, Tobias sends Raphael to recover his father's money. After the feast, Tobias and Sarah return to Nineveh. There, Raphael instructs Tobias to use the fish's gall to cure his father's blindness. Raphael then reveals his true identity and returns to heaven. In conclusion, Raphael is the archangel who heals Tobit and conquers Asmodeus.

Where does Saunière fit in this story? It is obvious that he was familiar with it, but it is equally clear that his interest in this story extended far beyond this initial observation.

The Book of Tobit was cherished by La Sanch: it is one of the prime showcases of the archangel Raphael, who is linked with Abdon and Sennen, those Babylonian saints who, like Tobit, shared a preoccupation with funerary rituals. But it is in Saunière's church where we see the priest take the story of Tobit one step further: he links the stoup (linked with Raphael) with Asmodeus (linked with Raphael), together with the inscription of "By this sign you will conquer", which is linked with the "X,I" or the Tau. Saunière's stoup is therefore primarily linked wih the archangel Raphael and this is another straightforward link with Arles-sur-Tech, where on October 24, Abdon and Sennen's relics were deposited in the Sacred Tomb. And, of course, we note that a tomb and relics are primarily linked with a cult of the dead. Lest we forget: La Sanch was an organisation that took care of those who were condemned to death, accompanied them during their final hours, and made sure that they would be buried. Just as Tobit made sure that those who fell dead, were given a proper burial, so La Sanch made sure that the condemned received a proper burial. The link between Tobit and La Sanch is therefore as straightforward as it could possibly be.

Funerary magic
The Book of Tobit in its original Chaldaean version, which Saint Jerome used for his Vulgate, got lost. But several ancient versions of this book remain: The Codex Vaticanus, Alexandrinus, Venetus Marcionus[48], the Armenian apocryphal translation, the Sinaiticus, the Vetus Itala[49], and as we have mentioned already, the Vulgate.

---

48   i.e. the Marcion codex which is kept in Venice, Italy.
49   i.e. the Old Italic version, which is written in archaic Latin. Also called the "Old Latin" version, it is one of the translations of the Bible which was in use in Europe before St. Jerome penned the Latin Vulgate in the 4th century AD.

It is said that Saint Jerome accomplished his translation in a single day, but it is known that he allowed himself to make large cuts in the text, because he affirms that he was forced to include this book in his Vulgate. The immediate question that arises is why? The likely answer would be that he did not desire to do so, but others, perhaps popular opinion, saw the Book as a required ingredient.

In his "Open Letter", Saint François de Sales declares that among the Protestants and the Greek Orthodox, as well among the Jews, the book of Tobit was seen as apocryphal. For the Protestants, the Book of Tobit could not be accepted because:

1. The Jews did not have it in their Canon;
2. The Churches had no respect for this book;
3. Eusebius of Caesarea emphasises that these stories are "corrupt and distorted" (L. IV, c. 22);
4. Calvin and Luther removed "scraped Tobit away from the Canon", making fun of it and considering it a fable.

Furthermore, all books of the Holy Scriptures are written in Greek or Hebrew. But Tobit was written in Chaldaean, as declared by François de Sales: *"Saint Jerome vouches for the fact that he had translated it from Chaldaean to Latin, in the Epistle 'Epistola ad Chromatium et Heliodorum, Praefat. in Tobium'."* This makes the Book of Tobit unique.

Commentators of the Holy Scriptures have no hesitation in saying that it was written by Theodotion, a disciple of Marcion, a very erudite Manichean. Marcion of Sinope (circa 110-160), was a major 2nd century Early Christian theologian, founder of what would later be called Marcionism. He was one of the first to be strongly denounced by other Christians (who would later be called "Catholic" in the original sense, i.e. the Greek word for "universal", as opposed to Marcionite) as heretical. He created a strong ecclesiastical organization, parallel to that of the Church of Rome, with himself as Bishop. The *Catholic Encyclopedia*[50] says of the Marcionites that *"they were perhaps the most dangerous foe Christianity has ever known."*

Marcion claimed that he tried to base his doctrine on the pure gospel, which he claimed had been corrupted and mutilated in the Christian circles of his time. His reformation, according to Marcion himself, was to deliver Christendom from false Jewish doctrines by restoring the Pauline

---

50   *The Catholic Encyclopedia, volume IX, published 1910. New York: Robert Appleton Company. Nihil Obstat, October 1, 1910. Remy Lafort, Censor. Imprimatur: +John M. Farley, Archbishop of New York. Refer to the introduction of the article entitled "Marcionites", written by J.P. Arendzen and transcribed by Tom Crossett.*

conception of the gospel; Paul being, according to Marcion, the only apostle who had rightly understood the new message of salvation as delivered by Christ. According to the *Catholic Encyclopedia*[51], *"it is obvious that Marcion was already a consecrated bishop"* and *"we can take it for granted then, that Marcion was a bishop, probably an assistant or suffragan of his father at Sinope."*

Some of Marcion's distinctly non-Christian ideas reappeared with Manichaean developments among the Bulgarian Bogomils of the 10th century and their Cathar heirs of southern France in the 13th century. In fact, Marcion's claim to recover the "authentic Jesus" has been a constant claim of various Christian heretics.

What made Marcion distinct from the many who sought to recover the "authentic Jesus", was that he believed that, while the universe was created by Yahweh, the God behind Jesus and his teachings is not the same as the universal creator. This position has led many in Orthodox Christianity to label his teachings heretical, Gnostic, and Manichaean, as they make use of the concept of the Demiurge and a Docetic Christ. Marcion drew a distinction between the God of Love described in the Gospels and more generally in the New Testament on the one hand, and on the other hand, what he called a "Bad God", violent and vindictive, which he likened to the aspect of God described by Moses. The Cathars nursed a deep hatred of Moses, whom they called the Nocturnal Demon, the father of vice and son of Lucifer. As such, the God of Abraham, Isaac and Jacob was demonic and it was necessary to throw away or burn all the writings of the Bible, both Old and New Testaments, as heretical texts.

Thus, in order to establish his strange doctrine, Marcion decided to draw up his own independent canon. This he accomplished by 150 AD, even before the official creation of the Roman Church's Canon. His own, very peculiar "Canon", called the "Canon of Marcion" or "Marcionite Canon", is actually still honoured in the Syriac Church and consists of a rejection of all the books of the New Testament, except for the Epistles of Paul and a rewritten version of the Gospel of Luke[52]. For Marcion, the God of the New Alliance was not Jesus Christ, but "Christ" alone. In accordance with this doctrine, he prohibited all the books that made too many references

---

51   *Ibid. Refer to the first part "I – Life of Marcion" in the article quoted above.*
52   *Actually the Marcionite Canon doesn't even include all of the Pauline Epistles, but only 10 out of 14.*

to the name of Jesus (namely the Gospels) and began to "revise" the others to make them compatible with his dogma.

Marcion focused on Paul and Luke, who was said to be Paul's travelling companion. But why focus on Paul? We find the answer in the Acts of the Apostles and more specifically in the story of Saul, i.e. Paul.

Born in Tarsus in Cilicia (Turkey) circa 10 AD, Saul finished his studies in Jerusalem, where he was educated by Gamaliel. Initially, Saul persecuted the Christians, even taking part in stonings. Having obtained letters of reference that allowed him to seek and persecute the believers in Damascus, Saul is on his way there, when he suddenly became blinded by God. We note that blindness was also the illness that struck Tobit. Three days later, Paul was cured by a Christian called Ananias. Thankful for this cure, he converted to Christianity and was baptized, changing his identity to Paul, who would then go on to become one of the primary saints that made Christianity into the world religion that it is today.

Theodotion, the writer of the Greek version of the apocryphal book of Tobit, saw the similarity between Saul being cured of his blindness by the disciple Ananias, and Tobit's eyes being cured by the Archangel Raphael. But the parallel goes beyond this, for, as can be seen in the Vulgate, Raphael introduced himself to the young Tobias with these words: "I am Azarias, son of Ananias the Great." In another apocryphal book by Theodotion, "The Song of the Three Children in the Furnace", the names of Ananias and Azarias appear again, this time accompanied by someone called Michael, which may be a reference to the Archangel Michael.

Therefore it can be said that the Marcionite doctrine is also closely related to the Chaldaean Book of Tobit, since the theme as well as the name of some characters used in the Book draw inspiration from the history of St. Paul *before* his conversion to Christianism – which was a favourite theme of Marcion, and since Theodotion himself, who translated it into Greek, was one of Marcion's most die-hard followers.

What was it that Tobit – or Abdon and Sennen – performed on the dead that some seemed to treat with such horror? By delving into the Book of Tobit, we find details as to what specifically he did. One day, Tobias came home to his father, stating that a man had just been murdered and was lying in the street. Tobit went out and brought the man's body secretly to his home, to bury him during the night. At sunset (a moment of day that was important for the cult of Constantine's Sol Invictus), Tobit took the body from his house, for burial. But it is clear that he not merely buried the dead, as that in itself would not be treated with abject horror; he also performed certain rituals upon them, rituals that seem to be exhausting and which result in him, one day, falling asleep and becoming blind from a bird dropping.

The texts also make it clear that this is not a simple burial of the dead, as some have argued the intrigue away. First, his family, friends and neighbours repeatedly warn Tobit that his behaviour has caused outrage and that some have even called for Tobit to be executed for the things he had done. Furthermore, the Vaticanus and Codex Sinaiticus state that Tobit's blindness was punishment for his "transgressions" and his "sins". It is obvious that the Church has not focused too much attention on these rituals; like Saul, the story is there to show the errors of a man, before he changes his life for the better. But it is clear that Tobit did "something" to these dead bodies… very similar to what Abdon and Sennen performed several centuries later.

Finally, we note that the successor of Sargon, the Assyrian king, is Schennab[53], and it is he who, in the Book of Tobit, was the main cause of all the dead people in the streets, whom Tobit buried. In Hebrew, Asmodeus is Schenad – showing yet another link between Tobit and the demon.

There are further details of interest in this story: Tobit's wife, Anne, is a weaver, the profession practiced by the Manicheans… and later associated with the Cathars. Is it further evidence that Tobit's family – and his wife – practiced the same cults as Abdon and Sennen? It is at the very least suggestive.

Did Anne help Tobit, her husband, in his magic? Let us compare her role to that of Marie Dénarnaud. Just as Anne would be buried next to Tobit, Marie was buried next to Saunière. One of the best known and verified stories about Saunière and his maid is that they both often went into the cemetery, at night. Saunière had even installed a new iron gate door with lock and a retaining wall around the cemetery, apparently so that no-one could find out what the priest was doing throughout the night.

At first, Saunière explained his nightly activities as "making room in the cemetery" so that more people could be buried. But this excuse did not last for very long and the villagers soon lodged an official complaint against him. They knew that Saunière – often in the presence of Marie – did something in the cemetery at night, something which involved disturbing the bodies of the dead. When the villagers tolerated it no longer,

---

53 *Often mistranslated as "Sennacherib" in modern editions of the text. See note 47.*

Saunière seems to have stopped doing whatever it was that he and Marie had been doing. To quote Gérard de Sède[54]: *"Rumours circulated about this behaviour: even for the less religious, graves were sacred. In the cemetery, the abbé was no longer welcome because, in 1895, the town council ordered him to leave the dead to sleep in peace."*

Many have interpreted these actions as being part of Saunière's search – or removal of evidence – with regard to his treasure. The testimonies given to the town council, as well as to the police station, during the years 1891 till 1896, make it clear that the villagers complained of the desecration of graves and Saunière's practice of strange rites. When he was forced to explain, he merely stated that *"several parishioners die each year; the cemetery became too small to give them a decent grave. I made the ossuary, which you can clearly see, with the remains of the old dead."* So Saunière was unable to hide the fact that he was digging up and transporting corpses, but he gave a mundane explanation for it.

René Descadeillas is one of the most distinguished authorities on the enigma and is considered to be a sceptic. Still, even he notes that this episode is "a mystery": *"The priest had caused several of his fellow townsmen to complaint to the Prefecture. Saunière locked himself in the cemetery at night and caused strange upheaval. The order was given for Saunière to stop turning the cemetery upside down. But what was he doing there? Why did he damage the graves? It's a mystery."[55]*

Descadeillas did not believe the story that Saunière had found a great treasure. Descadeillas was the chief librarian of the Municipal Library of Carcassonne and a leading member of a local historical society[56] and thus inti-

---

54   *Gérard de Sède, « Le Trésor Maudit de Rennes-le-Château », "J'ai Lu" (1972). For the English translation, refer to "The Accursed Treasure of Rennes-le-Chateau", DEK Publishing, 2001, translated by Bill Kersey.*

55   *René Descadeillas, « Notice sur Rennes-le-Château et l'abbé Saunière » (Notice on Rennes-le-Château and abbé Saunière) (1962). This famous writing was subjected to several modifications before being finally included in « Mythologie du trésor de Rennes », the full reference of which follows.*

René Descadeillas, « Mythologie du Trésor de Rennes: Histoire Véritable de l'abbé Saunière, Curé de Rennes-le-Château » ("Mythology of the Treasure of Rennes-le-Château : the Real Story of Abbé Saunière, Priest of Rennes-le-Château"), in « Mémoires de la Société des Arts et des Sciences de Carcassonne » (Research Bulletin of the Arts and Science Society of Carcassonne), 1971-1972 years, 4th series, volume VII, 2nd part; published in 1974.

56   *Elected a member of the Société des Etudes Scientifiques de l'Aude (Society of Scientific Studies of the Aude region) when he was 29, René Descadeillas (1909-1986) became chief librarian of the Municipal Library of Carcassonne in 1950, and then in 1964, chairman of the Musée des Beaux-Arts (Museum of the Arts) of Carcassonne. Meanwhile, in 1957, this*

mately aware of the myths, legends and history of the region. But although he did not believe the treasure story that Gérard de Sède and Noël Corbu attributed to Saunière, the above quote makes it clear that he did not think that Saunière's actvities were free of mystery either.

The archives in the possession of Laurent Buchholtzer shed further light on this episode, as they contain the text of several formal complaints against Saunière lodged by the villagers before the town council:

> "Rennes-le-Château, March 12, 1895.
> Mr. Prefect,
> We have the honour to inform you regarding the agreement of Rennes-le-Château's town council, during the meeting which took place on Sunday the 10th of March at 1pm in the townhall.
> We, the voters, protest their decision; the said work which they[57] allowed the abbé to carry out, is of no service; and we emphasise, in support of the first complaint, our wish to be free to, and in control of, the care for the graves of our ancestors lying there, and M. l'Abbé had no right, after we had put crosses or crowns, to move, lift or dislodge anything."

> "Rennes-le-Château, March 14, 1895.
> Mr. Prefect,
> We are upset about the work being carried out in the cemetery, above all in the conditions it has been up to now. Crosses have been removed, as well as gravestones, and at the same time this said work is neither for maintenance, nor for anything else.
> We join our signature: Faure Joseph, town councillor, Clottes Isidore, private guard, witnessed by Messrs. Garouste, Tysseire and Mis, not knowing how to sign."

> It is "our wish to be free to, and in control of, the care for the graves of our ancestors lying there."

This first hand evidence paints an even more dramatic picture than the reports of Descadeillas or de Sède. It shows that the entire town is furious about what is happening and that they do not accept the explanations that Saunière is giving them. Furthermore, it makes it clear that Saunière

---

erudite scholar had seen his talent recognised through his promotion as President-elect of the Société des Etudes Scientifiques de l'Aude.

57   "They" refers to the town council of Rennes-le-Château.

is rearranging and disturbing the dead, leaving the villagers incapable of decorating the graves of their family members as they please. It is equally clear that Saunière's actions are totally at odds with the will of the villagers. And the villagers do not believe Saunière's explanation as to why he is doing it either.

The first hand accounts do not mention the presence of Marie during these nocturnal activities, but then they are not expected to. Both de Sède and Descadeillas did include her. We note that Saunière was a tall, powerful man and would not have needed the help of Marie in anything that he did… except, of course, if he did more than move graves.

We do not know what rituals Saunière performed on the dead, but could it be that they were very similar to the Consolamentum that was performed by the Cathar priests in medieval times? J.M. Vidal in his book *Doctrine et Morale des derniers Ministres Albigeois*[58] emphasises that this was administered *"to the dying, even to the dead, when they cannot sin anymore."* Did Marie perform the role of the "socia", i.e. the assistant, as there was required to be one to help the Cathar priest; these assistants could be male (socius) or female (socia)?[59] Let us finally note that Saunière performed his work at night, as did Tobit. Rummaging in graveyards at nighttime is not immediately recognisable with proper Christian customs.

A fish on a grill

When Tobias is on his voyage to get money for his father, Raphael and Tobias have a rather curious and magical incident with a fish. When a huge fish appears, Raphael says to Tobias: "Take it by the gills and pull it to you." He thus pulls the fish onto dry land. The angel declared: "Clean this fish, but keep the heart, the bile and the liver; because if you put coal on it and smoke it, it will repel Asmodeus and the bile will give back life to your father, and he will regain his sight." Tobias obeyed and put the fish on a grill.

In *The Accursed Treasure of Rennes-le-Château*[60], Gérard de Sède writes about how he was able to consult some of Saunière's personal papers. One

---

58   Vidal, Jean-Marie, « Doctrine et morale des derniers ministres albigeois » ("Doctrine and Morality of the last Albigenses Ministers"), in Revue des Questions Historiques (Magazine of Historical Questions), LXXXV (1909), pp. 357-409, LXXVI (1910), pp. 5-48. Duplicated in fac-sim: Impr. C. Lacour, RediViva, Nîmes, 2002.

59   It is certainly a possibility, given that one the main characteristics of Cathar couples was that the perfects were not allowed to marry, let alone to have sexual relationships, with their sociae (plural of socia).

60   Gérard de Sède, « Le Trésor Maudit de Rennes-le-Château », "J'ai Lu" editions (1972). For an English translation, refer to "The Accursed Treasure of Rennes-le-Chateau", DEK Publishing, 2001, translated by Bill Kersey.

particular piece of paper attrached his attention: it was a strange pictogram, which has entered the chronicles of the mystery as *Le Sot Pêcheur*, (The Foolish Fisherman). In the various editions of his book, the pictogram changes its appearance and varies in the assembly of signs and letters, which are arranged around a few sentences, which in themselves are perfectly comprehensible. There is a reason for this obfuscation: De Sède felt that the text without a code was too easily identifiable... though no-one seems to have noticed from where it originated: the text is an extract from the Book of Tobit. So, what De Sède did was very odd: he found an apocryphal text, an extract from the Book of Tobit, but for him this was too clear and so he surrounded it with letters and signs and transformed it into a coded message, leaving the reader with the belief that this is a genuine code and that it will reveal something – other than the actual apocryphal text.

The text of *Le Sot Pêcheur*, once its coded coating has been cleared away, reads: "*P.S, Sot Pêcheur à l'embouchure du Rhône, son poisson sur le grill deux fois retourna. Un Malin (Asmodée) survint, et 25 fois le goûta. Cuit, il ne resta que l'arête. Un ange veillait et en fit un peigne d'or. B.S. Cur.*". - "P.S., at the Rhone's mouth, the Foolish Fisherman turned his fish over twice on the grill. An Evil One (Asmodeus) arrived and tasted it 25 times. (When it was) Cooked, only the fish bones remained. An angel was watching and made it into a golden comb. B.S. Cur."

Here, we have the true context of the message that Saunière set forth in the group of statues at the entrance of his church: Asmodeus, with the angels conquering "him". That group – or "hieroglyph", as De Sède saw it – also has the inscription B.S., which is assumed to be a reference to Bérenger Saunière. And we note that the inscription of the "Foolish Fisherman" also finishes with B.S. and "Cur.", which could be a reference to "Curé", i.e. abbé. The text and the statues thus show that Saunière truly did see himself in the role of Tobias – and also by extension, with the work he performed in the cemetery, in the role of Tobit. If we were ever in doubt about Saunière's allegiance, it is clear that he followed in the footsteps of Tobit and his Chaldaean ritual; he saw himself as a Babylonian priest of the dead.

We also note certain parallels between the Book of Tobit and Saunière's adaptation: Tobias went to the banks of the Tigris; the "Stupid Fisherman" – Saunière? – went to the mouth of the river Rhône. The Rhône rises as the effluent of the Rhône Glacier in Valais, Switzerland, in the Saint-Gothard massif, at an altitude of 1753 m. Up to Martigny, the Rhône is a torrent, after which it becomes a great mountain river, flowing through Lake Geneva (in French, Lac Léman) before entering France. It is joined by the river Saône at Lyon, before going south. At Arles – Arles! As in Arles-sur-Tech? – the Rhône divides itself in two arms, forming the Camargue delta, with all branches flowing into the Mediterranean Sea. One arm is called the "Grand Rhône", the other one is the "Petit Rhône" – so we do not know exactly to which mouth Saunière is referring.

In the Book of Tobit, we know that Tobias "puts the fish on a grill". Saunière turns the fish twice. In the Book of Tobit, the smoke will repel Asmodeus; Saunière speaks of Asmodeus tasting it 25 times.

Saunière provides further detail, but it is equally clear that this detail is twofold: at one level, the extra details clearly are ritual in nature: turning over twice, tasting it 25 times… such repetitive actions are key indicators of magical rites. At a secondary level, it is equally clear that the fish is supposed to be symbolic of something else: the fish symbolises the human body. In Saunière's interpretation of this event, the human body is devoured by the Evil One, Asmodeus, the man who kills Sarah's husband in the Book of Tobit. What Saunière is saying is that by performing this ritual, under the protection of Archangel Raphael, the corpse became gold – it was purified; taken away from evil, hell[61].

So, in one short verse, we have an allegorical summary of the rituals performed by Saunière, based on or identical to the cult of Tobit, both of them performing these rituals on the dead[62].

Things have come full circle, but one aspect still needs to be underlined: it is now quite clear that Saunière was practicing heretical rituals, perhaps on the corpses in his cemetery. Though this may raise eyebrows, it is clear that Saunière was not alone. Knowing that what he did fits perfectly within the framework of the cult of Sts. Abdon and Sennen, it is logical to ask whether such funerary rituals were also practiced by La Sanch in Arles-sur-Tech,

---

61 *"Hell" being seen as physical death in this sense, and "evil" as the putrefaction of the body or the destruction of the bones. The main characteristic of the Chaldaean conception of the afterlife is that life after death is not the production of resurrection, but rather of reincarnation. Therefore, the Chaldaean concept of death does resemble the Egyptian one: the body, or at least the bones, must be preserved so that another soul, or even sometimes a demon, can inhabit it. The notorious symbolic notion of the "living dead" stems from this particular Chaldaean-Egyptian worldview.*
62 *The process described in the "Sot Pêcheur" (Foolish Fisherman) extract – transmutating flesh into gold –, points to a connection at some level between the alchemical experiments of the Middle Ages – the goal of which was to change lead into gold – and the rituals performed by the Chaldaean Magi on the dead.*

the bailiwick of his good friend Grassaud[63]. If Saunière was a member of La Sanch and a heretical priest – "one of them" – then it also suddenly makes sense as to why he would be entrusted with the education of a "miracle child", Abdon. It also explains why La Sanch would donate money to him and why they came to his rescue when he was attacked by the bishop[64] and also later, after he himself had died, when Marie needed money[65].

Equally, we should not necessarily single out La Sanch in Arles-sur-Tech since we know that there is a network of penitent organisations elsewhere… and we know that these were the organisations that also donated money to Saunière. In short, Saunière was a heretical priest, part of the penitent tradition. That is how he made his "gold": his fellow believers, who wanted to have such a rite performed upon them, were the ones who made contact with him, no doubt paying him generously to perform the rite, or to receive the secret details as to how such a rite could be performed.

The parallel between Saunière and Tobit extends into the enigmatic source of his –Tobit's - wealth as well. We note that Tobit, the magician, has a lot of money that he has left at Gabael's house[66], in Rhages, in Media. He sends his son to collect this money… which is a long and perilous journey. We note how Tobias needs to hand in a type of note that will be recognised by the person who will have to give the money to him … no doubt for services rendered by Tobit? Tobias thus collects a deposit paid in by someone; and it is the same model that Saunière used to become wealthy. Saunière lived the life of Tobit… except that his helpmate's name was not Anne, but Marie.

---

63   *Eugène Grassaud was the priest of Amélie-les-Bains at that time. However, it is simply inconceivable for Grassaud not to have taken part in the ceremonies organised by La Sanch, especially since Amélie-les-Bains, formerly known as "Arles-les-Bains", was the former location of the "Sacred Tomb" worshipped by La Sanch, which is now in Arles-sur-Tech's abbey; Amélie-les-Bains is only 3 kilometres away from Arles-sur-Tech.*

64   *In the context of his association with La Sanch, let us remember that Eugène Grassaud was a very close friend of Saunière, who recommended him to ask Eugène Huguet for his defense in the court trials from 1910 onwards.*

65   *According to French researcher Pierre Jarnac, it was also Grassaud who lent money to Marie Denarnaud after Saunière's death.*

66   *Concerning the character of Gabael, it is advisable to refer to a note written by Voltaire in the French "Encyclopédie" (XVIIIth century): "Note_29: There was indeed the Jew Gabelus who had money quarrels with that fellow Tobias, and several very sensible and knowledgeable people trace back to Hebrew the origins of the word "gabelle", for we know that it is from the Hebrew language that the French one originates."*
The "gabelle" was actually a burdensome tax on salt collected from the peasants by the French lords before 1790, the origins of which are more intriguing than is apparent at first glance…

So this is how Saunière's "death trade" worked: he sent an "offer of a funeral mass" to a religious hospital, a convent, a monastery, a retirement home. Not just any, but one that was part of the penitent – or Chaldaean – circuit. Saunière thus cashed in on the deposit the deceased had left with the institution. And here is the final parallel with Tobit: Tobit had deposited that money in Media for his own funerary ritual. He is blind and is preparing for his funeral. He sends his son on a mission to instruct the people in Media that the time has come… that his time has come. The same happened with Saunière: he did not go around all of these places, but used the postal system. The person whose relative had received the rite which Saunière had performed requested a note, which showed that Saunière had performed the ritual. In return, the money was transferred to Saunière.

The "Villa Bethania" is often seen as Saunière's own estate and many tourists believe he lived there. But that is not true. For the whole of his time in the village, he lived in the presbytery, a much smaller and less elegant home, next to the church. It is known that he built the villa for other purposes: as a retirement home, for elderly priests. It is therefore clear that Saunière wanted to establish himself on this "route"; rather than take money from elsewhere, he wanted to give certain people the whole treatment: retire and take their money directly.

Pierre Jarnac and Laurent Buccholtzer have both discovered evidence that Saunière had been working on this project for a very long time. Buchholtzer notes that "during his trial, Saunière confronted his prosecutors with this argument", the argument being that the Villa Bethania had been built as a retirement home. In one of the letters he sent to the prosecution during the trial, he explained that for many years, he had spoken to the previous bishop[67] about this initiative and that he – unlike his successor – had never raised a single objection. Apparently, nobody at the diocese denied that this was not the case.

From Saunière's surviving records, it is clear that his income came from areas far outside the region[68], and this increased from 1899 onwards. That

---

67 The "previous bishop" refers to Monseigneur Billard, who was Saunière's bishop before Monseigneur de Beauséjour.

68 Laurent Buchholtzer, referring to the Villa Bethania:
"In [Saunière's] correspondence, we can notice that before he begins to build the villa in Rennes[-le-Château], Bérenger does research in the region in order to find a house. This fact proves in my opinion that abbé Saunière had never intended to live in or use for himself this building, which must have had another purpose. I rate as "probable" its utilisation as a retirement home for elderly priests, but the lack of oversight from the hierarchy of the diocese lets us suspect that it was actually not destined to the priests of the diocese." From the above

is the same year that Saunière began the Villa project, which was built between 1901 to 1905, or 1907 if you consider the completion of the Tour Magdala as the end of it. Intriguingly, and little known, is that the building was hit by a fire in 1903, but the police archives reveal that their enquiry could not find a cause, and hence they do not conclude whether it was an accident or a criminal act. Half jokingly, we can only wonder whether Saunière had been practicing the rite of Tobit – which may involve burning the body, like the fish is grilled – and the ritual got out of hand, resulting in a fire.

Finally, of all the possible names, Saunière gave his Villa the name Bethania. There is an apparent link with Mary Magdalene, to whom the local church was dedicated. But there is a more subtle hint: Bethania is specifically known as the location where Jesus raised Lazarus from the dead! And we note that this "rise from the dead" was performed in the presence of Mary Magdalene, whom many pseudo-Christian sects have identified with Isis, but whom they could also perhaps compare to Anne, Tobit's wife. As such, Jesus raised Lazarus from the death in the presence of Mary Magdalene; Saunière, too, used his "Mary" – Marie Dénarnaud. And speaking of Isis: the Tau symbol in Egypt means "new life" and "resurrection"; the rise.

---

elements, we can clearly see that the Villa Bethania, as a retirement home, was an integral part of Saunière's "financement plan".

Chapter 4

Angelic magic

The ritual that Tobit, Saunière (hypothetically) and La Sanch performed relies on casting out Asmodeus, by the power of Raphael; it is Raphael who transforms the dead bones into gold. It is the angel that is the active agent, and so Saunière's rituals would sit within the so-called "angelic rituals", i.e. rituals involving the angels.

Using angels in magic is common. In England, John Dee used angels and "Enochian magic" to perform his rituals. In the late 19th century, an entire movement of magic, often involving the assistance of angels, was all the rage in Parisian occult circles. For a man like Saunière, aware of the fashions and customs of his time, dabbling in "the occult" would thus be not out of the ordinary, or be seen as unique. But rather than "dabble", Saunière may have had "genuine" magic at his disposal and may have performed "real magical acts", unlike much of the mumbo-jumbo that was all too common then and is nowadays.

In the Book of Tobit, we read how Tobias called the angel and said: "We have gone a long way together, now take with you some beasts of burden… and go find Gabael[69] in the Rhages mountains. You will give him the note of recognition and he will give you another one, with the money deposit in return. Then, I will take the money he gave you, because you know that my father is counting the days for his grave."

Raphael then went to the Rhages mountains, found Gabael, returned the note and received the entire sum.

It is clear that Tobit was preparing for his own funeral, but it is Raphael who intervenes and shows that it is not yet Tobit's time to journey to the other world. As to the sum of money, this was fixed at ten talents and was apparently not debatable. It is a large sum of money, the equivalent of more than 7,000 dollars today. It is difficult to do a price comparison with the services Saunière offered, but it is clear that in Tobit's days, such services were expensive… and represented a life's savings. And it is clear that the "death rites" are definitely much more profitable than the ordinary trafficking in masses that is normally used to explain Saunière's wealth. Indeed, when we look at the "income" Saunière received from his donors, we see the cost was roughly 50 francs per month; or the equivalent today of 750

---

69   *See note 66.*

dollars per month. This extraordinary sum was not paid to him throughout the life-time of the donor, but for a period of between six to twelve months, resulting in a sum of approximately 7,500 dollars. It seems that since ancient times, the cost for this type of ritual had not suffered from inflation.

There is one final detail that should not be overlooked. We know that Saunière transposed the River Tigris onto the Rhone. So did he do the same for the Rhages mountain? If so, where is the local Rhages, the mountain of the angel? For Saunière, Rhages was Buga-Rhages… Bugarach, one of the highest and most impressive mountains, just to the east of Rennes-les-Bains. Bugarach is pronounced Boug-a-rak; Rhages is also known as Rakkan[70], or Rak. Of course, we need to ask whether this was just Saunière transposing one landscape onto another… or whether there was more to it than that.

A visit to the church of Bugarach – a village at the foot of the mountain – reveals that Saunière was not "just" transposing landscapes. Others seem to have been aware of this overlay as well. One stained glass window in the Bugarach church shows a scene from the Book of Tobit. Let us emphasise immediately that such a representation is excessively rare, and to find one so close to Saunière's Rennes-le-Château is spectacular; to find it in the Bugarach church is an improbable coincidence. Yet, here it is: a stained glass window, showing a faceless angel, guiding a young person who is known to be Tobias. The faceless angel is Raphael.

A Concise Guide to the Penitent Symbolism

This depiction of Tobias in the church of Bugarach is a straightforward identification that anyone can make. It is "hard" evidence. Other signs, such as that on the side of the Sacred Tomb in Arles-sur-Tech, are more difficult to interpret. We should add some details to our already quite extensive study about the symbolism of the Tau, the Mihir.

Very often, one can visit a church or a monastery's cloister, and go wandering through the halls and rooms of these places without ever noticing some engraved stones, strange figures, sometimes prominently displayed, sometimes hidden from view. A symbol engraved in the stone of a church is really a confession when it contains a thousand-year-old message, or when it professes a heretical faith foreign to any Christian interpretation.

---

70   *The ancient town of Rhages (in Greek, "Rhagae" in Latin, and "Rakkan" in the Medic language), today known as "Rey" or "Rayy", is the most historic town of the Tehran province, in Iran.*

Those signs of recognition, intelligible only to the initiated, thus betray the presence of penitents scattered into numerous organized and active groups, dwelling in sanctuaries which have all the features of Christian buildings but are, in reality, dedicated to Manichean rituals and Chaldaean deities.

It would be difficult to make an inventory of the many signs in use among penitent brotherhoods, since each sect has been adapting them over the centuries, either to the history of their region, or to the evolution of their own beliefs. This should not cause us to lose sight of the fact that originally, these symbols did have a similar iconography. It explains why nearly every graphic design, among the huge quantities of symbols that are engraved on our religious buildings, can be related to some primitive form of the Mihir, the Tau or, indirectly, the Persian Triad.

Almost all of these figures, which are of crucial importance due to their profusion, as well as the significance of their symbolism, are described in a short article written by Louis Charbonneau-Lassay in January, 1929: *Les Graffites hermético-mystiques de la chapelle des Carmes de Loudun (Vienne) (fin du XVe siècle - XVIe)* [The hermetic and mystical graffiti in the Carmelite Chapel at Loudun (department of Vienne, France) (end of the XVth century – beginning of the XVIth century)], which we shall comment upon below.

Born in 1871 from a Vendean family (i.e. stemming from the Vendee region in Western France), Louis Charbonneau-Lassay grew up in a religious environment from an early age, since he was educated by, and later entered, the congregation of the Brothers of Saint Gabriel at Saint-Laurent sur Sèvres. Charbonneau-Lassay proved to be a brilliant student and scholar. He dedicated his life to archaeology and Catholic symbolism, became a publisher and a member of various scholarly organisations, such as the "Société des Antiquaires de l'Ouest" [Antiquarian Society of Western France], the "Société Archéologique de Nantes" [Archaeological Society of Nantes], and the "Ecole Nationale d'Anthropologie" [French National School of Anthropology]. In addition, Charbonneau-Lassay participated in the Universal Exhibition which was held in Paris in 1900, and he is well remembered for his masterpiece about Christian symbolism, the title of which still resounds in everyone's ears: *Le Bestiaire du Christ* (The Bestiary of Christ)[71]. This means that the author, who was an historian, an archae-

---

71   First published in French by the Belgian publishing house Desclée de Brouwer in 1940, and then translated in English by D. M. Dooling: New York, Parabola Books, 1991.

ologist and a monk all at once, could boast of being a leading expert in the field of religious graphical symbols, or at the very least, was able to credibly lay claim to knowledge as to the secret meaning of certain figures.

Ever in quest of ancient and forgotten symbols, Charbonneau-Lassay had been informed by abbé Dupuis, priest of the parish of Saint Hilaire du Martray, of the presence of graffiti in the chapel of Notre-Dame de Recouvrance (Our Lady of Recovery), in the town of Loudun (in the Vienne department, near Lyon).

Amaury, baron of Bauçay, who owned more than a third of Loudun during the Middle Ages, had ceded pieces of land near a place called "Le Martray", for Carmelite penitent monks to settle there. These Penitents built a chapel called Notre Dame de Recouvrance (Our Lady of Recovery). It has been destroyed on several occasions, notably by the Protestants who set it on fire[72]. The chapel was reconstructed with the help of payments made by Louis, lord of Amboise[73], and later by René, Duke of Anjou, King of Sicily and lord of the town of Loudun.

Thus it was inside this building that became "the centre of an active cult", that Louis Charbonneau-Lassay noticed "on the lower parts of the wall, inside this chapel of Notre Dame de Recouvrance, several old and peculiar graffiti". In his article, he added that abbé Dupuis had allowed him to continue his research in "the spiral staircase of the small tower that leads to the old bell turret, […] and which contained a great number of engraved signs and inscriptions". After having identified "the modern inscriptions, generally simply workers' names […]", he noticed the presence of "hermetic and religious signs, among which several of Oriental origin". Surprised and perplexed by these graffiti, Charbonneau-Lassay came progressively to suspect the existence, among the Carmelite Penitents of Loudun[74], of "more ancient traditions, […] originating from the religious centres of Chaldea, Turan[75] and India."

---

72 They burnt the Carmelite monks' monastery itself as well. The « Huguenots », as the Protestants were being called at that time in France, considered this chapel and the cloister of the Carmelite monks as places of perdition, and did not hesitate to categorise the Carmelites as "heretics" and as "adepts of the Devil".

73 In order that masses be said for the resting of his soul, and to buy his salvation. Could it be a case of a Cult of the Dead?

74 As Louis Charbonneau-Lassay points out, the Penitent Order of Carmelite monks has been subjected to strong Oriental influences. Although they have adopted the Latin liturgical rite, Carmelite monks have indeed been allowed to keep the rite of the "Holy Sepulchre". At this point, the readers would greatly benefit from consulting the specific chapter dealing with the Order of the Holy Sepulchre.

75 "Turan" is the ancient Persian (Iranian) name for Central Asia.

We have to agree with him on this point. However, our key interest in his article lies in its catalogue of the graffiti. The first signs noticed by him, he explains, are *"engraved on the inner wall of the chapel"*. These are two I.H.S. acronyms, which, according to him, would only be *"an abridged form, with the two first letters and the last one, of the Greek name IHCOYS, Jesus"*. The author adds that "the three nails of the Crucifixion" are depicted under the second acronym.

Reproduction of the second "IHS" seal engraved in the Carmelite Chapel of Loudun, as drawn by Louis Charbonneau-Lassay in his article: notice the three nails located under the central "H".

Charbonneau-Lassay's interpretation seems to be too narrow, or at least, that is our opinion. It is indeed hard to conceive that this so-called "monogram", which is specific to the penitent brotherhoods, would have a Christian origin, or even acknowledge any sort of Christic interpretation. That seems to defeat the purpose of it being a secret marker of a penitent movement.

One can indeed read in the *Catholic Encyclopedia*,[76] in the "IHS" article, that *"towards the close of the Middle Ages* [the acronym] *IHS became a symbol, quite like the chi-rho[77] in the Constantinian period. Sometimes above the H appears a cross and underneath three nails, while the whole figure is surrounded by rays. IHS became the accepted iconographical characteristic of St. Vincent Ferrer[78]* [...] *and of St. Bernardino of Siena[79] (died 1444). The latter holy missionary, at the end of his sermons, was wont to devoutly exhibit this monogram to his audience, for which some blamed him; he was even called before* [Pope] *Martin V. St. Ignatius of Loyola adopted the monogram in his seal as General of the Society of Jesus (1541), and thus it became the emblem of his institute."* Let us note that Vincent Ferrer was the founder of La Sanch in Perpignan.

Thus the Christian interpretation of this so-called "monogram" composed

---

76   *The Catholic Encyclopedia, volume VII. Published 1910. New York: Robert Appleton Company. Nihil Obstat, 1ˢᵗ June 1910. Remy Lafort, S.T.D., Censor. Approved by John Cardinal Farley, Archbishop of New York.*

77   *Chi-Rho, that is to say "XP" or "PX", also written as "Pax", and anciently represented through the Babylonian Tau.*

78   *Died 1419 and Founder Saint of the "La Sanch" penitent brotherhood.*

79   *From the religious family of Saint Francis of Assisi.*

of three letters, did not appear self-evident to the Church, and neither was the devotion to this symbol, or its assimilation into the Chi-Rho. It should be mentioned here that the worship of the I.H.S.[80] by some monks, among them Bernardino of Siena, was condemned by the Augustinian monk Andre de Biglia in his treatise.[81] Andre de Cascia, another Augustinian, even wrote to Pope Martin V, arguing that *"this heretical cult destroyed the faith in the Holy Trinity, lowered the dignity of Christ's humanity; annulled the worship of the Cross"*.

If, as some ecclesiastics thought, the letters I.H.S. did not really mean "Iesus Hominum Salvator" (Jesus Saviour of Men)[82] and were not the ill-understood abbreviation of the Greek letters ΙΗΣΟΥΣ (Jesus), what might their correct interpretation be?

As mentioned, the founder of the Jesuits, Ignatius of Loyola, used to combine the letters I.H.S. with a star, a lunar crescent and another star in his seal. It seems that this acronym was related to astrological notions, probably stemming from Chaldaea, since it was the country where the Magi studied the stars.

But the most likely meaning of the I.H.S. is provided by a stone sealed into the wall of the church of the village of Prats-de-Mollo in the Pyrénées-Orientales [Oriental Pyrenees] region, a stone's throw away from Arles-sur-Tech. It depicts the I.H.S. acronym combined with a derivative form of the ansate cross including the "H" in its graphical shape.

The peculiar ansate cross engraved on the wall of the church of Prats-de-Mollo

80 Documentary sources: La prière de Jésus [The Prayer to Jesus], a book written by « Un moine de l'Église d'Orient » [a monk of the Eastern Church] (Father Lev Gillet), published by Chevetogne/Seuil editions (« Livre de Vie » - Book of Life collection), 1963.
81 « Le Mémoire d'André Biglia et la prédication de Saint Bernardin de Sienne » ["The Memoirs of Andre Biglia and the predication of Saint Bernardino of Siena"], a text with an introduction and notes from Father B. de Gaiffier in the Analecta Bollandiana, volume 53, 1935, pp. 307-365.
82 About the devotion of the Franciscans to the "IHS": see E. Landry, « Contribution à l'étude critique des Fioretti de saint François d'Assise » ["Contribution to a Critical Study of the Fioretti of Saint Francis of Assisi", in Les Annales de la faculté des Lettres de Bordeaux et des Universités du Midi [Annals of the Faculty of Literature of Bordeaux and of the Universities of Southern France], IVth collection, volume I, 1901, pp. 138-145).

This emblem was engraved in 1652 by "La Sanch", the confraternity of penitents founded by Vincent Ferrer. And thus we have almost come full circle.

Further confirmation comes from a note from the "Catholic University of America"[83], in which we learn that as early as the 8th century, the following inscription was found on Roman gold coins: *"dn IHS chs rex regnantium."*[84] *This inscription came as a replacement for the ancient PAX (the Tau) engraved on the Roman coins dating from the time of Constantine the Great, "because it became customary to draw three nails in the shape of a 'V' underneath the 'H', [and] it was also said that 'IHSV' stands for 'In Hoc Signo Vinces' (in this sign you shall conquer), the words Emperor Constantine saw emblazoned in the heavens under the sign of the cross[85] in the year 312."*

It is thus remarkable that the Christic interpretation that is usually given to the I.H.S. is actually an error, and that these letters are originally a representation of the Persian Triad and of the emblem associated with it, i.e. the Tau.

As to the three nails that are often depicted under the I.H.S. acronym, and notably present under the "monogram" described by Louis Charbonneau-Lassay in the Carmelite chapel of Loudun, these should not be associated with the nails "of the Crucifixion". These particular three nails form the shape of a "V" crossed by a vertical line, forming a symbol that adds the V to the acronym "I.H.S.", to form the initials of "In Hoc Signo Vinces". The renowned penitent Anne-Catherine Emmerich provides us with a striking example of this symbolism in her visions of the Passion of Christ. She writes: *"the cross received the symbolic form under which I had often contemplated it. The two arms deviated from the trunk by rising like the branches of a tree, and the cross itself resembled a 'Y', in which the inner line*

---

83   Excerpt of "St. Bernardino of Siena, Preacher of the Holy Name of Jesus", a text published on the website of the Catholic Information Center on the Internet (http://www.catholic.net) and written by Peter A. Kwasniewski, Ph. D. Philosophy concentrating on medieval philosophy, now Assistant Professor in Philosophy at the Catholic University of America.
84   An inscription, one of the interpretations of which follows: "Lord Jesus Christ, King of Kings". As early as the VIIIth century, the letters I.H.S., which were replacing the ancient P.A.X., appeared to be particularly appreciated by the sect of the Arians (a sect of which certain members of the family of Constantine the Great confessed frankly to being adepts). These heretics, although non-Christian, had contrived these three letters into a Christic symbol so that its worship would be accepted among the people.
85   This so-called "cross" was not the Christian right-angled cross, but rather a Chaldean Tau (an intertwined "XP" or "PX", i.e. the symbol from which the Egyptian ansate cross – ankh – derives).

[the trunk] *was extended to* [reach] *the same height as the two other ones* [...].["]⁸⁶ The "patte d'oie" ("goose foot") shape of the cross described above oddly conflicts with the one transmitted through Christian tradition.

Contrary to the conventional representation, which consists in drawing the Cross of Christ as a "Latin" cross (i.e. a right-angled cross, constructed after the geometric pattern of a cube), Anne-Catherine Emmerich associates the shape of a "V crossed by a vertical line", i.e. the shape of the three nails often seen under the I.H.S., with the representation of the Cross. From the Christian symbol of the redemption of mankind and of the victory of Christ over death, the cross became, according to Anne-Catherine Emmerich and the Penitent movement of which she was part, the pagan image of a Chaldean idol: the Babylonian Tau, the shape of which can either be a "V crossed by a vertical line", or take the more complete form of an "X crossed by a vertical line". (That is to say the shape of the so-called "cuneiform tetragrammaton", the depiction of the Persian Triad, which is composed of wedges or... nails.)

Thus in the I.H.S., we have, combined into one acronym, several symbols that have been used by the Penitents, sometimes alternatively and sometimes in conjunction, so as to mark their places of worship. Let us list some further examples: At "Puente La Reina" in Spain, a Penitent Christ can be seen, crucified on a Y-shaped cross located at the end of the "Iglesia del Crucifijo" (Church of the Crucified One) built in the 12th century. This church is currently located near the convent of the Order of the Padres Reparadores (Devotees of the Sacred Heart).

As for the "In Hoc Signo Vinces" (I.H.S.V.), it can be found either on works of art dedicated to penance, or on the liturgical ornaments worn by penitents, or even in their dwelling places.

Finally, the three nails are commonly encountered, either in combination with the I.H.S. in order to form the "In Hoc Signo Vinces", or with a pair of pliers and a hammer (i.e. the instruments needed to fix nails), as in the Basilica of Santo Cristo in the town of Lezo in the Spanish Basque country, not far from the French border, where one can see in addition to these signs, a hairless Christ with a shaved skull, an extremely rare depiction of a deity which is probably Chaldaean in origin, and androgynous. (There are only four such depictions in the world, one in the town of Kra-

---

86   « *Les Visions d'Anne-Catherine Emmerich* » *["The Visions of Anne-Catherine Emmerich"], Editions Tequi, volume III, page 287.*

kow in Poland, another in the town of Eibar, equally in the Spanish Basque Country, and the last one in the town of Segovia in the Castile-Leon region, in Spain.)

Now that we have revealed the significance of the I.H.S. acronym, let us get back to Louis Charbonneau-Lassay and his inventory of the symbols present in the chapel of the Carmelite Penitents of Loudun. The author lists four very similar forms of a "combination of lines" which, to the profane, "*is only the abbreviated acronym of the Virgin Mary's name, reduced to superimposed letters.*" To support this statement, Charbonneau-Lassay explains that during the 18th and 19th century, these letters were translated as "Ave Maria", or even that, by adding "*a point over each* [of the two] *downstroke*[s] *of the* [capital] *'M', it was interpreted as 'Jesus, Maria, Joseph'*".

But, as this scholar argues, the real meaning of this monogram is quite remote from this, as in "*Loudun we have* [...] *evidence*" that the penitent "*author of the graffiti, saw in the superimposed 'M' and 'A', the famous sacred syllable of Central Asia, the A.V.M. or O.M. If indeed one deconstructs the said monogram, in it can be found the three letters A, V, M, which, once reunited, form AUM.*" Besides, Charbonneau-Lassay adds, "*in the series of Carmelite graffiti of Loudun, the number VI*" is thought by him to "*express the fact*" that the engraver "*has, quite intentionally and clearly, meant to separate, or rather to render distinct from one another, as much as possible inside a monogram, the three letters A, V, M.*"

We have to agree. We should also add that the A, V, M acronym could also be a depiction of the Mihir or the Tau, in short, a symbolic equivalent to the I.H.S. and to the three nails associated with it. On this matter, Charbonneau-Lassay relates that "*during the revision of the Armorial Général* [the heraldic registry of the region] *in 1696*" the monastery of the Carmelite monks of Loudun had the following coat of arms officially registered: "*Argent, two interlaced letters M and A Sable, topped by a crown Or, and accompanied with a heart pierced by three nails Sable.*"[87] There is a double combination of symbols in this coat of arms: the I.H.S. with its three nails, and the said three nails with the A, V, M acronym. Could it be

87   L. Charbonneau-Lassay, « Le cœur et les trois clous » ["The Heart and the Three Nails"], in Regnabit magazine, 1925. p. 13 and following (« L'iconographie ancienne de Jésus-Christ, postérieurement à la renaissance. I. Le cœur et le Monogramme I.H.S II. Le cœur et les trois clous » ["The ancient iconography of Jesus Christ, after the Renaissance period. I. The Heart and the I.H.S. Monogram. II. The Heart and the Three Nails"], in Regnabit magazine, 5th year, no. 7, December 1925, pp. 10-22.)

that here we are presented with equivalent symbols?

We will close our analysis of the inventory of signs made by Louis Charbonneau-Lassay with the description of graffiti in the shape of a reverse swastika, or the combination of a swastika with "the Rose". It would be pointless to extend this chapter here with tedious historical detours, all the more so, since Charbonneau-Lassay makes use of reliable critical thinking in his study. Therefore, we will content ourselves with summarizing his opinion, which is that these figures are Chaldaean symbols. He declares that the origin of the swastika is located in the Orient, and that *"the best authors seem to concur with one another to acknowledge that this sign, assuredly of an astronomical nature already at the time of its creation, would have originated among the Chaldeans, and from their country, would have spread out to the high plateaux of Tibet and Turan*[88] *on the one hand, and towards Assyria, Europe and Egypt on the other hand."*

For us, the most remarkable feature present in one of these swastika graffiti discovered at the chapel of Loudun lies in the fact that the four gamma letters of the (in this case reverse) swastika are interwoven with an "X", i.e. a Chi-Rho, i.e. the emblem of the Babylonian Tau. Therefore, apart from the opinion of Louis Charbonneau-Lassay, we add that the swastika is one of the multiple forms the Tau took among the penitent movement.

Finally, since this is not mentioned in Louis Charbonneau-Lassay's article, it is appropriate to add that the presence of penitents can also be detected through other signs of recognition which almost always go unnoticed in the eyes of the profane. We are referring to the profusion of statues dedicated to Mary Magdalene, or the presence of her relics, or even to the mere fact that the said "holy" place happens to be dedicated to her…

The *Dictionary of Phrase and Fable*, in the article "Mary Magdalene"[89], states that she is the *"patron saint of penitents, being herself the model penitent* […]. *In Christian art she is represented either (1) as a patron saint, young and beautiful, with a profusion of hair, and holding a box of* [burial] *ointment or (2) as a penitent, in a sequestered place, reading before a cross or skull."*

Apart from Mary Magdalene, any sculptures or paintings of Saint Francis of Assisi, Saint Anthony of Padua, the profusion of ornamental angels in a

---

88 *The ancient name for Central Asia: see note 75.*
89 *Dictionary of Phrase and Fable, E. Cobham Brewer, 1894, "Mary Magdalene" article.*

church, the representations of the Holy Family inside a grotto or cave, the Magi, the engravings or frescoes depicting monks holding a skull in their hands, or statues of Black Madonnas, when such statues are located near a subterranean crypt, or near a water well, all of these, were used by the penitent network to signal out churches that were "nodes" on their map of "heretical France". As any visitor the Church of Rennes-le-Château will have noted, several of these "signals" are on display in Saunière's church.

Chapter 5

Heretics everywhere...

How might Saunière have discovered this ritual and how did this secret network survive, across centuries, even millennia? On the surface, it would seem that we are breaking new ground and that no-one has ever written anything on this secret tradition. Although a lot has indeed been written about this priest and how he may have possessed a secret doctrine somehow passed on from ancient times, most authors have argued that this was a doctrine involving Mary Magdalene and her role in "original Christianity", which these authors believe was later excised from the official Church doctrine.

That Saunière may have possessed knowledge of a secret tradition that is definitely un-Christian and which has survived in this region since recorded time, will seem strange at first; but if one is able to assume, based on no evidence, that Saunière was part of a secret tradition involving Mary Magdalene, then one should be able to believe, based on evidence, that he was part of a secret tradition – of a different nature. If you believe that unorthodox information about Jesus was able to survive in this region for 2000 years, then believing that a secret Eastern tradition could also survive here for all that time is merely a change in contents of what that secret tradition contained.

But it is not virgin territory that we are exploring here. Jean-Daniel Dubois is a specialist on the Manichean religion[90] and has written an article[91] on the transmigrations and influence of this religion in Medieval Europe and the rest of the world. He writes: "The Manichean religion was born in Iran [...] and has spread in the East and in the West from the 3rd century AD onwards. Arriving in the West by the western fringes of the Roman Empire, the first Manicheans were seen as Persian spies coming from Iran."

He then adds that the Manicheans suffered persecution from the Roman

---

90   *Jean-Daniel Dubois is a director of studies at the Religious Science department of the Ecole Pratique des Hautes Etudes (EPHE) in Paris. He publishes Coptic, Gnostic and Manichean texts. He is the head of "Apocrypha", the international journal of studies on apocryphal literature, which is published by Editions Brepols, in Belgium.*
91   *Jean-Daniel Dubois, « Mani, un fou de Dieu » ("Mani, a Rebel to God"), an article published in the 2006 issue of the Revue Historia Thématique (Historia Thematic Magazine) entitled « Les hérétiques » ("The Heretics"), under the section « Les premiers dissidents » ("The First Dissidents").*

Empire, in 302 AD, on the eve of the Great Persecution against the Christians (from 303 AD onwards). As Manicheism continued to spread despite the persecutions, it was forced to suffer a second wave of discriminatory measures.

Once they were accepted as the official religion, the Christians themselves declared Manicheism to be a heresy (although it is "an altogether different religion"), beginning with bishop Eusebius of Caesarea, who wrote in his *"The Ecclesiastical History"* in the beginning of the 4th century: *"At this time, the fool who gave his name to the demonic heresy summoned upon himself the reason's perversion, [and] the Devil, Satan himself, God's enemy, pushed this man to ruin a good many people. He was demonic and insane. He tried hard to counterfeit the Christ. [...] And from the Persian country, he spread [his disciples] in our days to inhabit Earth as a mortal poison."*[92]

Amongst the heretics, Mani is without any doubt the most inspired and the most dangerous. Still, that does not make him the best known. Some argue that he was at the origin of all heresies, but it is difficult to identify conclusively the first person who described the dualistic doctrine that lies at the foundation of these heresies – many of which have come to be known as "Manicheism".

The Persian Magi seem to have been amongst the first to take up this dualistic doctrine. Some claim that they received it from the Hittites, a group that could be described as Palestinian Arabs. But other researchers argue that the heresy is far older and that its roots could be found in the time of Abraham and that it resulted from the promiscuity of the Hebrews with the Chaldeans at that time.

Whatever the true origin, it is clear that for a "heresy" to take root, the heretics themselves must have been inspired originally by a Biblical doctrine, which they saw as a perversion of the "true message". Of course, those who continued to adhere to the official doctrine considered the heretics to be the perversion. We should also not see the heresy as a sudden dramatic shift, but as a gradual development that occurred in stages: a first emergence at the time of Abraham, a second at the time of the Hittites and a third phase when the Jews were in captivity in Babylon. At the time, there were laws that forbade the Jews to read certain sacred books, for fear that the Magi would understand and would thus alter their contents. Still, this approach is only a hypothesis and the actual development remains obscure.

---

92   *Eusebius of Caesarea, "Ecclesiastical History", Book VII, 31.*

There is, fortunately, more information available about Mani himself. He was born in Persia around 240 AD. According to church historians, he was still young when he was bought by a wealthy widow, who brought in an Arab by the name of "Scythian" to educate him. Scythian knew the secrets of the Magi, as well as his disciple Buddas (Buddha)[93]. Mani learnt this system and believed that he could perfect certain of its aspects.

However, there are other sources that state that this is not exactly how Mani acquired his knowledge. They declare that Mani had always been a Magus, living in the Zoroastrian tradition. In both versions, it is clear that Mani was a well-educated man. It is stated that he studied geometry, astronomy and medicine. With all this knowledge at his disposal, it is said that he set out to embarrass Christianity. He saw it as his mission to reform Christianity and "enrich" it with the doctrine of the Magi. Mani looked at other heretics who had challenged Christianity in the past, amongst them Basilidius, Valentinus, Bardesanes, as well as Marcion the Apostate. All of these heresies had been quashed. He hoped his mission would meet with success.

Mani studied the Holy Scriptures for details that he could use in his quest for reform: statements that would provide a justification for his doctrine. One evening, his spirit was apparently lifted by profound nocturnal meditations. He believed that he saw how in the Bible there was confirmation that God was not all powerful. Suddenly inspired, he felt the presence of a demon who is named "the power of the shadows", the "prince of this world" or the "author and father of sin". Lucifer? Satan? Who knows? He realised how this discovery could lead to a conclusion that God was limited by the sphere of the demon, and that it was the latter who had given birth to our reality. He thus declared publicly that God could not stop evil and that the demon was in principle the autonomous, powerful, ruler of this world. He claimed that the Old Testament was, as such, the work of the devil and could under no circumstance be considered as "right". Only the New Testament was, in his opinion, worthy of any interest.

As in most new religions, there is a need for a New Messiah and it is Mani, who feels he is overwhelmed by a supernatural force, who took on the role of the prophet who had previously been announced by Jesus to his apos-

93   Cyril of Jerusalem, "Sixth Catechetical Lecture", Chapter 22-24:
"Terebinthus, [Mani's] disciple in this wicked error, inherited his money and books and heresy, and came to Palestine, and becoming known and condemned in Judaea, he resolved to pass into Persia: but lest he should be recognised there also by his name, he changed it and called himself Buddas."

tles. He stated: "I am the Consoler, it is I, Mani, who is this Envoy from Heaven, this mysterious preacher predicted by Christ." He thus convinced numerous followers; and his preachings that his was "the Second Coming" took him to various regions. One day, far from his homeland, he came across Archelaus, the bishop of Cascar in Mesopotamia. The two had a heated discussion and both decided that they should settle the contest with a public debate. In 277, Archelaus thus set out to demonstrate both to the disciples of Mani and his own followers that Mani did not have a divine mission to fulfil and that his doctrine directly contradicted the Scriptures.

The debate is well-documented[94], but we can of course debate the objectivity of the scribes. Still, it seems that Archelaus won the argument. The documents were used by Socrates of Constantinople[95] to draw a portrait of Mani, whereas St. Cyril of Jerusalem[96] consulted them to refute any possible opinions that were aired against Christianity. As for Mani himself, he did not understand why his theory had so little success, so he returned to Persia. He approached Shapur I, King of Persia[97] and lobbied the monarch, telling him he should have greater faith and declared that he, Mani, had the power to heal and resuscitate. As the son of the king was on his deathbed, Shapur had the perfect candidate to test Mani's claims. Mani failed and one would expect that, with the death of his child, the king would condemn Mani. Instead, it seems that the king forgave Mani for not being all-powerful. However, Mani is reported to have died in prison awaiting execution by the Persian Emperor Bahram I[98], while alternative accounts have it that he was either flayed to death or beheaded.

Despite these prominent setbacks, many were inspired by his doctrine and his followers quickly multiplied. Their preachings had far more success

---

94   *"Acta Disputationis cum Manete Haeresiarcha" ("Acts of the Controversy with Mani the Heresiarch"), also known as "Acta Archelai" ("Acts of Archelaus") written by one "Hegemonius" (probably a pseudonym) in the 4th century. The first version of these accounts was originally written in the Syriac language and belongs to the Oriental Christian Sources (Comp. Jerome, de Vir. III. 72). However, the full text only remains in their Latin translation (which seems to have been made on the basis of a Greek translation). The full Latin text has been published by Zacagni ("Collectan. Monum. Vet., Eccl. Graecae et Latinae", in-4°, Roma, 1698), and Routh ("Reliquiae Sacrae", vol. V., pp. 3-206). An English translation of the dispute can be found in the "Ante-Nicene Library" published by T. & T. Clark (vol. XX., pp. 272-419). [Am. ed. vol. VI. p. 173 sq.].*

95   *Socrates of Constantinople (c. 380 – 450 AD), was one of the authors who continued the Church History started by Eusebius of Caesarea (c. 260 – 340 AD).*

96   *St. Cyril of Jerusalem, "Sixth Catechetical Lecture".*

97   *Shapur I ruled from 241 to 272 AD.*

98   *Bahram I, who was Shapur's successor, ruled from 272 to 273 AD.*

than Mani's own mission, spreading to Syria, India, Egypt, throughout Persia and even in the Far East. Even though we have termed this movement "Manicheism", it is known that while his followers had respect for Mani, it was not a blind following; in fact, some of his theories were altered. As such, Manicheism was a movement in which various people saw Mani as their main inspiration, but each teacher had adapted Mani's doctrine to suit his own opinions and teachings.

By 450 AD, there were apparently seventy groups following him and the evidence suggests that the Manicheist groups were closely linked with the Gnostics[99], another "Christian heresy" that at the time was a serious religious threat to what would become mainstream Christianity. It is believed that many of these groups united and in fact that Manicheism and Gnosticism became one. It shows how the original message was adapted repeatedly, and with each adaptation, was able to expand.

The Heretical Expansion

Manicheism was brought into the Mediterranean area through Palestine and Egypt, certainly from the middle of the 3rd century onwards, though it was already frowned upon in Egypt by the Ecclesiastical authorities before the end of the 3rd century. A papyrus dating from the years 280-300 AD (The Greek papyrus Rylands 469) is a letter from an Alexandrian Bishop warning against the missionary efforts of the Manicheans. At one time, the Roman Emperors were Manicheism's greatest opponents. The reason may be that the Persians in general were held in disregard by the Romans, and Manicheism, a child of Persia, failed to inspire the Romans. The Emperors found the doctrine odious and believed that it originated from the religion of the Magi.

Thus, between 285 and 492 AD, Manicheism was banned. Jean-Daniel Dubois[100] describes it best: *"But the most rigorous refutation of Manicheism would come at the end of the 4th century (381-383 AD), from the decisions of the Christian Emperor Theodosius aiming to stop several heresies all at once, which included Manicheism, on the pretext that Manicheans hid themselves among the ranks of the Christian Churches, appearing to be monks or ascet-*

---

99   According to Theodoret. Theodoret (c. 393- c. 466 AD) was a bishop in Cyrrhus, not far away from Antioch. He wrote many biblical commentaries. He is most famous for having continuated Eusebius of Caesarea's Ecclesiastical History where Eusebius left off.

100   Jean-Daniel Dubois, « Mani, un fou de Dieu » ("Mani, a rebel to God"), published in the 2006 issue of the Revue Historia Thématique (Historia Thematic Magazine) entitled « Les hérétiques » ("The Heretics"), under the section « Les premiers dissidents » ("The First Dissidents").

ics". Perhaps little changed between the 3rd and 19th century!

At the beginning of the 4th century, in Saint Augustine's time, Manicheans are said to have spoken Greek or Latin[101]. Saint Augustine himself fought them tooth and nail in Africa, but despite his tactics, they continued to multiply, often in the obscurity of catacombs or other secret hideouts.

Spain, Gaul, Armenia, Egypt… each region became populated by these dualist zealots. By the 7th century, we find some in China, where they have to explain their doctrines to the Imperial authorities. From the 8th to the 11th century, we meet the Manicheans on the roads of Central Asia's steppes, even becoming the official religion of the Uighur Princes. Marco Polo, in his travels at the end of the 13th century, still encountered some of them in southern China[102].

Jean-Daniel Dubois provides us with a very surprising glimpse of Manicheism and its ability to spread in the East (China, India, Iran, Persia), in Africa (Egypt), in Northern countries (Russia and the steppes of Central Asia) and in the West, this from the 3rd century onwards. Furthermore, Dubois makes interesting observations on Manicheism and Christianity. He writes[103] that *"we can understand why some primitive Christians saw Manicheism as a Christian heresy."* Dubois himself nevertheless makes a clear distinction between the nature and origin of Manicheism and Christianity. The two religions look alike, they share similarities, but do not pursue the same purpose and are in their structure, formation and dogma, very unlike, in fact even completely foreign to each other.

Dubois has written, in our opinion, one key observation that stands out amongst the rest: that at the end of the 4th century certain Manicheans were hiding *"among the ranks of the Christian Churches, appearing to be monks or ascetics"*. It is equally clear that despite continued and repetitive persecution, Manicheism continued to spread, entering the West. As they were persecuted, they decided to go undercover, hiding in the very structure that was trying to suppress them. Hence, they infiltrated their enemies: rather than hide in underground catacombs as the early Christians did, the Manicheans became members of religious congregations… and continued to thrive and expand as such. They had become "the enemy within"[104]. The technique chosen by the Manicheans was not to form a new

---

101   *Ibid.*

102   *The Manicheans of Southern China were called "Zaitoun".*

103   *Ibid.*

104   Jacques-Bénigne Bossuet, « *Histoire des Variations [...]* » ("*History of the Variations*

block and try to fight as such, but rather to infiltrate, operate undetected and survive, if not convert, from within – like a virus.

When Emperor Theodosius failed to kill this "infection", he wrote that they called themselves "ascetics". An ascetic is defined as a person who devotes himself to piety and mortifications. In line with the notion that this reality was created by "the Evil One", they saw the human body as devilish and hence subjected it to terror and pain; only the mind was divine, but was caught inside its evil coil; penitence was there to liberate the soul from the body.

In the Middle Ages, the Church once again ran into trouble with people who were then labelled penitents and flagellants. Like the Manicheans in the 4th century, we find that these penitents were found to live within religious communities, often monastic communities, and tried to live in extreme poverty, performing mortifications. Little has changed, it seems, between the 4th and 14th century, when these penitents – or should we just boldly write "Manicheans"? – live in the monastic communities of northern Spain and Southern France. The same situation applied to Italy, in the 11th and 12th century, where Manicheans had also entered religious orders.

Bergier, in his *Theological Dictionary*[105], mapped their progress, stating that Manicheans *"took refuge in Bulgaria, where they were known as Bulgarians or Bougres."* He adds that others had indeed entered Italy, building religious communities in Lombardy, who then sent preachers out to France and other regions. In the Languedoc, these missionaries adopted the name of Cathars[106]. Bergier's scenario of the spread of this heresy is supported by Bossuet[107], who confirms that the Cathar heresy was linked

[...]"), published in 3 volumes by Charpentier, 1844, chapter XI, § 203:
"It is the sect [Manicheism] that has infected Christianism for the longest period and in the most dangerous manner; for the longest period, because it has been witnessed as active for so many centuries; and in the most dangerous manner, for it did not seek any clear-cut schism like the other [sects]..."
105 Abbé Nicolas Bergier, « Dictionnaire de Théologie » (Theological Dictionary), published in 8 volumes by Chalandre & Petit, Besançon, 1826.
106 Further confirmation of the Bulgarian (i.e Manichean) origin of the Cathars can be found in « Le Recueil » of Etienne de Bourbon, a Dominican monk from the 8th century, according to whom *"the Cathars were also called Bulgarians, because their Occidental birthplace was located in Bulgaria."* Interestingly, let us point out that Etienne de Bourbon's words imply that Catharism also had another, presumably more ancient, birthplace in the Orient... Refer to « Recueil Inédit d'Etienne de Bourbon », published by Lecoy de la Marche, Paris, 1887.
107 Jacques-Bénigne Bossuet, « Histoire des Variations » ("History of Variations"), published in 3 volumes by Charpentier, 1844.

to Manicheism and adds that Lombardy was the epicentre for the spread of this religious doctrine. Pfister[108] notes that even though the Manicheans had installed themselves first in Northern Europe, it was in Lombardy and the adjoining regions in the north of Italy that the cult took on considerable proportions and that it was here that it had – once again – successfully infiltrated medieval religious orders. Italy, it seems, sat at the crossroads of the Manichean mission.

In *The Cathar Council's acts of Saint Felix Da Caraman*[109], quoted by Nicolas Vignier in *Church History since the baptism of Our Lord Jesus Christ*[110], the writer gives us a glimpse of this religion's diffusion in this country: *"As we find it written by an ancient author, the heresy has been brought from overseas territories, namely, from Bulgaria. From there it spread through other provinces [...] to the country of the Languedoc, Toulouse and Gascony, (the so-called Albigensian heresy) or Albigensians who were similarly called Boulgres from Bulgarians and 'Cottereaux' for 'Cathars'."*

The writer adds, speaking about the origin of this heresy: *"At first, the Cathar's heresy began to spread in Lombardy. They had a bishop called Marc, and under his authority were the whole of Lombardy, Tuscany and the Marches of Trevisa. This Marc received his orders from Bulgaria. There also came from Constantinople to Lombardy a certain heretic named Pope Nicetas."*

The regions of Tuscany, the Marches of Trevisa and Lombardy and more generally the whole of Northern Italy, therefore had certain Manichean churches. But this account remains inadequate to get a precise idea of the exact number of these Manichean establishments in Italy. The presence of one or several Cathar churches, in itself, does not mean that there had been an infiltration of Manicheism throughout society. Hence, other documents provide us with a more detailed inventory of the settlements of these religious organisations, and above all of the scale and magnitude of the infiltration.

---

108 Christian Pfister, « Etudes sur le règne de Robert le Pieux (996-1031) » "Studies on Robert le Pieux's reign (996-1031)", Bibliothèque de l'Ecole des Hautes Etudes (Library of the School of High Studies), Paris, 1885, page 326.

109 For a full-fledged scientific study of these precious documents, refer to: Antoine Dondaine, « Les Actes du Concile Albigeois de Saint Félix de Caraman. Essai de critique d'authenticité d'un document medieval » ("The Acts of the Albigensian Council of Saint Félix de Caraman. An Attempt at a Critical Study of a Medieval Document's Authenticity"), Miscelanea Giovanni Mercati, Roma, 1946, pp. 324-355.

110 Nicolas Vignier, "Book of the Church History since the Baptism of Our Lord Jesus Christ", Leyden 1601, page 268.

Vittorio Sabbadini[111] of Bologna University and archivist of the Mantua State Records reports that in the *"De Heresi Catharorum in Lombardia"* (1210)[112], it is stated that the Lombardian Manichean Church was made up of six dioceses: the Church of Concorezzo, the Church of Desenzano, the Church of Bagnolo San Vito, the Church of Marca Trevisiana (The Marches of Trevisa), the Church of Florence, and finally the Church of the Valle Spoletana (The Spoleta Valley). To this, we must add another document, which provides a revealing glimpse of how the heresy was rooted in these populations. It is the testimony, dated 1250, of Raniero Sacconi[113], a former Cathar who had become a Dominican, which adds some details concerning the exact number of Cathar heretics. He states that there are *"thirteen Cathar Churches, 500 'perfects' (Cathar Celebrants) for the Church of Desenzano in Italy, at least 1,500 for the Concoresians still in Italy, about 200 for the Church of Bagnolo San Vito, maybe 100 in the Marches of Trevisa, 150 'perfects' for the French Church, and finally almost 200 in the Churches of Toulouse, Carcassonne and Albi."* (The County of Toulouse, at that time, was not part of France.)

In his statement, the witness says that 500 Manichean Churches are located in Constantinople, in Romania, Lydia and Bulgaria. His analysis of the Cathar population only takes into account the presence of Cathar priests, the "perfects", because the number of heretical believers in Italy and the other countries is not only difficult to list, but at the same time was said to reach "infinite numbers" – which must probably be read as "extremely widespread".

Penetration

This testimony is a rare document, which was not available in Bossuet's time, because the archives at that time had not yet been examined. The exhaustive search through the works of the Inquisition and other historical texts was mainly achieved by the Dominican monk Antoine Dondaine[114],

---

111 *Vittorio Sabbadini, "Gli eretici sul lago : Storia dei Catari Bagnolesi" ("The Heretics on the Lake: History of the Bagnolese Cathars"), San Nicolo Po, May 2003.*

112 *This anonymous manuscript from the 8th century, currently kept in Basel, is the main historical witness with regard to the Cathar hierarchy in Italy.*

113 *Raniero Sacconi, "Summa de Catharis" ("A Numbering of the Cathars"), 1250.*

114 *Dondaine, A., "The Cathar Hierarchy in Italy, II: The Tractatus de hereticis of Anselmus of Alexandria" in: Archivum Fratrum Praedicatorum (The Dominican Order's Archives) 20, 1950, s. 234-324. Dondaine A, "The Cathar Hierarchy in Italy, I: The De Heresi Catharorum", in: Archivum Fratrum Praedicatorum, 19, 1949, s. 280-312.*
And finally, "De Heresi Catharorum in Lombardia" in A. Dondaine, "The Heresies and Inquisition during the 8th and 9th centuries" Norfolk 1990, III, pp. 306-312.

in the 20ᵗʰ century. What it reveals is that the infiltration was much more widespread than previously believed. By the 13ᵗʰ century, the infiltration seems to have been a complete success; the virus had, in certain regions, actually taken over and was using the power of the Church against the Church itself.

Vittorio Sabbadini[115] states that *"in the Council of St. Felix Da Caraman, in 1167, Nicetas came from Constantinople to Italy to unify Catharism in the Latin countries."* The main Cathar reformer, the Bishop Nicetas, moved from Constantinople, went to Thracia, crossed to Albania, no doubt making a detour via Bosnia and finally arrived in Italy to take possession of his Church. It shows the extent, geographically, of one man's control and how well-organised it was over an area that was actually larger than that over which the Catholic Church exercised dominance at that time. As to its origins, the Dominican Anselmus of Alexandria in his treatise *"The beginning and the origin of the dualistic heresy in the Middle Ages"*, written in 1270, maintained that Manicheism and Catharism originated in Asia Minor, spreading in the Byzantine Empire as far as Thracia, before it reached the West. These writers, who write in the immediate aftermath of the Albigensian Crusade, therefore identified Catharism with Manicheism: they shared the same geographical origin and both were a dualistic religion.

As to Italy, it is clear that the country had an important Manichean population, visited by the bishop of Constantinople himself. It means that Italy was not some isolated enclave, where a local, corrupted or diverse form of Manicheism existed; it was mainstream Manicheism and was widely popular, judging from the reported numbers of perfects that existed in the country. The Manichean penetration was so profound that in some cities, Florence in particular, it had largely overtaken Catholicism as the dominant religion.

Although the Albigensian Crusade had apparently been a success in eradicating the religion in Southern France, forcing the local lords to show their allegiance to the papal troops, or lose their territory, elsewhere, and specifically in Italy, the situation (from the perspective of the Church) seemed to be worse. The census takers had decided it was impossible to repress the heresy, as it appeared to be too widespread, too varied and too well organised. To try to eradicate the "evil" from France, it had taken

---

115   *Vittorio Sabbadini, "Gli eretici sul lago: Storia Dei Catari Bagnolesi" ("The Heretics on the Lake: History of the Bagnolese Cathars"), San Nicolo Po, May 2003.*

a long and painful crusade; to remove the cancer from Italy might have meant the total destruction of Italian society; and as Italian society was the foundation of the Church itself, it would mean that not only would the heresy be eradicated, but that the Church would be committing suicide

Indeed, we do need to ask the question as to whether the Catholic Church was still alive as such at the end of the 13th century. In Italy, the sect had penetrated various regions, which were actually thought of as the centre of Catholicism. When we ask whether Catholicism was still alive, we know that there was a Pope; there were bishops and priests, monks and people going to church. But how many of these "Catholics" were actually "double agents"? The situation in Italy seems to have been so dire that no-one knew the extent of the heresy – except to say that it was "extensive" – and no-one knew how to remove the cancer. With any substitution of one bishop for another came the very real risk that a Manichean adept would be pushed into a position of power. We note that, at that time and throughout most of the Catholic Church's history, popes, cardinals and bishops were tradition-ally Italian, so the danger of an infiltration into the highest ranks of the Catholic Church was even more real: the recruiting grounds were infested with a virus.

In the final analysis, the Church decided to persecute the Cathars of the Languedoc, and also hunt them down in other regions; but it was unable to reduce their numbers in Italy, in the heartland of the heresy, where the Ca-thars were most numerous and where it would therefore be the easiest to to make some or many arrests. How can we accept that the Roman Catholic Church deals with the Cathar problem of the Languedoc first, before even trying to remedy the Lombardian heresy, which posed a direct threat? In-stead, it waits until 1281 to start a campaign in northern Italy, four decades after laying siege to Montségur, which housed the last vestige of Catharism; but few people have probably ever heard of this "Lombardian crusade". The reason? There was very little to it: it was a subdued repression, which only reached certain areas and was not very profound in impact.

The Manichean-Cathar movement was also present in Germany, Flan-ders and in the Champagne region, as well as Burgundy – the regions from where Saunière received large donations. Many of these regions remained unaffected by the Albigensian crusade when it occurred in the 13th cen-tury. In Italy, we know that the heresy was still alive in the 14th century, as was the case in Bosnia. But even though the Cathars in Germany, Flanders and the Champagne were not the subject of a crusade, they did suffer from persecutions.

Philippe Martel, of Paul Valéry University[116], wrote that *"Catharism is a European phenomenon. [...] It grew on a permanent basis [...] in far-away Bosnia [...] and had twin bases [...] which are in Occitania and northern Italy. While the Occitan Cathars were persecuted from the beginning of the 13th century, their brothers in Lombardy enjoyed good fortune: we must wait until 1281 to see their own version of Montségur, the Sirmione Castle, on Lake Garda. Meanwhile, the Cathar communities of northern Italy served as a solid rear-guard for the Occitan Cathars. [...] It was to their Italian brothers [that they came] to perfect their religious education, which was no longer possible to ensure in Occitania, controlled by the Inquisition."*

It seems that we need to draw two conclusions. First, that the Roman Catholic Church did not want to intervene in Italy – but when finally it did, not forcefully – because of the extensive infiltration of Manicheans within the Church hierarchy. Secondly, that the delay of 100 to 150 years before any action was taken meant that the Italian heretics had more than ample time to prepare themselves for a possible attack and make sure that the impact would be as minimal as possible[117].

For some readers, there will no doubt be an apparent contradiction in the above conclusion: if the Manicheans had taken over control of the Church and were able to fend off a crusade against themselves in Italy, why did they attack their brethren in the Languedoc? The reason is that the persecution of the Languedocian Cathars was not an initiative from the Church;

---

116   *Philippe Martel is a researcher at the French CNRS (Centre National de la Recherche Scientifique) and a professor at the Paul Valéry University in Montpellier, France.*
117   *This gap of almost 100 years between Italy and Languedoc in the repression of the Cathar heresy, suggests that the Manicheans of Italy have had more than ample time to take precautions to escape the unpleasant fate that may have been reserved for them. How else can we explain that Italy's huge Cathar population ("innumerable", as reported by Raniero Sacconi in 1250) managed to literally vanish before 1281, even when the retaliatory measures taken against these heretics were far less severe and frequent in that country than in other places? There is an obvious contradiction here, and one which can only find a solution by concluding that the Manicheans did assimilate progressively into the Roman Catholic Church. In other words, the Manicheans became part of the ecclesiastical clergy, by infiltrating it as well as by participating to it, "under the guise of monks or ascetics" (said Emperor Theodosius – already – in his time). This infiltration of the Catholic Church by the Manichean clergy can only have occured, for the most part, between the end of the 7th century and 1281, between the first persecutions in the Languedoc and the Northern countries (i.e. modern Belgium, Flanders, Germany, the Netherlands), and the date corresponding to the inexplicable disappearance of the sect in Italy.*

the instigators were nobles from Northern Europe, who had taken it upon themselves to repress the heresy; only later did the Church engage in, and take over the offensive. Julien Havet, in *The Heresy and The Secular Arm in the Middle Age until the XIIIth Century*[118], observes that it was King Robert the Pious who, in 1022, sentenced the Cathars of Orléans to the stake, a punishment that was not used by the Catholic Church. In fact, Robert had to "invent" this type of torture for the occasion. It shows that the initial reaction came from the lay, not the religious powers.

The birth of the penitent movement

What became of the Italian Cathars between the end of the 11th century and the beginning of the 14th century? They developed into the penitent movements.

At the time, Italy was a Christian possession; having taken over from the Roman Empire. The Church governed the whole of Italian society, which, at the time, was largely feudal and agriculture-based. The clergy were a worldly power, on par with the Roman Emperor; they spoke in Latin, the language that continues to be the official Catholic means of communication, and had litttle if any contact with the population. The latter did not use or understand much Latin, speaking instead the language of the region.

The feudal social model imploded at the end of the 11th century. Lombardy and central Italy saw radical social changes: the cities began to trade increasingly with the East and a new social class began to appear, which soon became an economic, and therefore a political force: the merchants. The countryside became victim to rural depopulation, with people flocking to cities, where there were jobs and a higher standard of living.

On an intellectual level, the cities saw an influx of foreign ideas. Chief amongst these were ideas that floated about from the Eastern world to the eastern shores of Europe, where Manicheism was an important religion. Turning to the West, we find that serious problems threatened the continent: the plague, as well as incessant quarrels between the papacy and the German Empire, each vying for political supremacy.

Faced with this option, it is clear which side was more appealing for the

---

118   Julien Havet, "The Heresy and the Secular Arm in the Middle Ages until the 13th century", Paris, 1881, pp. 488-517. Also refer to Ladrierre A., « L'Eglise – Une esquisse de son histoire pendant vingt siècles » ("The Church – An Overview of its History for Twenty Centuries"), Editions Bibles et Littérature Chrétienne, Chailly Montreux, for more information on how these Cathars of Orléans are actually related to Oriental missionaries called "Poblicans" (a distortion of "Paulicians").

northern and central Italian cities. Indeed, they let go of the already fragile bond with the Catholic clergy and became entranced by the "heretical" thinking that hailed from Asia Minor.

It was at this period that the whole of Europe, but particularly northern and central Italy, western Germany, northern France and the Languedoc, was settled by groups of penitents and flagellants – Manicheans. Voltaire, in his *Philosophical Dictionary*[119], noted his amazement at the strength of these religious movements: *"At the start of the 13th century, Brotherhoods of Penitents had formed in Italy, in Perugia and in Bologna. Almost naked young people with rods in their hands [...] flogged themselves in the streets. Women were watching them through window shutters, flogging themselves in their bedroom."* Meteren[120] wrote about the Franciscan, Adriacem, a preacher of Bruges, who flogged totally naked female penitents. In many of the convents, the monks and nuns whipped themselves on the buttocks. Such open displays of pain and nudity obviously did not go down well with all branches of society and quite often, some type of veil had to be drawn over these practices; hence the reason why women in Italy seemed to be flogging themselves in the privacy of their bedroom, rather than walking around naked through the streets of Italy.

It should not come as a surprise that the "morality" of these people was often the topic of discussions. Today, we would probably qualify their practices as a morbid obsession of mortification of the flesh (masochism), or a "pain fetish". Although the penitent movement has survived to this day, over the last two centuries, it has been specifically their displays of the willingness if not the actual desire to suffer pain in public that have been muted, facing demands that their public demonstrations of their faith occur instead in peace and tranquillity. Of course, we can only wonder whether, like the monk Silas in *The Da Vinci Code*[121], self-mortification continues to be practiced in the privacy of their homes.

How many penitent brotherhoods came to settle in the European cities is known: in France, they were present in Marseilles, Toulouse, Nice, Limo-

---

119   Voltaire, *"Philosophical Dictionary"*, part 1, in the article entitled *"Austerities, Flagellations, Mortifications"* [1764].
120   *Emanuel van Meteren, "Historia Belgica" ("Belgian History"), anno 1570.*
121   *Dan Brown, "The Da Vinci Code", published by Doubleday Books, 2003.*

ges, Limoux, Provence and Monaco[122]. They were present in Cologne[123] and in most cities of Flanders, western Germany, eastern and Southern France[124]. But "worst off" was, once again, Italy, which had an exceptional density of flagellant brotherhoods, with Calabria, Florence, Perugia, Venice and Piedmont chief amongst them[125].

Voltaire[126] also noted that these self-flagellations were not specific to penitents, but were also practiced in the more mainstream confraternities, such as the Franciscan community. In Umberto Eco's *The Name of*

122   Source material for the presence of these French confraternities can be found in:
Marseilles: Allier, R, "The Society of the Very Blessed Sacrament of the Altar in Marseille, A secret society in the XVIIth century", Champion, Paris 1909, and Barnes, Andrew E., "De Poenitentibus Civitatis Massilia" ("On the Penitents of the City of Marseilles"), Ph.D Princeton University, 1983.
Toulouse: Boursiquot, Jean-Luc, "Penitents and Toulousaine Society in the Age of Enlightenment", Review of Southern France, 1976.
Nice: Bordes, Maurice, "Contribution to the Penitents Brotherhoods' study in Nice in the 17th century" Review of Southern France, 1978.
Limoges: Cassan, Michel, "The Various Faces of the Devots Brotherhoods: the example of Limoges in the 16th centurty", Review of Southern France, 99, 1987.
Provence, Monaco, Limoux, etc.: Froeschlé-Chopard, Marie-Hélène, "The Popular Religion in Eastern Provence in the XVIIIth century", published by Beauchesne, Paris, 1980.
123   Gérard Chaix, « Les confréries à Cologne au 16ᵉ siècle » ("The Brotherhoods of Cologne in the 16th century"), Transcript of the 1983 Symposium of Rouen, published by F. Thelamon, Rouen, 1987.
124   Michel Vovelle, « Géographie des confréries à l'époque moderne » ("A Geography of the Brotherhoods in the Modern Era"), in Revue d'Histoire de l'Eglise Française (Historical Review of the French Catholic Church), 1983.
125   Source material for the presence of these Italian confraternities can be found in:
Calabria: Esposito, G., "Per la storia delle confraternite del Rosario in Calabria" ("On the History of the Rosary Confraternities in Calabria"), Rivista storica calabrese (Calabrese Historical Review), n.s., 1, 1980, p. 145-162.
Florence: Henderson, John, "The Parish and the Poor in Florence at the Time of the Black Death: The Case of San Frediano", Continuity and Change, 3 (2), 1988, and same author: "Confraternities and the Church in late medieval Florence", Studies in Church History, 23, 1986.
Central Italy: Henderson, John, "The Flagellant Movement and Flagellant Confraternities in Central Italy, 1260-1400", Studies in Church History, 15, 1978.
Piedmont, Perugia, Venice, etc.: Martini, G., "Storia delle confraternite italiane con particolare riguardo al Piemonte" ("History of the Italian confraternities, with a particular emphasis on the Piedmont region"), Turin, 1935 and Martinelli, O. "Le confraternite di Perugia dalle origini al S. 19", Annali, 291-544, 9-364, and 9-428, and Monti, G. M., "Le confraternite medievali dell'alta e media Italia" ("The Medieval Brotherhoods of Northern and Central Italy"), Venice, 1927, and finally Richard MacKenny, "Devotional Confraternities in Renaissance Venice", Voluntary Religion, eds. W. J. Sheils and D. Wood, Blackwell, Oxford, 1986.
126   Voltaire, "Philosophical Dictionary", part 1, in the article entitled "Austerities, Flagellations, Mortifications" [1764].

the Rose[127], we see both the presence of such self-flagellation practiced by members of this enigmatic community, as well as a lapsed heretic, screaming "penitence" at the young Franciscan Anselmo. Also, we note that Meteren[128] wrote that the flagellations he had observed in Bruges were performed by a Franciscan father, Adriacem[129].

Jean Chélini[130], professor of Law and Political Sciences at the University of Aix-Marseille, wrote that the penitents went out of their way to encourage craftsmen and traders to join their movement: they targeted the new social class. These men worked and lived in the markets, where they were stall-keepers or assistants. They were the force of the street, a militia, which also was able to defend the city and which sometimes controlled access to it. Chelini adds that the meetings of these organisations sometimes took place in a church, but they were just as likely to occur in the public square of the cloisters of a convent. Each group had its patron saint and they all showed themselves in public, in their processions, during the Holy Week.

This was the situation in Italy and the rest of Europe from the 13th century onwards; we note that La Sanch existed in Perpignan in the early part of the 15th century. As peaceful as the La Sanch procession is today, at other times and elsewhere, the public self-flagellations often resulted in such public disorder, that the authorities were forced to clamp down on the processions, its participants and members of the audience. As Jean Chélini puts it, the processions often led to "anticlerical and sectarian demonstrations… [or worse.] In 1454, 22 flagellants were condemned to be burned at the stake in Ascherleben, Thuringen[131]. Those who had "repented" and

---

127   Umberto Eco, *"Il nome della rosa"*, *Bompiani, Milano, 1980. "The Name of the Rose", English translation by William Weaver Jr., published in 1983 by Harcourt, New York, and Secker & Warburg, London.*

128   Emanuel van Meteren, *"Historia Belgica" ("Belgian History"), anno 1570.*

129   *This episode is also quoted by Voltaire in his "Philosophical Dictionary", in the same article as above.*

130   Jean Chélini, *« Histoire religieuse de l'Occident médiéval » (A Religious History of the Medieval Occident), republished by Hachette Pluriel, 1997. The history and customs of the penitents are also prominently on display in another writing by the same author, actually the article « Entre confrères, faut s'entraider ! » ("Among friars, one has to help one another!") in Revue Historia Thématique (Historia Thematic Magazine), no. 65 from 01/05/2000, p. 53, under the column : « Un Moyen Age inattendu » ("Unexpected Middle Ages"), in the "Jean Chélini" section. Jean Chélini is a professor at the Faculty of Law and Political Science of Aix-Marseilles III, and the director of the Institut de Droit et d'Histoire Canonique (Institute of Canonical Law and History) of Aix-en-Provence.*

131   Ascherleben, *is a town located in modern Germany, in the Land (county) of Thuringen.*

had foresworn their alliance to the movement were forced to wear special clothing, which allowed the population to recognise them for who they had been".

The spread of the penitent movement towards northern Europe was assisted by its implantation within the trade and merchant community. Italy became an economic power, which spread its economic influence far afield. Florence, for example, relied heavily on the dying of wool. The wool came from sheep bred as far away as the Borders region of Scotland. It was shipped to Bruges, which soon became the Venice of the North. Thus, not only did Bruges become a town where there was a major Florentine presence, but it also became an important centre for these penitents. Equally, we note that some of the Manicheans were later referred to as "weavers", the wool and related trade and products being one of the main pillars of the new economic model.

With the spread of a trade economy across Europe, the Manichean doctrine expanded too, and by the 14th and 15th century, the situation had grown worse than ever before; Manicheism had infiltrated the religious orders, but now it had also infiltrated the new and emerging powerbase of the economy. This meant that the penitents were not merely influential in the corridors of the Church, but were also becoming rich – which is an important observation to make as Saunière is of course known as a rich priest, thus fitting both aspects.

This "new power generation" made the penitent movement an important player in local politics; and in the aftermath of the Albigensian Crusade, it was clear that many felt extremely upset with nobility and the clergy, who even then were beginning to be seen as the old establishment. One example was Jean Le Bel, born in Liège, around 1290, in the family of the deputy mayor of the town[132]. He noted that the resident penitents wanted to topple the Church and to replace the rituals and liturgy with a penitent sacrament (focusing on self-flagellation). He believed that plans were afoot to try to accomplish this within a number of cities in Flanders and its neighbouring areas.

As to the nature of this "sacrament": in his *Vrayes Chroniques*[133], written

---

132   *Jean Le Bel (c. 1290 – c. 1390) was a Canon at the Saint Lambert Cathedral of Liège, who nevertheless led a worldly life. He actually served as a soldier in the army of Edward III, king of England, and fought at the side of his friend and protector Jean de Beaumont, the younger son of the count of Hainaut.*
133   *Jean Le Bel's « Vrayes Chroniques » ("True Chronicles"), deal with the beginning of the Hundred Years War in an accurate and concise style, covering specifically the 1329 -1367*

at the request of Jean de Beaumont, the younger son of the earl of Hainaut wrote that *"during the great plague in Germany, the penitents gathered in a location where they undressed, keeping on only their underwear, to flog themselves twice a day, using lashes and needles that they stuck into themselves, as much as they could, hoping that as much blood as possible flowed from their shoulders. When some of these penitents came to Liège, everybody ran out to see them. […] To everyone, they seemed to be Holy People. […] Some inhabitants of Liège learned their practices, translated their chants and joined their group; they travelled all over the regions of Liège, Brabant, Hainaut and elsewhere. […] This fashion increased to such an extent that all cities were full of these people who call themselves scourgers and fellow members."*

In the end, it was left to the Pope to pass sentence on them, for they were in a position *"to destroy the Holy Church. They had already begun to disturb services and the offices of the Church, claiming in their stupidity that their self-flagellation and chanting was more worthy than the Church rituals."*[134] There were fears that they would perhaps soon begin to kill priests or the clergy, as a fast and relatively easy method to turn the situation to their advantage – again underlined in *The Name of the Rose*, where one converted "Dolcenite" was said to have killed priests before his conversion.

The flagellants were not seen as some aberration of Christianity; they were seen as a heresy. Jean Le Bel and his fellow chroniclers emphasise the movement's heretical nature and the sentences passed by the Pope and the local lords, such as Pope Clement VI in 1349, the German Emperor Charles and the French king Philip le Bel, all stressed the heretical nature of the movement. Many of the charges against them report attempts on the life of priests and clerics, as well as more "moral charges" such as practicing vice in groups, renouncing the Church's sacraments, rejecting the Church hierarchy, as well as papal authority, and claiming self-flagellation as the only mechanism through which salvation could be obtained.

Pope Clement VI denounced the flagellants not only as heretics, but also called them superstitious, debauchers and declared that he believed them to be guilty of diabolical beliefs; he forbade anyone to provide accommodation to penitents, or to participate in any way in their rituals. The Pope was not alone in his condemnation. Dezobry and Bachelet wrote that the *"penitents were rebellious, looters, murderers, who lived a debauched life with various forms of excess"*. The *Catholic Encyclopedia* described the penitents

---

period.
134   *Ibid.*

as *"a fanatical and heretical sect which increased in the 12ᵗʰ century and during succeeding centuries. The terrible plague of 1295, the tyranny and endless anarchy in the Italian states, the prophecies regarding the arrival of the Antichrist and the end of the world by Joachim de Fiore [allowed the] Brotherhood of the Disciplinati di Gesu Cristo in Umbria to extend rapidly into the centre and north of Italy. [...] These cults spread beyond the Alps, as far as the Alsace, Bavaria, Bohemia, Poland, Austria and Hungary.*

In 1347, the Black Death swept across Europe [...] and with an extraordinary immediacy, the flagellant brotherhoods resurfaced.

In Italy, the movement [...] spread rapidly to all social classes. Its diffusion was signalled and helped by the popular songs of the Passion of Christ and Our Lady of Sorrows. [...] All of them founded 'Case De Dio', Houses of the Lord[135], which acted as their meeting places."

The picture that these authors sketch reveals that the penitential movement was a heretical, geopolitical force present, if not unified, all across Europe. We note that like the Cathar-Manichean movement of the previous centuries, the origin and spread across the continent of the penitent movement occurred from Italy, towards Flanders, western Germany and the Languedoc. Just as the Manicheans infiltrated the Church, so the flagellants infiltrated both the Church and the new merchant communities. Like the Cathars, the flagellants seemed very popular with the local population, who flocked to see their processions through the streets. But unlike the Cathars, the flagellants were of a clearly visible, highly controversial and bloody appearance. Cathars did not like the flesh and looked upon the body as a work of evil. Perhaps they flogged themselves, to liberate the soul from the body. But if they did, they showed greater restraint than the flagellants, who brought the message visually, in front of everyone who wanted to see – and it seemed that most did want to see it!

Dress code

The medieval penitents were ascetics and practiced mortification. They were seen as lay monks; in fact some of them were real monks. Although the mainstream historians of the history of the Church have largely neglected them, they did exist and were a powerful force. Unfortunately, historians tend to focus on wars between two clearly defined political entities (nations), rather than on internal, ill-defined "terrorist activity". As the *Catholic Encyclopedia* noted, these confraternities adapted themselves,

---

135   The "Case De Dio", interestingly, were hospitals.

and made sure that they fell in line with the Church authorities as much as they could. They sought approval from the Church, which could often do little else but grant it to them. There were, nevertheless, frequent reviews and bishops often demanded changes in their liturgy and processions. To some extent, of course, the Church knew that if it approved and brought them under its umbrella, it also meant that it did have at least have some control over the cancer that was destroying its organisation.

Largely, we see two clearly defined features which the penitents held central to their belief: their clothing, and the practice of mortuary rituals – in a sort of parallel to the Cathar consolamentum.

Jean Chélini[136] already highlighted that "repenting penitents", those who had seen "the error of their ways", were forced to wear special clothing, so that they could easily be identified. This was similar to the Yellow Cross the Cathars had been forced to wear beforehand. Statute 10 of the Council of Toulouse stated that Cathars were forced to wear *"two crosses, sown on the chest, one on the right and one of the left side"*. The Council of Béziers in 1233 confirmed the requirement for this identification and in 1242, a meeting of the council of Tarragona, in Spain, reached the same conclusion.

Other documents[137] show that the members *"wore a sort of coat [...] with a red cross on the front and back, and their head covered with a cowl."* To get an impression of what this looks like, we merely need to look at the penitent procession in Perpignan or Limoux, or elsewhere, to see a likeness of the typical dress of the penitent. The Ku Klux Klan's dress was directly inspired from the penitent dress code. The Council of Béziers once again had to stipulate that – this time – three crosses had to be sown on the sentenced penitent's "bag". A relapsed heretic, i.e. one who had committed a second offence after being sentenced, was identified by no less than four crosses, of varying colours.

As it entirely hid a person's features, the dress code was meant to enforce the notion that each member was equal and indistinguishable from any other. During their processions, there was no way to identify who walked in front or last in the procession... or who was actually participating; total anonymity was and remains guaranteed.

But the type of dress that was chosen by the authorities for sentenced

---

136 Jean Chélini, « Histoire religieuse de l'Occident médiéval » (A Religious History of the Medieval Occident), republished by Hachette Pluriel, 1997.
137 "General Dictionary of Compared Biography and History", Ch. Dezobry and Th. Bachelet, Paris, 1857.

heretics to wear also guaranteed that no-one saw what the body looked like underneath. Indeed, mortifications, flagellation, sticking needles into the flesh could still be practiced in private, without anyone being the wiser when they walked about in public. When treating someone who self harms these days, making sure that the areas of self-harm are made visible is a key ingredient to guarantee that the self-harm has stopped; this was not the case for the flagellants. So, again, although the Church apparently came down hard on these penitents, in truth, it assisted them in continuing their practices. Either the Inquisition was not manned by the brightest of men, or it actually condoned that which they were trying to eradicate. In fact it is highly likely that it was the latter, for we can read in Cathar documents[138] that the ritual of the consolamentum "was carried out in appropriate clothing, the celebration consisting of an obligatory heretic's livery made from black clothing or a simple thin cord of linen or wool worn around the waist, on the shirt for men, or on the flesh for women". As the Inquisition were aware of this… it seems they allowed what they were meant to forbid[139].

The penitent monks were ascetics and practiced mortification, but they also were not allowed to own anything. Again, we see this debate parodied in Umberto Eco's *The Name of the Rose*[140], where the religious debate is about whether or not Jesus owned the clothes he wore. On the surface, it seems a ridiculous debate, but the outcomes of such debates – which did occur – were of importance for the various movements. The Church had many possessions; the heresies stated a truly religious person should possess nothing. If the consensus was that Jesus did not own the clothes he wore, it would have been seen as a victory for the penitents.

For the penitents, anything that was required was owned by the community – a form of communism. But mostly, they were forced to beg or to pool their resources to survive. The fact that they did not have worldly possessions was a key ingredient in their "survival of the soul", for money was seen as a prime incentive for people to love worldly possessions. There is, of course, a clear contradiction in the success that the movement had with recruiting the merchants, as these were quickly accumulating wealth; the "nouveaux riches" of their times. But many of these "nouveaux riches" also

138   Doat, XXV.fol 60; ms 609 from the Library of Toulouse, fol 50, Guiraud P, CV.
139   All the more so, since the goal of inquisitorial procedure was precisely to "incite the heretic to acknowledge himself guilty", and if need be, to do "penance".
140   Umberto Eco, "Il nome della rosa", Bompiani, Milano, 1980. "The Name of the Rose", English translation by William Weaver Jr., published in 1983 by Harcourt, New York, and Secker & Warburg, London.

donated large sums back to the community, often in projects that resulted in employment, or shelter for the homeless… shelter for the penitents.

Furthermore, the penitent was known to fast and abstain from certain types of foods, specifically meat, and in other instances diary products. Only that which had been grown in the Earth was deemed to be good to eat.

As mentioned, it is not known whether the Cathars practiced self-flagellation or any other types of mortification. But it is known that they saw the body and the material world as a creation of the "Evil God". Edmund Hamer Broadbent in *The Pilgrim Church*[141] states that *"the dualism that under the appearance of Manicheism had so many supporters in the first centuries and which was also professed by the Paulicians, reappeared in the shape of Catharism. The [doctrine] was based on the antagonism between two principles, one good, one bad. According to this absolute dualism, it was the bad principle that had created matter, and the good, only the spirits, some of those dragged down to the Earth and trapped in their bodies."* As mentioned, these movements saw their soul as being a prisoner of the body and the body had to be punished for this vile seduction to which the soul had fallen victim, in a moment of weakness. Hardening the soul to withstand the torments of pain was another key ingredient in mortification. But, in fact, the Chaldean cult of the Dead is not intended to provide any form of resurrection or "ascension" in Heaven, as opposed to an endless cycle of reincarnations if one doesn't receive it. According to the Chaldeans, humans have no soul, so apart from their bodies, a physical soul (i.e. instincts and emotions, often ascribed, in origin, to the "soul of a cast-out angel") is all we possess. Hence, the Chaldean Cult of the Dead is meant to allow their physical souls to reincarnate on Earth, thus avoiding the certain unpleasantness of eternal ennui, at the very best, or eternal chastisement, at the worst, in the after-life.

Humans very much resemble animals in the Chaldeans' worldview. They believe that humans are former fallen angels, *forever* sentenced by God to wander on Earth as atonement for their sins. The key word here is "for-

---

141 *Edmund Hamer Broadbent, "The Pilgrim Church", first published by Pickering & Inglis Ltd., London, 1931. Interestingly, the title was translated as follows in the French edition of the book: "The Painful Pilgrimage of the Church through the Ages" (published in Yverdon, Switzerland, in 1939). Refer to chapter VII, "The sects" and paragraph 57 "Sects who distort Christianism: The Cathars" for the source of the quotation. Note: the quotes used here are based on the French edition of this book.*

ever", which means that there can be no resurrection or "ascension to heaven" for them.

Therefore, when they die, and since they are not fit for heavenly resurrection, they should normally stay imprisoned in the underworld, i.e. the world of the dead. Chaldeans are therefore anxious to have their mortuary rites executed, since they believe it is the only way not to suffer forever, to snatch them away from the jaws of Hell.

It is in this doctrine that we distinguish most clearly the Cathar/penitent doctrine from the Christian doctrine, in which there is no room for reincarnation. We also note that the Hermetic doctrine, which was introduced into Florence in the middle of the 15th century also has similarities with the Cathar and penitent doctrine, though the Hermetics did not practice mortification.

Edmund Hamer Broadbent adds that *"Around 1260, a craftsman of Parma, Gerardo Segarelli [...] formed a congregation of Apostolic Brothers belonging largely to the lower classes and travelling all over the country, begging and urging the people and the clergy to do penance. In 1286, Honorius IV banned them and in 1290, Nicolas IV renewed this interdiction. In 1294, Segarelli was sentenced to life imprisonment; in 1300, he was burned as a relapsed heretic."*[142]

Segarelli's dualistic doctrine preached penitence and advocated castigating the clergy for its ostentatious wealth. It is Segarelli who was the direct inspiration for the character of Salvatore in Umberto Eco's *The Name of the Rose*, for Segarelli was known to say "Penitenziagite", instead of the correct Latin "poenitentiam agite", "to do penance".

His successor, Fra Dolcino Di Novare, carried on his penance work, within an apocalyptic vision inspired by Joachim de Fiore. We note that Vincent Ferrer also preached within an apocalyptic framework. According to de Fiore, the end of the world was close and mortification and self-flagellation were the only way to escape the dreadful divine wrath.

Later, the sect took the name of Dolcinian Confraternity (the Dolcenites of *The Name of the Rose*) and distinguished itself for its desire to cause

---

142   Edmund Hamer Broadbent, "The Pilgrim Church", first published by Pickering & Inglis Ltd., London, 1931. Refer to chapter VII, paragraph 55 for the source of the quotation. Note: the quotes used here are based on the French translation of Broadbent's book, entitled "Le douloureux pèlerinage de l'église à travers les âges" ("The painful pilgrimage of the Church through the ages"), and first published in Yverdon (Switwerland) in 1939.

social upheaval and bring about greater equality among the people. Similarly, the Florentine Renaissance was noteworthy for its creation of various social models, which were seen as social experiments that would bring "Heaven to Earth" and which would obviously, through the administration of the Rite, ensure the cycle of incarnation on a "heavenly earth", and avoid the certain eternal sentence to the Dantesque underworld of their beliefs.

The Mortuary Rite

Apart from a dress code, the movement was also known for its mortuary rites. Death is an essential moment for all of us. Within the Christian doctrine, however, it is not the most important passage, in spite of what one may think; a Christian believes that death is the end of life and that at death, the soul is largely "ready and waiting" for the Second Coming and the Resurrection to come – hopefully soon. For the penitents on the other hand, death was a special occasion – literally once in a lifetime – a test to withstand (quite comparable with what some near-death-experiencers have described as a "life review"), which would provide the verdict as to whether the soul would have to dwell eternally in the underworld, or could return to Earth for its incarnation.

Mortuary rites, in general, have received little to no attention from historians and archaeologists. Egypt was a country obsessed with death and mortuary rituals, yet little is known about the actual details, leaving various popular authors to make their widely diverse interpretations of what could have, but not necessarily occurred. We know that the Cathars had a mortuary ritual, known as the consolamentum, but apart from some basic observations, little is known. The same applies to the mortuary rites of the Manicheism.

Did the flagellants have a mortuary rite? It seems likely that they did, if only because they would spend the final day with those that had been condemned to death. We know that Manicheans and Cathars had a mortuary rite, so if the flagellants did not have one, it actually would have defeated the purpose of their organisation, for their doctrine was all about death and focused specifically on death as a key event. As to details of this rite, to our knowledge, it was first written down in the Apocryphal Chaldaean Book of Tobit – and this should not come as any surprise.

As mentioned earlier, the Book of Tobit is not acknowledged by the Protestant or Orthodox Churches, nor was it ever part of the Jewish Bible. It is one of several such books, including the Books of Judith, Esther, Bel and the Dragon, the Prayer of Azarias and the Song of the Three Children in the Furnace, the Prayer of Manasseh, Baruch, the Wisdom of Jesus son of Sirac, the Wisdom of Solomon, etc. It has, however, been singled out by some commentators such as Daniel Lortsch[143], who note its unbiblical, superstitious and "devious" nature. Among them, Pastor L. Randon even considers the book to be a pure fabrication, writing things like *"The Book of Tobit is merely a fiction in which they tried to imitate the poem of Job without great success. Its only interest to us lies in the fact that it provides some insight into the superstitions of the Jews of Palestine at that time, and probably into the ones of the Jews of Babylonia as well, [specifically] about [their belief in] angels and demons."[144].*

We have discussed many of details earlier and the full text can be read at the end of this book, but to summarize the story as briefly as possible now: Tobit is taken captive in Assyria, where he practices a specific burial of the dead, for which King Sargon sentences him, as the ritual is prohibited. Tobit thus seems to stop this practice, but when his son Tobias runs into the house during a party and shouts that a child of Israel has just been killed and is lying dead in the street, Tobit jumps up from the table and collects the body. He brings it into his house, so he can bury it after sunset, which he does, but his neighbours and his wife tell him off, saying that he will soon be condemned to death if he continues. However, continue he does, until one night he is so tired of performing these burials, that he falls asleep on the way home, upon which a bird's dropping makes him blind. The Codices Vaticanus and Sinaiticus both state that the Lord struck Tobit with this disability (blindness) for his sins, i.e. the burial rites he performed upon the dead. Indeed, Tobit declares: "Your punishment is severe because I broke your precepts", suggesting that what he is actually doing is somehow contradictory to the "Divine Doctrine".

God was accusing him of not believing that Man can be in the image of God, and of refusing to believe in resurrection. Tobit thinks that humans are former fallen angels, forever sentenced by God to wander on Earth

---

143   *Pastor Daniel Lortsch, « À propos des Apocryphes de l'Ancien Testament - Comment ces livres sont entrés dans la Bible. Pourquoi ils n'auraient pas dû y rester. Comment ils en sont sortis. » ("About the Apocryphal Books of the Old Testament: How these books came into the Bible. Why they should not have stayed there. How they went out."), published by Librairie Delachaux & Niestlé, 1917.*
144   *Pastor L. Randon, « Les livres apocryphes de l'Ancien Testament » ("The Apocryphal Books of the Old Testament"), published by Société Biblique de Paris (Biblical Society of Paris), 1909.*

as atonement for their sins. Tobit believes that the mortuary rites will allow corpses to reincarnate on earth, so that the fallen angel – i.e a human being, according to the Chaldean doctrine – may avoid the sentence of imprisonment in the underworld, the world of the dead.

Finally, we need to underline that the story of Tobit is built in two stages: at first, it is the king who intervenes and forbids Tobit, who nevertheless perseveres. He does not listen to the advice of his neighbours, not even of his own wife, which means that in the end, it is up to God himself to intervene and stop him. But Tobit interprets his blindness as a "death penalty": he no longer wants to live and it is clear that he begins to make preparations for his own death – which we can only assume will involve someone else performing the mortuary rite upon him. This is why his son is sent to Media, to inform a contact there to release funds and soon thereafter no doubt perform the ritual. The second stage is when Tobit sets this sequence of events into motion, and the archangel Raphael intervenes and makes sure that Tobit will not go through with it, knowing that this means the restoration of Tobit's sight. Thus only if God is able to show that in the end it is he who is much more powerful than Tobit's magic, only if God can show to Tobit that though he punishes, he also heals and only if Tobit repents, will the desired outcome come about. And, of course, the Book of Tobit was there to show that God was more powerful, and benign, and even helped those that practiced the mortuary cult – even the most ardent magicians, such as Tobit.

Tobit practices a mortuary rite, a cult of the dead, which we have called "The Rise". In the full versions of the Book of Tobit, Tobit states that during this ritual, he purifies himself and strives to be closer to the will of the Lord – which is exactly what the Manicheans considered – or hoped – would occur at the moment of death: a Rise.

Although Tobit is a Jew, it is clear that, because this book was incorporated into the Septuagint and because of its emphasis on his (Jewish) neighbours' horror, the ritual itself was not part of the Jewish tradition. The Book itself is in fact a warning against such "foreign" traditions. In fact, we could go one step further: the Book of Tobit was included in the Jewish Bible, for the Jews of Alexandria, who lived amongst the Egyptians, and who were renowned for their funerary rituals, some of these involving the Book of the Dead. Did the Jews of Alexandria feel, in the 3rd century BC, that their religion had become infiltrated by Egyptian funerary practices, and was this the reason why the Book of Tobit was included in their literature? To serve as a warning to the Jews that they might fall prey to the same temptations that were Tobit's downfall?

At some level, the "crimes" that Tobit committed can indeed be interpreted within a smaller framework, namely that Tobit touched corpses, which was a legal prohibition, as dictated by Moses himself. The Greek Septuagint itself incorporates this notion, stating that "that night, when he was lying motionless, being unclean" – "unclean", because he had been touching corpses, which in Jewish law was only allowable for the most immediate family members. But obviously there is more, for similar versions make it clear that, whereas others see Tobit as "unclean", he himself considers that these rituals "purify" him. It is therefore clear that what Tobit was doing was anathema to Jewish doctrine, which is particularly stringent in its rule about touching dead bodies. It could perhaps be argued that the Jewish doctrine was so strict because it originated - if we follow the popular story of Moses, who grew up in Egypt – amongst the Egyptian people, who practiced elaborate mortuary rites upon the dead, a practice against which Moses – and the Jews by consequence – rebelled.

For the Jews, the burial of the dead was of no importance and not a condition for the soul's salvation, and – of course – the same is true of Christianity[145], in which salvation can only be obtained through personal acceptance of the sacrifice of Jesus Christ on one's behalf. In the Book of Psalms LXXIX, v 2-3, the Psalm of Asaph reads how "nations have given the dead bodies of your servants as meat for the heavenly birds; the flesh of your beloved to the earthly beasts, they spread their blood like water around Jerusalem; and there was nobody to bury them". The uselessness of burial is also repeated in Deuteronomy XXVIII, v 26: "And the dead bodies will be food for all the heavenly birds, and the worldly beasts."

As a basic Jewish practice, a dead Jew in the street was not allowed to be touched, other than by his most direct family; letting him lay dead in the street was insignificant; whether buried or not did not matter to the Jews. But it did matter to Tobit, for he believed that a dead person that was not buried according to the Rite of the Dead, could not escape the underworld.

We see the same preoccupation with La Sanch, in Perpignan, who made sure that those who were condemned to death would be buried.

---

145   *Refer to the following note.*

The early Church struggled with burial too. In the *City of God* and *De Cura pro Mortuis Gerenda*, written in 422 by Saint Augustine, he provides Paulinus, Bishop of Nole, with an answer to his question as to whether *"the offering we allocate to the Clergy for the dead, does it bring forgiveness for the sins of the soul?"* Saint Augustine replies that *"For the ancient people, the deceased's Fate after death was conditioned by mortuary rites and burial. But as a purpose of salvation, these rites are totally useless."* He then quotes the Psalm of Asaph and Deuteronomy. Further on, he writes: *"'Leave the honouring of the dead to the dead', answered Christ to a man who wanted to pay tribute to his deceased father before following him*[146]. *Also in Gaul, the martyrs' bodies were given to the dogs. The fragments of their limbs left by the dogs and their bones were burned to the last piece. This destruction, we must believe, has been allowed by God only to teach to the Christians that their contempt for life must be accompanied by an even bigger contempt for burial rites."* It shows the Jewish influence on the practices of the early Christian Church, which today is actually typified by its extensive cemeteries – but perhaps these should be seen as evidence of how successful Manicheism infiltrated and converted Christianity?

In short, it shows that not only has the cult of the dead no biblical foundation and was condemned amongst the Jews, but burial itself was not considered to be of any importance either by them or by the early Christians. Although it was written down in the Book of Tobit, it is clear that the cult predates this book and is likely to be of Chaldaean origin. Saint Jerome wrote that the text of the Book of Tobit came from Chaldaea, from Babylon in fact and that *"he translated this book in only one day from a Chaldaean manuscript which an old Jewish erudite scholar interpreted for him in Hebrew"*. It shows that the Book of Tobit itself was of Chaldaean origin and probably detailed a Babylonian tradition. It is from this ancient Babylonian tradition that it later became adopted by the Magi, as well as Manicheism, which in turn influenced Catharism and the penitent movement.

The Cathar Belief
It seems that with the Cathars, as well as with the Manicheans, Good and Evil were independent, autonomous principles. God was only "a god" and he found himself confronted with another powerful entity, which some

---

146   *The exact quote reads "But Jesus saith unto him, Follow me; and leave the dead to bury their own dead" (Matthew VIII, 22; Luke, IX, 60). Saint Augustine rightly uses it to demonstrate that the cult of the Dead is not only prohibited by the Old Testament, but by the New Testament as well. Hence, this practice goes against all biblical principles.*

thought was even more powerful than him: "the demon". The dualistic approach of Manicheism stated that the body was made by Evil and the soul by Good. The soul was a partial emanation from the Divine Entity, a tiny speck of light that had escaped from the Divine Abode ruled by Good, to inhabit a body crafted by the Demon; there is thus a perpetual struggle between both forces inside each of us.

This forms the foundation of all dualistic traditions, which speak of two opposing forces. The doctrine also argued that this opposition had a profound and direct influence on Mankind, specifically the notion of Free Will. Manicheans argued that we should not choose one or the other force, but that instead we should submit, if not surrender, ourselves to dual influences, for our Free Will would, by default, lose to these two powerful entities. Resistance to Evil was futile and it was considered to be at odds with the innate order of things. It offered followers of dualism a unique insight into evil and sin, which was somehow not "their own fault", but considered to be largely the result of the power of evil upon the individual, willing a person to commit evil. It was an easy escape for those who perjured, lived a life of vice, crime, etc. Everything seemed pardonable, for the individual was not responsible for his mistakes[147], he was merely a ship being rocked on the sea of good and evil.

In short, the ordinary human was seen as a being that was deprived of consciousness and true Free Will. He was but an emanation from a collective "mind", which directed his entire existence. He was responsible neither for his crimes, nor his good deeds. The Perfect Guilhem Bélibaste stated that "the ordinary believers need not fear to devote themselves to all turpitudes, because they have to be persuaded that their sins will be forgiven at the final hour, by the reception of the sacrament (Consolamentum)."[148] A "sacrament", of course, for which he would have to pay large sums of money.

An ordinary Cathar worshipper was therefore allowed to kill animals, swindle, steal, smuggle, disobey the religious obediences such as fasting for Lent, indulge in lust, all of this without any need to feel bad or remorseful, for at the final moment, the Consolamentum could wipe his slate clean. As such, the Consolamentum was a magical rite. Already, we see a clear social distinction, in which several educated people no longer believed in the

---

147   *Art. Her. B. Franc, XII; Art. Her. P. Maurini, XLIX.*
148   *Art. Her. P. Maurini., XXIII, "Sermo. Jac. Auterii" ("Sermon of Cathar perfect Jacques Autier"), Fol. 251 C, "Guilhem Belibasta" ("Sermon of Cathar perfect Guilhem Bélibaste").*

power of magic and thus were not swayed by such doctrines. The logical, educated mind suggested that for every action, there had to be a reaction, or repercussion, whereas the dualistic preaching suggested that this was a fallacy: doing evil in life did not mean the divine powers would condemn you to evil in death. Preachers such as St. Bernard remarked on how hard it was to persuade "ordinary people" away from the attraction of the Cathar thinking. He stated that *one cannot convince them through reasoning, they cannot comprehend it, it remains to them unintelligible. Not a single authority corrects them, they cannot accept it, nor submit themselves to it. Persuasion is useless, for their hearts remain hard and bold. The dice are thrown, they prefer to die than to convert. What awaits them, will be the flames.*[149]

This was in contrast with the Perfect, the "Good Men". They distinguished themselves from the rest of the community because of their lifestyle, as well as the administration of the Consolamentum. They themselves had been given the Consolamentum, not at the moment of death, but after a probationary period.

They were called preachers, prophets and were often seen as the "Son of the Holy Spirit". The Perfect was not allowed to touch the blood of any animal. They lived off alms, gifts and offerings and often exchanged blessings and other prayers against various material needs. Food was chief amongst their needs, though it is known that many Perfects often fasted. They seemed to imitate the lifestyle of the most devout Christians and often lived amongst them. The Holy Communion, though they felt reluctant to take it, was nevertheless not forsaken; instead, it seems that they carried the host with them, to play with it and mock it after the service had finished. They were to be found in the churches on Sundays and the other feasts imposed by the Church, so that no-one had any idea that they were not truly Christians. They frequently had to make the sign of the cross so that they would not give away their true allegiance, but as they detested doing it, they pretended that they were merely chasing away the flies from their face[150]. But such conformism comes at a price and Guilhem Bélibaste is on record as stating that on certain occasions, he had an intense desire to break all the crucifixes with an axe. But as he knew he had to restrain himself, he hit them and insulted them.

---

149   *St. Bernard of Clairvaux, Sermon LXVI no. 2, "Rusticani homines et idiotae".*
150   *Raniero Sacconi, "Summa De Catharis", 1250, published in 1764 in P. Garcias, Bonaccorsi 209, Art. Her. P. Maurini, XVII. Conf. A. Sicredi. Fol. 127 B : "A known heretic is far less harmful than a pseudo-Catholic" [Serm. LXVI, n°4, LXIV, n°9, Serm. LXV, n°8]*

The Perfects were known as great preachers. The improvisation, the sharp and innovative use of expressions, the melancholic ambiance and often mysterious surroundings in which they preached all added to incite and ferment the devotion of their audience. Admission to the Cathar belief was easy: after listening to the preaching, the Perfect placed his hands on the person, and he became a Cathar. To become a Perfect, it took more than a year in the company of superiors to learn all that was necessary, before receiving the sacrament. It seems that most Perfects became powerful public speakers, this from contemporary sources, as well as some original material, such as one speech by the Perfect Pierre Autier. Autier attacked the Eucharist virulently, debating how it could be possible that The Lord (Christ) can be present inside the host. *"The Church states grotesquely that Jesus Christ is present in the host. I want some proof of this enormous and monstrous impossibility, for even if the body of Christ had the height of a mountain or the length of a whale's bone, the priests would have eaten it long ago."* It is simple, yet powerful argumentation that could – and still is able – to move people. It highlights how easily a religion can be attacked if the Church states that the host is the physical (rather than symbolical) body of Christ, and the Perfects used this swaying of emotions and doubt to lure these people into their own flock.

The Cathars stated: "Jura, perjura, secretum prodere noli." "Swear, perjure yourself, but never tell the secret."[151] The secret indeed remained well-guarded, for only some details about the Consolamentum are known to us. The Perfect, as mentioned above, received the sacrament of the Consolamentum. Once someone became a Perfect, union of the sexes was condemned. For some, this was "clear evidence" that the Church was right in describing the nature of the sacrament as orgiastic and satanic. Only the Perfects were held to such tyrannical standards (which they hardly ever observed, according to witnesses) and the general population was free to simply do whatever the alternating prevailing forces of good or evil dictated, since all would be magically cured by the Consolamentum at the time of death. Furthermore, there were rumours that these men practiced sodomy amongst themselves and were repulsed by women. It is clear that then as now, such attacks on the sexuality of the priests was commonplace, and more often than not totally unjustified.

When the Perfect received the sacrament, there was a formula which they

---

151   *In. Cant. Serm. LXV n°2.*

had to recite. It is written down by Reinerius Sachoni[152]: *"I solemnly promise to render myself to God, to no longer touch a woman, to no longer kill an animal, not to eat meat, eggs or dairy product, to eat only plants, and not to eat without a companion."* It is not totally clear whether the vegetarian regime was the result of a belief in reincarnation and a return as animals, or whether it had to do with the dualistic principle; if animals were believed to have spirits, these may have been subject to the same good-evil contradiction and for a Perfect to be pure...

With no such "joys" to enjoy in this (evil) realm, life for the Perfect became a task of penitence, deprivation, a mortal coil that needed to be thrown off at death, facilitating and favouring the Ritual so that a better existence could be entered into through a new incarnation, as opposed to suffering the underworld.

St. Bernard nevertheless wondered: *"Why reject with such horror dairy products and everything that comes from the flesh? You limit, out of respect for the foolish opinions of Mani, the greatness and abundant benefits of God; you make a distinction between the things he has created and decide that some are unworthy, instead of receiving all of them graciously. I do not applaud your abstinence, I abhor your blasphemy, and it is you that I proclaim to be unworthy."*[153] Though they believed that this world was created by the evil God, it may seem that they would not have understood nor cared what St. Bernard was saying. However, Bernard's sermons were not intended to convince the true Manichean believers, but were rather designed as a means to try and hinder their progress, by trying to "immunise" the general population before the Cathars attempted to convert them.

Let us nevertheless note that the order that forbade to kill and eat animals only applied to the Perfects. Those who had not been given the Consolamentum, were free to do as they pleased. This distinction should also be seen from a magical perspective, in which "bodily cleanliness" is a key factor in the successful execution of certain rituals.

It was the Consolamentum that upset the Church most: if the ordinary Cathar was allowed to do very much as he pleased, it was because his "salvation" was assured by this spurious "sacrament", and by this alone. It was a complete negation of the New Testament's fundamental message, the "Good News", that the only way of redemption for mankind was by

---

152   Raniero Sacconi, *"Summa De Catharis"*, 1250.
153   St. Bernard of Clairvaux, *Sermon LXVI, no. 6 and 7.*

the sacrifice of Jesus Christ, which was available for the taking simply by acquiescing to it in Faith.

The Consolamentum was generally received by Cathars on their death-bed, when it was certain that they were terminally ill, and that consequently they would not be able to commit any more sins. If, against all odds, they ever came to recover, they were frequently deprived of food and starved to death.

From a logical point of view, the Consolamentum is the closest thing to mortuary baptism, since it was given either to the dying, or to the dead themselves, in which case this ritual prescribed that the corpses of the deceased should be plunged into barrels filled with water (cf. Marcion)[154]. Sometimes however, the Consolamentum was given when the person was still alive. The one who had received this "sacrament" was then called a "Perfect", i.e. a heretical priest who had wilfully chosen to buy his "salvation" by receiving the Consolamentum. As such, the "Perfects" could receive large amounts of money as "mortuary offerings", and in exchange grant "salvation", the heretical way, to the souls of the dying and the dead, no matter what these people had done during their lives.

In theory, the Cathar "Perfects" should no longer sin, for the Consolamentum had allegedly "cleansed" them from all their wrongdoings. However, there was no real imperative to comply with this obligation, since it was always possible for the wrongful ones to have a fellow "Perfect" give them the Consolamentum once again, so as to "start anew".

Apart from the purification of sins, this "sacrament" was believed by the Cathars to have several dualistic effects (i.e. a struggle between the opposites: men/women, Good/Evil, the rich/the poor, etc.). The "Perfects" were formally forbidden to even touch any woman, for the Cathars considered women as impure beings. Every aspirant to the status of Cathar "Perfect" was required to take a solemn oath never to touch a woman again, as part of the Consolamentum ritual.[155]

Moreover, the Consolamentum annulled the marriage, and the new

---

154   Voltaire, « Philosophical Dictionary » [1764]: « Saint Epiphanius and Saint John Chrysostom declare that […] among the Marcionites, it was customary to put a living person under a dead one's bed, to ask him whether he wanted to receive baptism, the living person answered yes; then the corpse was taken and immersed in a tank [filled with water]. That custom was [later] banned." Also refer to St. John Chrysostom, 40ᵗʰ Homily on the First Epistle to the Corinthians.
155   The actual text of this oath can be found in Raniero Sacconi, Summa de Catharis, 1250.

"Perfect" gleefully disavowed his wife and children, and all that made of him a father. But he then attached himself to another woman, with whom he lived without being allowed to touch her.[156] Still, several Cathar "Perfects" are known to have had illegitimate children, which further demonstrates, if need be, that these so-called "Perfects" did not always abide by the obligations pertaining to their office.

The Cathar liturgy was scant, containing very few religious books. It was largely composed of the beginning of the Gospel of John and certain epistles. The Cathars rejected the entire Old Testament; the religious writings used in Churches were seen by them as diabolical. Specifically Moses was treated with disdain, if not hate, for he was labelled by these Manicheans as a "demon of the night", "the father of vice" and "the son of Lucifer". Furthermore, it seems that their version of the Gospel of John, a copy of which can be found in the archives of Carcassonne, contained some strange features. However, it is also believed that the Gospel of John was only a relatively late inclusion and that previously, the Cathars cherished another book.

The Perfect Guilhem Bélibaste, who declared his loathing of the Old Testament, did not hold the New Testament in any higher regard either, it seems: *"I have nothing but contempt for the Evangelists, and I affirm that I have as much, if not more power than the apostles themselves and the son of Mary."*[157] Harsh words about Jesus, and yet he and other Cathars *appeared* to acknowledge the authority of Jesus' own teachings, or, more exactly, so they pretended. Indeed they claimed that Jesus himself had given them their knowledge and precepts. Their own teachings stated that Christ had, in secret, written an *"Epistle to the Cathars"*, which is also sometimes called *"Epistle to the Bogomils"*. This book was "the true doctrine" according to these Manichean heretics, whereas the *"Epistle to the Romans"*, like the entire Old Testament, was in their opinion "promulgated by the Devil". It suggests that the Cathar "Perfects", at some point, had in their possession a secret book, probably of Bulgarian origin, which they seem to have guarded jealously. As to the nature of the object or its contents, nothing is known. Of course, its very existence may well be entirely mythical, and the product of legends.

As to the man of our legend: Bérenger Saunière. It may seem strange to see a man receive money from far away places, to perform rituals for the

---

156   *Art. Heret. P. Maurini, XXXVIII. Conf. A. Sicredi., fol. 128 b.*
157   *Raniero Sacconi, Summa de Catharis, 1250.*

dying or the dead. But this is precisely what Tobit describes: he sends his son off to Media, to tell someone to perform a ritual, whereby a substantial sum of money is turned over to this person, who, upon completion of the ritual, sends Tobias back with a note, evidence for Tobit that the ritual had been performed.

A key ingredient of magic is the negation of space, if not time. Distance was no problem, as is underlined in the popular depictions of voodoo magic, in which a part of a person, a swatch of hair, or nail clippings for example, is attached to a small doll, which then acts as the proxy for that person's human body, which is somewhere else; the ritual done to the doll is then transferred by magic to the human body wherever that may be. It is within this context, that it is possible that Saunière was an operating magician, working with the dead, even though as often happened, he did not have to be physically present with the body; all he may have required was some personal possession, or part, of the deceased person, to perform his "magic"[158].

---

158 *Perhaps a skull or some bones? If Saunière actually praticed the Cult of the Dead, it means that he fully subscribed to the basic teachings of the Chaldean Magi. According to this doctrine, man is deprived from the Holy Spirit. According to the Magi worldview, human beings literally have no mind, and all they have is a physical soul (i.e animal instinct and emotions) and most importantly, inside their bones is where their soul lies. This is where reincarnation came in handy for the Chaldeans, and it also explains why preserving the integrity of the skeleton was crucial to the Cult of the Dead. And every indication seems present to believe that Saunière did indulge in the Chaldean Cult of the Dead, especially when he gave the following poor excuse to the villagers of Rennes-le-Château in an attempt to justify his rummaging of the graveyards in the cemetery:*
"Several parishioners die every day; the cemetery had become too small for them to receive proper burial. With the remains of the old dead, I therefore made the ossuary you can see here." It is apparent here that Saunière had a "crush on bones", shall we say, or a fondness for bones, which he tries to dismiss as merely "tidying" the remains, when his true goal was actually to gather the bones of the deceased in a single place.

Chapter 6

Paying the price for Heaven

Most people pray that they are admitted into Heaven, but it seems that some were willing and able to pay for it. Seven thousand dollars, to get into Heaven: it seems a small price to pay – provided of course, that it is possible, or that Heaven actually exists. The Mortuary Rite did not come cheap, though the exception may have been made for the Cathar Perfects. In the Book of Tobit, it is clear that Tobit had set aside substantial funds for the service and, of course, Saunière's obvious wealth, if that is where it came from, makes it clear that he did not come cheap either.

In the Book of Tobit, Tobit had set aside 10 silver talents, with Gabael, and it is his son Tobias who is asked to collect it. Intriguingly, it seems that upon his return, Tobias is also carrying a "talisman" with him – no doubt certain artefacts linked with the rituals that are going to be performed.

In another Apocryphal book, Maccabees II, chapter XII, verse 40 and following, there is another reference to the Mortuary Rite, where the price for the redemption of the deceased soul is stipulated:

> *"40: Then under the tunic of every one of the dead they found sacred tokens of the idols of Jamnia, which the law forbids the Jews to wear. And it became clear to all that this was why these men had fallen.*
>
> *41: So they all blessed the ways of the Lord, the righteous Judge, who reveals the things that are hidden;*
>
> *42: and they turned to prayer, beseeching that the sin which had been committed might be wholly blotted out. And the noble Judas exhorted the people to keep themselves free from sin, for they had seen with their own eyes what had happened because of the sin of those who had fallen.*
>
> *43: He also took up a collection, man by man, to the amount of two thousand drachmas of silver, and sent it to Jerusalem to provide for a sin offering. In doing this he acted very well and honourably, taking account of the resurrection.*
>
> *44: For if he were not expecting that those who had fallen would rise again, it would have been superfluous and foolish to pray for the dead.*
>
> *45: But if he was looking to the splendid reward that is laid up for those who fall asleep in Godliness, it was a holy and pious thought. Therefore he made atonement for the dead, that they might be delivered from their sin."*

It is clear that this text inspired the debate as to whether or not offerings given to the clergy for the dead forgave the souls of the dead for their sins.

For Saint Augustine, the answer was no. The Bible and Mosaic Law agreed. Still, we note that the saying of masses for the salvation of the souls of the dead is a well integrated Catholic tradition, still widely practiced. Again, it is evidence of the infiltration of the ideology of the Cult of the Dead and its almost unnoticed transformation of the Christian doctrine.

The "payment" for passage into Heaven is a typically pagan symbol. In Greece, there was the symbolic coin that needed to be given to the ferryman Charon to cross over the River Styx. The ritual is much older; in fact, the entire system of paying for the souls of the deceased is a Chaldaean invention. Again, Maccabees was written by the Jews, in Greek and not in Hebrew, upon the return from the Babylonian Captivity. We thus see both Chaldaean and Greek preferences. This reference to the Cult of the Dead did not make it into the Bible. Furthermore, the Mortuary Rite itself was specifically banned in the Bible and the canonical books and Maccabees was obviously considered to be too heavily influenced by the Chaldaean ideology to be widely circulated, let alone approved, by the Jews. The Book shows that during the captivity, some Jews had adopted the local fashions, rituals and religion.

To sin or not to sin, that's not the problem

The Cult of the Dead can be described as such:

- the worship of the mortal remains of the deceased, his grave, other relics;
- the need to bury the deceased;
- the unconditional faith that its followers have in the ritual;
- the payment of a high price for the ritual's performance;
- the belief that the rite itself is able to grant access to Heaven, without regard for whether a person has sinned or not during his or her life.
- The belief that these rites are the condition for the salvation of the soul.

These conditions seem to apply to several ancient religions, but it is also clearly present in the much more recent Manichean doctrine, as specified in the lecture of Archelaus, the Bishop of Charcar (Mesopotamia), who preached against Manes[159]: *"Manes admitted two principles [...] One,*

---

159   Collectan. Monum. Vet. Eccl. Graecae et Latinae, in-4°; Romae, 1098, acts of the Archelaus conference against Manes, St. Cyril of Jerusalem, Catech; 6 and St. Epiphanius, Haer, 26, Cotelier volume 1 "On the Apostolics Fathers" p. 543 and following.
Instit. Hist. Christ. 2nd part, chapter 5, p. 351. St. Augustine, "Contra Advers. Legis and Proph." ("Against the Adversaries of the Law and Prophets"), 1, 2 ch. 12, n 39. St Augustin, "

a good God, a God that created the souls, the other bad, the creator of the world and Mankind." This doctrine has been termed dualism or ditheism. One interpreter, Father J.B. Bergier[160], concluded that this meant that "*us [human beings] thus have nothing to fear from our crimes [...] there is no more good or bad.*

This doctrine is destructive of any law and all societies, because as Man has been created by the evil God, his acts are beyond his control, his free will seems to be non-existent, and he is merely under the influences of the good or the bad God. Free will is denied, Man is not responsible for his sins, and it is not up to him to be good or bad, nor is he able to redeem himself for his mistakes."

Bergier and others have interpreted the Mortuary Rite as going against the very "Will" of God. Most religions preach that in order to enter Heaven or return to God, we need to live justly and correctly – live "good". What is Good and Just is then set down in a religion's doctrine, which equally becomes the backbone of the laws of a society.

The Cult of the Dead did not necessarily suggest unlawfulness or stipulate that people should sin as much as possible; it was not "evil" in that sense. In fact, we see that the Cathars and the Penitents lived largely exemplary lives, with devotion, and a belief in God. The people felt that Cathars in the South of France were deemed to be of higher morals than the Catholic clergy in the region.

What was instrumental to the Cult of the Dead was a belief that whether you lived "justly" – without sin – or not, a "just life" was not important to gain entrance to Heaven. Equally, it seems that its followers did not believe that for those who had lived an exemplary life, this would automatically mean that entrance to Heaven would be accomplished. In either case, it completely ignored the central tenet of Christian faith, the redemptive sacrifice of Jesus Christ and His resurrection. And that was where the doctrine ran foul of the Christian clergy.

Many religions and societies have, of course, frowned upon the beliefs of the Cult of the Dead, for they make social control extremely difficult. At the core, these people, whether Cathar, Manichean, Chaldaean or penitent, felt that our reality had been created by an evil God (though they would

---

De Morib. Manich." ("On the Morals of the Manicheans"), ch. 12, n 25, etc.
160   "*The Doctrine of the Church, its life, its works, its era, and the influence of its genius*", by abbé J.B Bergier, missionary of Beauprès, published by Ambroise Bray, Paris 1856.

never call him "God"). They rejected anything material and any pleasure in life, which they felt were temptations to the soul, placed in this reality by the Evil One, to lure us in to enjoy this reality. Instead, they trained the soul to abstain from worldly pleasures, which the penitents emphasized by self-chastisement, both in the belief that self-harm strengthened the soul, as well as hoping that such practices would lead to what we would call "out of body experiences", in which the soul, during life, is liberated from the body – "Heaven on Earth". To achieve access to Heaven, they also relied on magical rituals, which in their opinion, bypassed any form of "last judgment" and any question as to whether or not a person could enter Heaven.

It is here that their "blind faith" – an expression quite appropriate in the case of Tobit – in their religion becomes apparent: how did they know that a certain ritual was able to accomplish a feat that seems to have been a loophole in God's Will? Similarly, how could they know, or their priests guarantee, that the ritual was performed correctly? In magic, the execution of the ritual is vitally important, for errors or omissions are catastrophic: if you deviate in the slightest manner from the instructions and procedures, the end result is not guaranteed and most likely not achieved.

The Cult of the Dead relied on the Mortuary Rite, which was believed to guarantee the soul's salvation. Some commentators have argued that the ritual itself was thus seen as being able to erase "sin", but it is not altogether clear whether the cult followers "cleansed" themselves of their sin or not, or whether instead the ritual was "just" a bypass for the last judgment of the dead; in short, on the Highway to Heaven, most souls seemed to have to pull over, to be "judged" – have their papers checked – and only those whose "sins were forgiven" were allowed to continue. It seems that for the cult followers, there was no stopping at the "judgment office" but rather, they just continued on, because through the enacting of the ritual, they were able to pass through the toll booth and continue on the Highway to Heaven.

The Mortuary Rite was practiced in Mesopotamia and Egypt and, no doubt, other ancient civilisations as well. It may seem surprising in this day of Egyptomania that it is Mesopotamia that influenced several nations, rather than Egypt. Throughout its Dynastic Rule, Egypt was largely self-contained and wary of foreigners. Mesopotamia, on the other hand, was a more dynamic empire and it was, of course, a key location for the Jews. It was Mesopotamia that gave rise to Manes, who was instrumental in popularising and spreading the cult, but he was not alone. Marcion, a dualistic and Gnostic Chaldaean (born in Sinope in the second century AD) spoke and used the same Mortuary Rite. In the story of St. John Chrysostom, the Archbishop of Constantinople, it is stated that *"the Arian heretics, the Anomeans and Sabellians were not the only sectarians that Chrysostom's zeal had to fight. The Antiochean Church was devastated by all the mistakes that are born out of pride. Marcionites, Valentinians, Gnostics, Manicheans, Macedonians [...] all sects, all of the old and new mistakes had their followers in the patriarchal city [...] Chrysostom fought them [...] He exclaimed: 'Would you like me to explain to you how Marcion's disciples understand the Scripture regarding the necessity of baptism? Amongst them, when a follower died without having been baptised, some found a way to baptise him after his death. One got close to the deceased's bed, talked to him, asking him if he wanted to be baptised; the deceased did not answer, but somebody hidden under the bed answered for him, and said that he wanted to be baptised. The deceased was then immediately baptised instead of the person who answered for him."* [161]

Marcion was a dualist, believing in the good and the evil and agreed that Man had been created by the Evil One. Like all other dualist doctrines, Marcion and his doctrine were soon condemned by the Church.

Despite not being the origin of this cult, we cannot exclude Egypt, for it was still deemed to be of extreme importance. Gaston Maspero[162], professor of Egyptian Archaeology and Language at the Collège de France in Paris and Director of Egyptian Antiquities, noted that there existed strong and close bonds between the Chaldaean Magi and the religion of ancient Egypt, specifically on the teachings of the souls of the deceased: *"[Chaldaeans] had a legal system and a full-fledged religion. Their writing was originally hieroglyphic, like the Egyptian writing. [...] It seems that the first Chaldaeans had a similar view of our world to that of the Egyptians. The spirits, the "ZI", [were similar to] the origin of the Egyptian doubles who understand the souls of the dead. [Among the Chaldaeans], as well as among the Egyptians, the souls reached the foot of the great Western mountain [...] in the Kournoudé. In this religion, there is neither reward for the righteous*

---

161   *"The Doctrine of the Church, its life, its works, its era, and the influence of its genius"*, *by abbé J.B Bergier, missionary of Beauprès, published by Ambroise Bray, Paris 1856. For the original source of the quotation, refer to St. John Chrysostom, 40th Homily on the First Epistle to the Corinthians.*
162   *Gaston Maspero, "Ancient History of the Classical Eastern People" (5 volumes) Paris, 1895-1908, Book II: "The Near East, before and during the time of the Egyptian Domination".*

man, nor punishment for the impious person." Maspero underlined that the concept of the Cult of the Dead existed from the dawn of Egypt's civilisation and there is indeed evidence from the First Dynasty – and before – that the ancient Egyptians practiced a complex system of funerary rituals – which of course soon began to involve the pyramid.

Amongst the various Egyptian rituals, we need to focus on one, the so-called "Ouag [or Wagy] Festival"[163]. Evidence of this festival exists from circa 2560 BC (the 4th Dynasty, the one that built the most impressive pyramids[164]). The Festival has clear parallels with the Mortuary Rite. The determination of the date on which it had to be performed followed the lunar cycle; it occurred 17 days after the New Year[165]. If we were to transpose this system onto our modern calendar, where New Year obviously falls on January 1, we end up with the festival occurring on January 17. We will return to this date later on. In ancient Egypt, "private worship of the dead", i.e. worship that seemed to sit outside the framework of "normal" religious services, was performed on that date[166].

Amongst the Chaldaeans, according to Fernand Nicolay[167], "*it was taught that the divinities had a mission to raise the dead and that the vital energy, the EKIMU [the soul], was loosened from the deceased body if the relatives worshipped it.*" In ancient Egypt, at the Wagy Festival, Nicolay[168] adds that the deceased had to resort to his family's prayers, because "*once he had surrendered his last breath, the soul could not do anything for itself; from now on, it had to obtain everything by means of its friends' and relatives' piety, or else through its own foresight to put some money 'by the side' [before death]*", money, of course, which had to be used to pay the Egyptian (or Chaldean) priests for performing these rituals.

According to these authors, in ancient Egypt, the deceased's salvation

---

163   Perpillou-Thomas, F. "*Ptolemaic and Roman Egyptian Festivals, according to the papyrologic Greek Documentation*", Universitas Catholica Lovaniensis; Lovanii, 1993, and "*Egyptian Festivals according to the Greek Papyri*", A.N.R.T, Lille, 1991.
Also: Altenmuller, H., "*Das Fest des Weissen Nilpferd und das Opfergefilde*", N° 1, pp. 29-44, "*A Tribute to Jean Leclanc*", IFAO, Cairo, 1994.
164   *The three Pyramids of Cheops, Kephren and Mykerinos are located in Giza, Egypt.*
165   *According to the lunar cycle, on which one of the Egyptian Calendars was based.*
166   *Moreover, the Wagy Festival was specifically dedicated to Osiris, the Egyptian god of the dead.*
167   *Fernand Nicolay, "History of Beliefs, Superstitions, Customs and Usages according to the Decalogue Plan", Book I, II and III, Editions Victor Retaux (3rd printing), Paris, 1900.*
168   *Fernand Nicolay, "History of Beliefs, Superstitions, Customs and Usages according to the Decalogue Plan", Book II, Editions Victor Retaux, Paris, 1900.*

The "Sacred Tomb" of Arles-sur-Tech

Abdon and Sennen, the two key saints of La Sanch (taken from the church of Peyrestortes, near Perpignan)

Wall painting in the church of Prats-de-Mollo, showing the sign of the weavers (Tisserands)

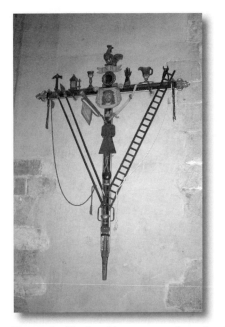

Two typical "La Sanch" crosses, one from the church of St James (Perpignan), the headquarters of La Sanch, the other from Arles-sur-Tech

Tiled decoration in the church of Arles-sur-Tech, showing images of the La Sanch procession

The La Sanch Procession in the streets of Perpignan (2006)

The statue of Asmodeus, inside the church of Rennes-le-Château

The cemetery of Rennes-le-Château

The village church of
Rennes-le-Château

Church of the Blue Penitents of
Narbonne

Church of Prouilhe

Stained glass window of Tobias, inside the church of Bugarach

The church of Notre-Dame-de-Marceille

The church of Bugarach, with Bugarach mountain in the background was dependent on neither the qualities of the deceased person, nor the manner in which he led his life, but largely it was the result of the Cult of the Dead, which involved his friends and family focusing their prayers on his mortal remains – and not forgetting the fact that money had been set aside so that his burial and prayers for his soul could be accomplished. As in Chaldaea, so in Egypt, it seems…

The Consolamentum

When Christianity spread westwards, so – as we have seen – did the Cult of the Dead. In the Middle Ages, the Cult was present in Europe largely as a result of Manicheism. With the Cathars, the Rite became known as the Consolamentum. Jean-Marie Vidal[169] highlighted how important and necessary this ritual was to the Cathars. It is known that after the Albigensian Crusade, Southern France had very few Perfects left; many had been killed during the Crusade and in 1244, several were sequestered at Montségur, and most of those decided to die in a funeral pyre, rather than repent.

Still, the Cathar community was relatively large. All authors, such as René Weis[170], agree that the most important aspect of the cult was the administration of the Consolamentum to the dying. This ritual could only be performed by the Perfects. There thus existed an underground network that had to know where the Perfects were (and sometimes in hiding), asking them to come to a certain village, to administer the rite to a dying person. Towards the end of the 13th century, sometimes the Perfects did not make it in time or had to make choices between whom to see, as they could not be in two places at the same time. The importance of the Consolamentum is underlined in the accounts that tell that sometimes, once the ritual had been performed, the person on his deathbed nevertheless recovered. But rather than deciding to live (after all, he considered this reality to be evil), he preferred to starve himself to death[171], so that he died under the

---

169   Vidal, Jean-Marie, "Doctrine and Morality of the last Albigenses Ministers", *Magazine of Historical Questions*, LXXXV, pp. 357-409 (1909), LXXVI, pp. 5-48 (1910). Duplicated in fac-sim: Impr. C. Lacour, RediViva, Nîmes, 2002.

170   René Weis, « Les Derniers Cathares: 1290-1329 » ("The Last Cathars: 1290-1329"), Editions Fayard, Paris, 2002.

171   Excerpt from Philipp Schaff's "History of the Christian Church", Volume V: "The Middle Ages. AD 1049-1294", § 80: "The Cathari": "The Endura, which has been called the cruelest practice the history of asceticism has to show, was a voluntary starvation unto death by those who had received the Consolamentum. Sometimes these rigorous religionists waited for thirteen days for the end to come, and parents are said even to have left their sick children without food, and mothers to have withdrawn the breast from nursing infants in executing the rite. The reports of such voluntary suicide are quite numerous." Source of the information

"influence" – the protection – of the Consolamentum.

The ritual was given not only to the dying, but also to those adults that wanted to become a Perfect. Vidal adds that "many wonderful effects" were linked with this ritual and that it was considered essentially an amalgamation of a baptism of the dead, as it were. We note that the sacraments should not necessarily be seen as being Christian in nature. They are "merely" rituals that the Church performs as well. Baptism was practiced in ancient Egypt and John the Baptist of course was not a Christian, as such, for Jesus was just one of several hundreds if not thousands of people that John baptised.

Amongst the sacraments performed by the Cathars, we note the key sacrament of penance, so cherished by the penitents. We also note that baptism of the dead, as practiced by the Marcionites[172]. Vidal adheres to the standard line, namely that the Consolamentum washed away the sins of the deceased: *"The heretication, i.e the consolamentum, if duly received at death's door, purified them of all sins, freed them of any return or compensation. Debts, robbery, usury stopped, were forgiven."*[173]

He also describes details about whether or not Cathars had to pay for these services. *"As soon as a Perfect was summoned to the bed of a dying person, he went in great haste [...] but above all, the dying person was required to pay his debts to the Cathar Church. If he refused to do so, he was deprived of the ritual."*[174] This is conclusive evidence that, within the Cathar community of France, this payment was a standard condition too, but payable to the Cathar community, rather than the Perfect himself. For the Perfect

for the above quotation: Alphandéry, Paul, Les idées morales chez les hétérodoxes latins au début du XIIIe siècle, Paris, Leroux, 1903, p. 51.

Döllinger, Johann Ignaz von, „Beiträge zur Sektengeschichte des Mittelalters" ("A Contribution to the History of Medieval Sects"), Munich, 1890, part II, 205. A most valuable work including original documents, in the collection of which Döllinger spent many years and made many journeys. Full reference for the quote: Schaff, Philipp, History of the Christian Church, Oak Harbor, Washington State, Logos Reseach Systems, Inc., 1997 electronic edition based on the first published version by Charles Scribner's sons, 1907, enhanced with corrections by The Electronic Bible Society, Dallas, Texas, 1998.

172   Refer to St. John Chrysostom, 40th Homily on the First Epistle to the Corinthians.

173   Vidal, Jean-Marie, "Doctrine and Morality of the last Albigenses Ministers", Magazine of Historical Questions, LXXXV, pp. 357-409 (1909), LXXVI, pp. 5-48 (1910). Duplicated in fac-sim: Impr. C. Lacour, RediViva, Nîmes, 2002. Vidal also refers to the following source material at the end of this quote: "Sermo G. Belibasta" (Sermon of Cathar perfect Guilhem Bélibaste"), folio 216c, Art. Her., P. Maur., VIII, LIV, et folio 117e,

Molinier, Charles, « L'Inquisition dans le Midi de la France », Paris, 1880, p. 283.

Schmidt, C., « Histoire et doctrine de la secte des Cathares ou Albigeois » (2 volumes), Paris, 1849, II, p. 84.

174   Ibid.

to receive it would blatantly have gone against the central doctrine of Catharism, which was that Perfects were not allowed to own anything.

Other documents also show us this Cathar custom. Reinerius Sacchoni[175] accuses the Perfects of meanness regarding the Consolamentum ritual, and in the "Cathar rite"[176] we read that *a believer who is ill or dying owes something, and if he can pay for it, he must do so.* Also: *"And if he does not want to do so, he must not receive the ritual."*[177] Jean Guiraud[178] confirms these observations: *"To recover the debts due to the Church by the believers, the Heretics even resorted to refusing the Consolamentum. [...] For the Perfects, death's door was also the moment to benefit from some inheritance."*

It underlines that if the believer could not redeem himself through his "right and just actions", the Cult of the Dead provided an alternative, in which his savings were there to allow the Rite to be performed.

This aspect of Catharism is seldom highlighted by the more popular books on the subject. It places them in a far less innocent light than that into which popular authors have cast them. But we should immediately emphasize that the Cathar tradition of taking money for the Mortuary Rite was not their invention; it was part and parcel of a tradition that had existed for at least two thousand years, if not longer.

We also note that penitents, themselves, were not allowed to have any personal possessions, and so, it seems, it was the case for the Perfects. Guiraud implies that the priests took the money for themselves, but he and others make it clear that the money was destined for the Church. Like the penitents, the Cathars shared their possessions and it seems that the Cathar Church made sure that the Perfects were supported in their needs, either directly (by giving money to them so they could buy food), or indirectly (by having Cathar believers provide it for them).

Flagellants everywhere

Although the Albigensian Crusade did not wipe out the heresy, it did have a severe impact on the Cathar Church. It brought Catharism in France to

---

175   Raniero Sacconi, *"Summa de Catharis"*, 1250.

176   *"The Cathar Ritual"*, published by Cunitz, Iena, 1852.

177   *"The Cathar Ritual"*, p, XXII.

178   Refer to Jean Guiraud, *"Questions of History and Christian Archaeology"*, Paris 1906, p. CLXXXIII. This work is quite revealing with regard to the Cathars' "moral standards". Another work by the same author: *"The Medieval Inquisition"*, Coll. *"Christian Life"*, No. 6, Ed. Grasset, Paris, 1928. Further confirmation of this can also be found in: Abbé Douais, « Les Albigeois, leurs origines », Paris, 1878, p. 247.

its knees, struggling for survival. But outside of France, there were no such troubles – or at least not on the same scale.

Around the 12th and 13th centuries, in northern and central Italy (and in Western Europe in general), the Cult of the Dead was transformed into the Penitent Flagellants. Whereas Catharism is seen, at least in retrospect, as a religion outside of the mainstream Church, the Flagellants infiltrated the community and the religious orders and structures, and were largely considered to be a part of them. Under the appearance of being monks, these confraternities took the care of the dead upon themselves; they sang the offices for the dead; they ensured humanitarian aid for those who could not pay for their own burials; they took it upon themselves to care for the dying.

Despite such apparently noble aims, certain confraternities soon became the subject of repressive measures. In 1389, a group of penitents, the Bianchis, came down from the Alps and spread throughout the whole of northern Italy. They began to approach the states of the Roman Church and the Pope seemed to consider them to be dangerous; he ordered that they should be burnt. As a result, in 1414, 127 flagellants were executed in Sangershausen, upon the orders of Grand Inquisitor Schoenfeld. At that time, the Council of Constance condemned them as heretics too.

Jean Gerson wrote *"Treatise against the sect of the Flagellants"* (main title: *"Epistola ad Vincentium"*, "Letter to Vincent")[179], which was directed towards none other than Vincent Ferrer, founder of the Penitents of Perpignan. Gerson firmly denounced the movement. Despite such preachings, it did not stop Ferrer or any other movement from continuing to expand. Although the Church continued to preach against them, the Mortuary Cult was now so widespread and popular that that it had clearly won the battle against the Church. Ferrer is now known as "Saint Vincent Ferrer"; each city in Italy had its resident penitents and a census listed up to fifty different brotherhoods, all of whom took responsibility for the burial of the dead.

In Florence, the Santa Maria Militia[180] helped the dying, as well as securing them a proper burial. They were founded as early as 1224, but they

---

179   Jean Charlier de Gerson, "Epistola ad Vincentium. Tractatus contra sectam flagellantium" ("Letter to Vincent. Treatise against the Sect of the Flagellants"), se. Opera, Dupin editions, vol. 2, p. 658, 660.
180   Now know as the "Archiconfraternita della Misericordia" (Arch-Confraternity of Mercy). Today, this penitent brotherhood is actually in charge of the ambulance services for all of the hospitals in Florence.

were in existence even earlier than that. The confraternity was officially founded to support the Guelfs, the Pope's partisans, during the war against the Ghibellines, who were backed by the Holy Roman Emperor[181]. The Cathars in the region, known as the Patarini, supported the Ghibellines. The confraternity's task was to try to assimilate the Cathars, so that the Patarini would shift their alliance. On 31st March 1329, the confraternity[182] was promoted by the Florentine Council to the rank of an independent "public organisation". Afterwards, it began to found subsidiaries in the city, each of which was responsible for care for the dying and the dead. Amongst these is the Order of the Red Cross, whose earliest origins may stretch back to Florence.

Elsewhere in Italy, in Naples, a text from Alexandre Dumas illustrates the role of the penitent brotherhoods in that city, as well as the "price" that had to be paid for belonging to it. In chapter VI of "The Corricolo, Story of the author's journey in Naples"[183], we read:

"Trials in Naples last three times longer than in Paris. [...] The day we passed through it, the traffic was congested; we were obliged to get down from our Corricolo[184], to continue on our way on foot, having to nudge past here and there. We had nearly passed through this crowd when we thought of asking the reason of why it was here. One person answered: there was a trial between the Pilgrims Brotherhood (Penitents) and Don Philippe Villani.' We asked what the trial's cause was about. 'The defendant, being buried a few days before at the cost of the Pilgrim's Confraternity, was summoned in order to prove legally that he was dead [...] We asked Francesco who this Don Philippe Villani was. At this moment he showed us a person running.

- Here he is, he told us.

---

181   *Frederick II of Hohenstaufen (1214-1250), Emperor of the Holy Roman Empire of the German Nation. He was the grandson of the infamous Frederick I Barbarossa (Redbeard) (1155- 1177), who himself contributed in no small part to the longstanding conflict between the Guelfs and the Ghibellines.*

182   *The Arch-Confraternity of Misericordia.*

183   *Although Alexandre Dumas is generally thought of as a novelist, his book « Le Corricolo » (1843), is not a novel, but a journey account, so the people, locations and events named in it are real. In this book Alexandre Dumas tells the story of the journey he made from Rome to Naples in 1835. It features colorful descriptions of the life and ways of the city of Naples and its inhabitants.*

184   *Dumas himself, elsewhere in this book, explained what a corricolo is:*
"What is a corricolo? A sort of tilbury that was originally intended to carry one person, and to have one horse harnessed to it. [Now] it can be harnessed with two horses, and carry from twelve up to fifteen people." Corricolos were of common use in Naples during the 19th century.

- The one buried eight days ago?

- Himself.

- Can this be possible?

- He will be raised.

- Is he then a wizard?

- He is the nephew of Cagliostro.

[....]

On 15th November 1834, the Pilgrim Congregation received the following notice: 'The Honourable don Philippe Villani having died of spleen, the Venerable Pilgrims Brotherhood is requested to give the appropriate orders for his funeral.'

In order to help our readers to understand the meaning of this invitation, it is necessary to say a few words regarding the way the funeral service in Naples occurs. By ancient custom the dead were buried in the churches. It is unhealthy, as it leads to 'aria cattiva'[185], the plague, cholera; but it doesn't matter, it is the custom, and from one end of Italy to the other, one bows before this tradition. [...] Each and every inhabitant, during his lifetime, takes the precaution to escape from the undertaker, the cart, and the Campo Santo [the common grave, the cemetery for the poor]. As a result, there are associations for funeral services amongst the citizens, and also mutual insurance companies, not providing life insurance, but a form of death insurance.

Here are the usual formalities to be accepted in one of the fifty mortuary associations in the happy city of Naples. One of the society members introduces the neophyte, who is elected brother by the vote of a secret ballot: from this moment, each time he wants to use any religious practice, he goes to his brotherhood's church; it is his adopted parish, which must, at the cost of a small monthly payment, [...] bury him after his death. If on the other hand, one has neglected this formality, not only is one forced to pay the high price for all the ceremonies fulfilled during life, but the parents must spend fantastic amounts of money to receive this funeral grandeur [...] On 2nd of November, the day of the deceased, each confraternity's catacombs are opened to the public.[...] The skeletons of the brothers who died during the year are raised up, they are dressed in beautiful clothes, placed reverently in niches prepared for the event, all around the hall; then, they receive visits from their parents, who are proud of them and take friends and acquaintances to show them the proper way in which their family members are treated after death. Afterwards, they

---

185   *"Aria cattiva" means "infectious air", "contaminated air", in Italian.*

are buried permanently in a garden of orange trees, called Terra Santa.

All the funeral corporations have income, rights and highly respected privileges; they are ruled by a Prior, who is elected each year from amongst the members. There are confraternities for all orders and all classes: for the nobles and magistrates, for the traders ,and the labourers. Don Philippe Villani belongs to this honourable Brotherhood [the Pilgrims] and he had so much felt the necessity to remain a member, that as low as the Wheel of Fortune might drag him [financially], he had always paid his share devotedly and scrupulously to the general and yearly contribution.

Twenty-four hours after the death, the time demanded by the police rules, the funeral cortège made way towards Don Philippe's house. An Earl, selected among the oldest nobility of Naples, held the Confraternity's gonfalon, then the Brothers, lined up in pairs and in red Penitents' dress, walked before a coffin."

Alexandre Dumas' report of his encounter in Naples leaves us in no doubt whatsoever: all the elements that are part of the Cult of the Dead were still present and practiced there. He notes that a citizen took out "death insurance" and that it was a custom that existed and was followed throughout Italy.

From Dumas' text, it appears that the Neapolitans considered "a proper burial" to be the highest honour a person could have and the family took great pride in the fact that one of their members paid a confraternity the money to look after them. The most important social distinction seems to be that they managed to avoid the common grave, or a burial without a ceremony (i.e. without a special ritual).

It is clear that Naples was in the hands of these brotherhoods: they had privileges and were regulated by law, and the city had no less than fifty such organisations – comparable in modern times to a town or city that has fifty undertakers. But unlike an undertaker, it is clear that the brotherhood was organised on the model of a secret society, with admission strictly regulated and the prior elected by a secret ballot.   Equally, it is noted that this service was not "local"; the faithful were likely to have to change parishes, as the brotherhood's church could be elsewhere. In short, these brotherhoods, whether you believe they were heretics or not, were an organisation within the Church, not reporting to the bishop, but self-sufficient and largely diverting funds away from the local church, towards the pockets of the confraternity. You can ask what these organisations did with all that money... perhaps give a bit to priests like Saunière?

As with Tobit, in Naples, the Mortuary Rite came at a cost and most, like Tobit, had saved up for it. There were two methods of subscription: annual or monthly membership, or a one-time payment (which seems to have been, for obvious reasons, much higher) when a person was dying. Dumas noted how most "took his precautions" during their lifetime. Still, it seems that the fees did not guarantee a membership as such; rather it was payment in instalments. It was therefore possible that when a person required the Mortuary Rite, if his payments were still not sufficient to cover the expenses, then other people would be asked to "top up" the account. In particular, if a person died young, that responsiblity would fall specifically on the parents. We can only hope that the brotherhoods had high morals, for it is clear that blackmail and false claims about insufficient funds were easy temptations.

In Naples, the Mortuary Rite was not merely about a ritual of the dead, it is also ostentatious display of the dead: a deceased person is raised up, dressed and then put on display in specifically designed niches, where he is admired by the family and friends.

Equally, we note a sectarian aspect of life in Naples – and other Italian cities – as people are initiated into a secret brotherhood, with membership largely anonymous, and with certain judicial privileges, as well as having money at their disposal. It sounds strangely similar to one typically Italian organisation, secretive, powerful and wealthy: the Mafia. And we are not the first to ask the question whether the Mafia originated from within the ranks of the penitent brotherhoods.

Finally, if anyone is still unwilling to accept that Naples was in the grip of the penitents, let us remember Dumas' words, how the fellow members of the brotherhood lined up in pairs and dressed as red penitents: in Naples, the domain of death and dying were the exclusive bailiwick of the penitent organisations.

Shrouds

Let us also note some other peculiarities of the penitent movement: its devotion to shrouds. We see the "Veil of Veronica" on the typical La Sanch cross in Southern France. Veronica's Veil is a legendary Christian relic. Veronica from Jerusalem encountered Jesus along the Via Dolorosa on the way to Calvary, where she paused to wipe the sweat (in Latin, suda) off his face with her veil. Christ's image was miraculously imprinted onto the cloth[186]. According to legend, Veronica later travelled to Rome to present

---

186   *In Latin, a shroud is called a "sudarium" and in Greek a "sudarion", from "suda",*

the cloth to the Roman Emperor Tiberius. Legend has it that it had miraculous properties, being able to quench thirst, restore blindness, and sometimes even raise the dead. No doubt it is the latter aspect that makes it even more of interest to the Cult of the Dead.

The story of Veronica and her veil does not occur in the Bible, though the apocryphal *"Acts of Pilates"*[187] mentions a woman called Veronica who was cured by touching the hem of Jesus' cloak. The name "Veronica" is a colloquial juxtaposition of the Latin word Vera, meaning "truth", and the Greek word Icon, meaning "image"; the Veil of Veronica was therefore largely regarded in medieval times as "the true image", and the truthful representation of Jesus, preceding the now more infamous Shroud of Turin.

We will return to the Shroud soon, but let us note that although it is not a legendary artefact we won't find the Veil of Veronica anywhere on display today. Its provenance prior to the 12th century is uncertain, but in 1297, the image was brought to Saint Peter's in Rome by order of Pope Boniface VIII. When the part of the Basilica housing the relic was remodelled in 1506, the veil disappeared. There are rumours that it is now in the hands of a confraternity... we may have a fair guess what type of confraternity. On a similar note, the Black Madonna of Notre-Dame de Marceille was "saved" by a penitent brotherhood at the time of the French Revolution.

The importance of Veronica's veil to the heretics is clear when we note that many artists created reproductions of it. But in 1616, Pope Paul V prohibited the manufacture of any copies unless they were made by a canon of Saint Peter's Basilica. In 1629, Pope Urban VIII not only confirmed this prohibition but also ordered the destruction of all existing copies. His edict declared that anyone who had access to a copy should bring it to the Vatican, under penalty of excommunication. Harsh words, surely, for something that does not require such strong treatment… unless, of course, we realise the importance of the veil in the eyes of the Cult of the Dead. In the churches of these confraternities, whether in the South of France or Northern Spain, we find the walls are adorned often with not just one, but several copies of Veronica's veil.

For a cult interested in burials, the burial cloth of Christ should be seen as an important relic. Enter the so-called Shroud of Turin. The Turin Shroud is an ancient linen cloth bearing the image of a man who appears to have

---

sweat.

187 *"Acts of Pilates"* is an apocryphal book written in the 4th century. It is also known as *"Gospel of Nicodemus"*.

been physically traumatized in a manner consistent with crucifixion. It is presently kept in the royal chapel of the Cathedral of Saint John the Baptist in Turin, Italy. The legend states that it was the cloth that covered Jesus of Nazareth when he was placed in his tomb and that his image was somehow recorded as a photographic negative on its fibres, at or near the time of his proclaimed resurrection. Sceptics contend that the shroud is a medieval hoax or forgery – or even a devotional work of artistic verisimilitude. It is the subject of intense debate among some scientists, believers, historians and writers, regarding where, when and how the shroud and its images were created.

From the point of view of the Cult of the Dead, the shroud itself is important: whether a forgery or a genuine burial cloth, it is a burial shroud and hence a key aspect of the Cult of the Dead. Unfortunately, the Shroud's origins are so nebulous and contested, that we cannot devote too much attention as to whether or not the Cult of the Dead was strongly involved in its preservation – or indeed its creation.

Finally, as described by Alexandre Dumas, the Neapolitan brotherhoods specialised in the "donation of the shroud" as well as "in the weaving of shrouds". Should we interpret these shrouds as the modern equivalents of – for example – the ancient Egyptian practice of mummification?

The Egyptian Wagy Festival and Saunière's preoccupation with January 17th

The private worship of the dead in Naples seems to bear direct parallels with the Wagy Festival in ancient Egypt. The festival of Wagy was celebrated in honour of Osiris, on the 17th day of the first month of the year. On that date, funerary gifts were given to the dead. In ancient Egypt, the New Year began on the day when Sirius, the brightest star in the sky, rose together with the sun – known as a heliacal rising. At least, that was the theory. In practice, the Egyptian calendar was not fixed (it did not taking the quarter day into account), which meant that every four years, the New Year moved one day. This meant that it took 1460 years (365 times 4) for the calendars to realign.

It was only in Ptolemaic times (3rd century BC) that the Canopus Decree stated that the New Year and thus the calendar should become fixed. New Year's day was fixed on July 20th; Wagy would thus have been celebrated on August 8th. If, however, as is now the custom, we begin the New Year on January 1st, then the feast is celebrated on January 17th.

The festival of Wagy was the day of the dead and is thus the parallel of November 2nd, the day of the dead in the Christian calendar, the day on which the Neapolitan brotherhoods performed their rituals. On that day, the families came to the tombs of the deceased, with offerings, performing rituals, specifically "fumigations". The ceremonies were often followed by a funerary meal. Raphaël Bertrand[188] has translated a contract found in Assiout, which states: *"Contract between the governor and director of the priests Djefaihapy, rightful in voice, agreed with the clergy of the temple of Upuat, lord of Assiout, to the effect that a loaf of white bread will be given to him by each person for his statue which is located in the temple, the 18th day of the first month of Akhet, the day of the feast of Wagy, and to leave [the temple] following his funerary priest, reciting the formulas of glorification for him [i.e the deity], [after] having lit a torch for him conforming to the manner in which it is [customarily] done, each time they perform the rituals of glorification for their own dead, the day on which the torch is lit in the temple."*

Wallis Budge[189] found references to the festival, which he calls "Uak" – a third way to transliterate the name. Budge gives many direct references to the Egyptian rites, which state clearly that the dead person is identified with Osiris and his star, Sah, "the lord of the vines in the festival of Uak". The ritual tries to bring the souls back to the Duat – the equivalent of the Christian Purgatory. *"You rise with the star of Sah in that part of the sky; you lay down the star of Sah in the western part of the sky. Your third is the star Septet, the seats of which are pure, and it guides you along the beautiful*

---

188 Refer to the following article under the section "4. Un contrat d'Assiout: traduction (Raphaël Bertrand)" ("4. A Contract from Assiout: translation by Raphaël Bertrand"):
Raphaël Bertrand, « Le culte funéraire en Egypte Ancienne » ("The Funerary Cult in Ancient Egypt"), in Papyrus Express (online magazine) vol. 1 no. 4, 1st October 2000.
http://www.egypteeternelle.net/papyrus/v01n04/article2.htm (French text)
Raphaël Bertrand is a French Egyptologist who specialises in the transcription of pharaonical documents from the Ancient Empire (c. 3100 – c. 2330 BC), the Middle Empire (c. 2064 – c. 1797 BC) and the New Empire (c. 1543 – c. 1078 BC). He mastered Middle-Egyptian, Neo-Egyptian, Hieratic and has basic knowledge of the Coptic language. He also teaches on the Egyptian language. His subjects of interest are the Ancient Empire, the study of administrative structures, economics, religion and philology.
189 E. A. Wallis Budge, "Legends Of The Gods - The Egyptian Texts, edited with Translations by E. A. Wallis Budge", London, 1912. Full electronic text (produced by John B. Hare and Carrie R. Lorenz) : http://www.fullbooks.com/Legends-Of-The-Gods.html
Also refer to: "Papyrus of Ani (Egyptian Book of the Dead) In Three Books, Translated by E. A. Wallis Budge" from Sunrise magazine, April/May 1982. Copyright © by Theosophical University Press. Full electronic text (transcript provided by the African Studies Center of the University of Pennsylvania): http://www.africa.upenn.edu/Books/Papyrus_Ani.html

roads in the sky towards the Reed Fields."

We thus find ourselves reading about a death mass, where the souls are commemorated by their families – with the light of the torch perhaps reminding us of the light of the souls. Little has changed between 2500 BC in Egypt and 1850 AD in Athens.

January 17th, the modern equivalent of the date of the Wagy Festival, is a famous date in the mystery of Rennes-le-Château. Intriguingly, it is linked specifically with death and the dying… this is not a coincidence.

Today, people flock to Rennes-le-Château to see the spectacle of the so-called "Blue apples" inside the church of Rennes-le-Château. The phenomenon, which is by no means unique – in fact it is very common – is created by the sunlight projecting parts of a stained glass window on the opposite wall.

Passing over this rather sad tourist attraction, we come to the tombstone of one Marie de Nègre Dables (Dame d'Hautpoul de Blanchefort), who died on 17th January 1781. Central to the mystery, her tombstone, which is in the cemetery of Rennes-le-Château is deemed to have been the key through which Saunière was able to acquire his wealth. But perhaps the key is not just the tombstone itself, but also the date on the inscription?

Bérenger Saunière himself suffered a stroke on 17th January 1917. Of all the dates on which to suffer a stroke, we can only wonder whether it was indeed a coincidence. Saunière had been ill for some years, sometimes being confined to his bed for up to a week at a time. Few were therefore surprised to find that he suffered a stroke and died shortly afterwards – on January 22nd. Still, might there be another specific reason why he had the stroke precisely on January 17th? Is it possible that he performed certain magical rituals that day – perhaps the most important magical day of the year for priests of the Cult of the Dead? Perhaps he had been close to dying for a long time, but willed himself to live on, until January 17th? After all, for a dying man, the Mortuary Rite and performing certain aspects on key dates may perhaps even have meant that he could perform the rite on himself?

Let us not speculate too much: all we are suggesting is that, knowing that January 17th could be an important date for the Cult of the Dead, an already seriously ill Saunière could have performed certain rituals that took too much energy out of a frail body… resulting in a stroke, from which he would die five days later. It makes one wonder whether Tobit's blindness was also not so much the result of a "coincidence" involving a bird's dropping, but perhaps a side effect of the magical rituals that he had just performed. While it is probably a coincidence too that Saunière himself was rumoured to have had one glass eye when he died... But perhaps the glass eye, the stroke, the blindness could be side effects of the materials involved in the ritual – or perhaps the outcome of the energy that was required in order to perform these rites; after all, Tobit was so tired that he fell asleep on his way home after one rite. Those upon whom the rites were performed, had to pay a price to enter Heaven, but it may be that the magicians that performed the Mortuary Rite paid a physical price too...

Chapter 7

Heretics everywhere

Before we can put the history of the Manicheans to rest, there is one final branch of this movement that needs further attention: the Humiliati. The Humiliati reveal a clear progression from a Manichean to a Penitential movement, which would later be integrated within the Catholic Church as if it was one of their own, yet did nothing to rid itself of any of its former heresies.

Let us return to the Book of Tobit and note that his wife, Anne, seems to spend the entire day doing nothing but weaving. This profession was typical for the Manicheans and it seems that whether it was 600 BC or 1100 AD, weaving was a telling occupation of these people. Bernard of Clairvaux[190] also noted that amongst the Manicheans and Cathars in the North of Europe, *"the members that formed this secret society were primarily ordinary people, among whom we recognise the weavers."* According to another commentator, Eckbert of Schönau[191], *"the weavers were so numerous amongst the Cathars, that they gave their name to the sect"*... which was indeed what happened: for most of the Middle Ages, the Cathars were known as "the Weavers"[192]. The first such mention was found in the North of France, written by the chronicler Baudry, bishop of Noyon Tournai (1097), when he spoke about Ramihrd, who was burnt in Cambrai in 1077: *"many of this cult still live in certain towns, up to this day. And living from weaving, they are named as such."* [193]

---

190   *Bernard of Clairvaux, "Sermo. In Cant. 65", N° 5.*

191   *Eckbert of Schönau, « Sermones Contra Catharos » (1165), Advers. Catharos, Sermo I.*

192   *Abbé E. Vacandard, who was a Doctor in Theology and second Chaplain at the Lycée Corneille in Paris (at the end of the 19th century), stresses the connection between Cathars and Weavers in "Cathares, les origines de l'hérésie Albigeoise" ("Cathars - The Origins of the Albigensian Heresy"), duplicated in fac-sim: Impr. C. Lacour, RediViva, Nîmes, 2001: "Among the sectarians appeared prominently weavers, who were known in the country under the name of 'Arrians'." Vacandard furthermore mentions in support of this statement several sources which underscore the fact that this opinion was very widespread: "De Textoribus, quos Arrianos ipsi nominant". [Gaufrid., ep. N° 4], and [Gaufrid]. Ep. Ap. Migne, E. CLXXXV, p. 410-415, N° 4.*

193   *Ed. Le Glay, chronique d'Arras et de Cambrai, Paris 1834, p. 356 à 35.*

Paul Frédéricq, "Corpus documentorum inquisitionis haereticae pravitatis Neerlandicae I" ("Corpus of Documents of the Inquisition on the Perversion of the Dutch Heretics, I"), Gand – La Haye, 1889.

So they were called Weavers, but also Lollards, Bogomils and various other names and nicknames[194]. In the French historian Jules Michelet's *Le Peuple*, at the chapter entitled "The Servitude of the Worker Dependent on the Machines" we read that *"The mystical weavers of the Middle Ages became well-known as Lollards, for as they worked, they lolled, singing with a low voice, or at least in spirit. [...] I have already spoken about the Weavers of Flanders [...] the Lollards, Beghards, as they were called. The Church often persecuted these people as heretics. [...] The real name of this class is the first one that was given to them in Italy, in the Middle Ages: Humiliati."*[195]

The Catholic Encyclopedia[196] has this to say about the movement: *"A penitential order dating back, according to some authorities, to the beginning of the eleventh, but more probably to the beginning of the twelfth century, to the reign of Emperor Henry V, who, after quelling a rebellion in Lombardy, led the principal nobles of the cities implicated back to Germany as captives. Converted from the vanities of the world, they assumed a penitential garb of grey and gave themselves up to works of [...] mortification, whereupon the emperor, after receiving their pledges of future loyalty, permitted their return to Lombardy. At this time they were often called Barettini, from the shape of their head-dress. Their acquaintance with the German woollen manufactures enabled them to introduce improved methods into Italy, thus giving a great impetus to the industry [...]. On the advice of St. Bernard, in 1134, many of them [...] withdrew from the world, establishing their first monastery at Milan. They exchanged their ashen habit for one of white. Some years later, on the advice of St. John Meda of Oldrado (d. 1159), they embraced the Rule of St. Benedict*[197], *adapted by St. John to their needs; they received*

---

194   Refer to Jean Duvernoy, « Le Catharisme : La religion des Cathares » ("Catharism: the Religion of the Cathars"), Privat, Toulouse, 1979, pp. 307-308 for more details about these nicknames: "The Cathar heretics received various designations in order to differentiate them from the rest of the population: 'Bonshommes' (Good Men) here, 'Patarini' there; in France, they were most commonly known under the nicknames of 'Albigenses' or 'Weavers'." Abbé J.P. Migne, Patrologia Latina, 195, Ch. 14: "They are the ones who are commonly called Cathars... The ones we call 'Cathars' in our Germany, 'Piphles' in Flanders, 'Weavers' in France, because of their practice of weaving."

195   Jules Michelet, « Le Peuple », Comptoir des Imprimeurs-Unis, Paris, 1846.

196   The Catholic Encyclopedia, Volume VII, 1910, published by Robert Appleton Company. Nihil Obstat, June 1st, 1910, Remy Lafort, S. T. D. Censor, Approved by: + John Cardinal Farley, Archbishop of New York. Refer to the article "Humiliati" written by F. M. Rudge.

197   St. John Meda was a Benedictine monk, and the Prior of the Humiliati Order (or rather, Brotherhood). St. Bernard of Clairvaux, who advised the Humiliati during their beginnings, was a Cistercian monk (from Cîteaux, an offshoot of the Benedictine Order). The Order of Saint Benedict does have a connection with penitent brotherhoods.

papal approbation from Innocent III about 1200 [...] The order grew rapidly, [...], formed trades associations among the people, and played an important part in the civic life of every community in which they were established. In the course of time, however, owing to the accumulation of temporal goods and the restriction of the number of members admitted (for at one time there were only about 170 in the 94 monasteries), serious abuses crept in, which St. Charles Borromeo was commissioned by Pius V to reform. His fearless efforts roused such opposition among a minority that a conspiracy was formed and a murderous assault made on him by one of the Humiliati, a certain Girolamo Donati, called Farina, which, though it was unsuccessful, was responsible for the execution of the chief conspirators and the suppression of the order by a Bull of 8th February 1571[198]. *The houses and possessions were bestowed on other religious orders, including the Barnabites and Jesuits [...]"*

The origins of the order's foundation seem to go far back in time. According to some sources, the confraternity was even older than the beginning of the 11th century, although others see it more in the beginning of the 12th century. The foundation could therefore have taken place between 1017 or 1178, the latter being the date which is accepted by most historians.

Philip Schaff in *History of the Christian Church*[199] states that:

"At a later date, a portion of the Humiliati associated themselves in convents, and received the sanction of Innocent III. It seems probable that they furnished the model for the third order of St. Francis."[200] As such, the founding of the Order of the Humiliati well before other congregations such as the Franciscans and the Dominicans means that these organisations may have been inspired by the Humiliati. As far as organisation is concerned, there is little contestation that this was the case; the big question, of course, is whether the Franciscans and the Dominicans were equally inspired by the doctrine of the Humiliati even though it is clear that they will fervently deny any such link. But if they were inspired, it would make the Humiliati the first Manicheans to be officially incorporated into the fold of the Roman Church under the guise of monks and ascetics.

---

198   *The papal bull of 8 February 1571, which ordered the official suppression of the Humiliati Order, was issued by Pope Pius V.*

199   *Schaff, Philipp, "History of the Christian Church", Oak Harbor, Washington State, Logos Reseach Systems, Inc., 1997, electronic edition based on the first published version by Charles Scribner's sons, 1907, enhanced with corrections by The Electronic Bible Society, Dallas, Texas, 1998.*

200   *"History of the Christian Church", Chapter X: "Heresy and its suppression", paragraph 84.*

We know that it was the hope of these Manicheans to infiltrate the Church and take it over from within. And we also note that the Humiliati wanted to "embrace the rule of St Benedict, adapted by John Meda to suit their needs"[201]. This seems to imply that the Benedictines too may have been a mechanism that the Humiliati used in their efforts to infiltrate the church.

Certain historians will – and can – argue that the conversion from the Manicheans and the Penitents, when they were integrated into the orders such as the Dominicans and Franciscans, as they would later be, was in fact a genuine conversion, with these people being welcomed within the Catholic Church. But the Catholic Encyclopaedia focuses purely on their heretical nature, including the statement that they were forbidden by Pius V. The worst case scenario is that the penitents had infiltrated all the above mentioned monastic societies, which could mean that they controlled up to seventy percent of monastic Catholicism.

This is what Marco Sommariva[202] says about the cult's recognition: *"[The Humiliati,] we see them in Milan and other Lombardian towns in the middle of the 12th century. They are groups of laymen who live in a community. [...] They refuse to take oaths in courts. [...] They consider themselves to be the true faithful, true Christians and true Catholics. They demand from Pope Alexander III confirmation for their common lifestyle. This they receive, but certain things do not reassure him [the Pope], seeing they are not allowed to make 'conventicula' [that is to say that they are forbidden to have reunions and assemblies] and to preach in public. [...] For the Humiliati, the condemnation of the Council of Verona of 1184 was just ahead, followed by a series of excommunications."*

So before condemning them officially, the Pope was already wary of the organisation, making sure that their ideology did not spread, by forbidding them to preach in public, or hold rallies or assemblies. But why? According to Madeleine and Roland Conte, in *Les Confréries de Pénitents*, the Humiliati had *"chosen to practice poverty [...] to preach penitence [...] and claimed to start to return to the primitive Church"*. The bull *"Ad Abolendam"* of Pope Lucius III, at the Council of Verona[203], makes it clear that for

201   *The Catholic Encyclopedia, Volume VII, 1910, published by Robert Appleton Company. Nihil Obstat, June 1st, 1910, Remy Lafort, S. T. D. Censor, Approved by: + John Cardinal Farley, Archbishop of New York. Refer to the article "Humiliati", written by F. M. Rudge.*
202   *"Ribelli, 1000-2000, Un lungo millennio" (Rebels, 1000-2000, A Long Millennium") by Marco Sommariva (Editions Malatempora, 2002, collection Perturbazioni).*
203   *Pope Lucius III, "Ad Abolendam", a papal bull quoted in: "The Disciplinary Decrees of*

the pope, the Humiliati were placed in the same category as the Cathars and Manicheans. In the eyes of the Church, they were guilty of the same crimes: heresy.

But after the condemnation, the Humiliati made amends with the Catholic Church and were recognised in 1201 by Pope Innocent III.

Richard Weber[204] adds that *"one portion of this group"* reconciled itself with the Church, but with one important *"distinction: those who would preach must become clerics and be ordained. They became a clerical Order of Humiliati. Those who remained as lay people would form a lay Order of Humiliati, dependent upon the clerical Order. The lay Humiliati are the first group to be described as a Third Order".* From 1201 onwards, the order had clear sailing. Only in 1571, under Protestant pressure, specifically to make sure that the Lutherans could not criticise certain aspects of the Church, were the Humiliati suppressed.

According to the Catholic Encyclopaedia, the Humiliati had committed "serious abuses". But of what nature? For Voltaire[205], *"the religious of this order, primarily established in the Milanese region, lived scandalously."* This is scant information, though it is known that other authors accused them of "depravities". It is in *La Lombardia nel secolo XVII*[206], a book from 1854, that we find further details: *"The brothers of the Humiliati, who introduced the manufacture of wool in our regions, had become extremely wealthy and corrupt. They possessed 94 houses, each able to house 100 brothers. [...] Saint Charles [Charles Borromeo, archbishop of Milan] tried to reform them [as] the Humiliati brothers received an income of 25,000 zecchini [gold coins] from the [wool] manufactures and were filled with depraved cravings[207]. [...] Manzoni has written as to how Frederic Borromeo [Charles' cousin] paid visits [to his clergy], as we retain 'Exordia plebanarum visitationum', which*

---

the Ecumenical Council", B. Herder Book Co., St. Louis, 1937, p. 242-243.

204   Fr. Richard Weber, O.P., "History of the Dominican Laity, Part 1". *An eye-opening confession on the true origins of the Dominicans by the Dominicans themselves, published on the official website of the Dominican Order for the Province of St. Albert the Great (Chicago): http://www.domcentral.org/oplaity/layhistory.htm*

205   Voltaire, « Essai sur l'histoire générale, les mœurs et l'esprit des nations depuis Charlemagne jusqu'à nos jours » ("An Essay on Universal History, the Manners and Spirit of Nations from the reign of Charlemaign to the Age of Lewis XIV"), (1756), Chap. CLXXVI.

206   "La Lombardia nel secolo XVII – Ragionamenti di Cesare Cantù" ("Lombardy in the 17th century – Reasonings by Cesare Cantù"), Milano, 1854. Refer specifically to the second part "I Borromei" ("The Borromei") for the exact source of the quote.

207   For more on this topic, see also Cesare Cantù, "Gli eretici d'Italia" ("The Heretic of Italy"), Turin, 1867, vol. II, p. 291.

are transcripts of the speeches that he held at the beginning of his visits. [...] Happy to find himself in the middle of his clergy, he nevertheless sees some of the disorder in which they find themselves, but of which he is not going to exaggerate the faults vis-a-vis the world. [...] He wanted [...] that they did not abuse mass, or that they left rubbish in holy places, that they did not financially speculate on the corpses or burials, [...] or that they spoke too much with their people, because too much discussion led to doubts and questions."

Borromeo adds words that we would ardently wish to see written in certain modern books: "It was not a faint blush, the blush I suddenly felt come upon me at the moment when I began to think that it would be advisable that I would reason with you at length on the subject of the horrible and abominable events that we have witnessed [...] I am archbishop, will I also be constrained to seek a method to persuade some of my priests so that they would diligently stop their ugly avarices about the dead? I am the archbishop of a very noble and very old metropolitan church, do I have to address myself to such things? My studies should be better, my works worthier: and I seek and ardently wish finer works from you, you who listen to me, you who are soaked in this vice. [...] Nevertheless, today it is upon me to demonstrate with powerful words, that even the barbarians observe this law that at no point should corpses be mutilated; and that the worldly philosophers, and not only the Gospels, should persuade you of that; that the care for the dead has been entrusted to you, in order for you to stay removed from any corruption through illicit profits. [...] And lately, I have found myself forced to compare these avid priests with savage beasts."

It seems that Charles and Frederic Borromeo had identified the main and illicit occupation in which the clergy of Milan were involved, especially the Humiliati: the cult of the Dead. The accusations cannot be misinterpreted: the clergy had "mutilated" corpses, as well as interfered with tombs, and even speculated financially on them. It is not a flattering portrait that the archbishop paints of the Humiliati. But it seems that his words were not well received. Indeed, Charles Borromeo would soon become the object of a plot, resulting in several assassination attempts on his life. If the Humiliati were behind this effort, we can indeed see this as the last, desperate attempts of an order that had been found out to be "fake" Catholics: despite claiming to be Catholic, in truth they had not changed any of their ways and they continued to practice the Manichean belief.

Seizing power

The nature and the power of the Manichean heresy in Europe was felt with the appearance and penetration of the Humiliati within the Catholic

Church. But they were not alone; other confraternities of Penitents would soon evolve and create their own religious orders... and not the least: the Franciscans and the Dominicans.

These orders had their origins within the Manichean cults, but in the 12th and 13th centuries would transform themselves into the most enviable and prestigious orders of Christianity. It shows how the penitents were perfecting their penetration methodology. In fact, they would soon set themselves up as the prime defenders of the Catholic cause. And the method used was particularly ingenious and vicious, for it would allow the heretic to do penitence[208], i.e. recognise the fact that he was guilty of heresy, after which he repented and often became a monk in one of these orders... if not an inquisitor.

The heretics appeared to abdicate their religion and pretended to convert to one of these Catholic monastic orders. But, in truth, these were heretics pretending to convert heretics, and the environment in which the "former" heretic ended up, was as heretical as the one he had just "abandoned". As to them rising to the rank of inquisitor, what better argument was there in favour of this than that a "former" heretic should go out and hunt down his former friends? That was in fact the argument that they used when they solicited the Pope for his approval, as well as the recognition of their orders.

Such techniques – basic once you see them for what they are – allowed the enemy of the Church to establish itself within the heart of the Church; soon, it would become the heart of the Inquisition (formed by the Dominicans and the Franciscans). But apart from the obvious plan which the Church either did not see, or did not want to see, or could not respond to, there are three other factors that played a role:

the number of heretics, which was countless, and their implantation within the general public;

their geographical spread;

their political influence within the German Empire.

We have focused a lot of our attention on Italy and Southern France, but the penitent presence in Germany should by no means be neglected. The German kingdom was born from the battle of Fontenay-en-Puisaye, after which the grandsons of Charlemagne divided the lands of their grand-

---

208   Gabriel Audisio, "The Barba and the inquisitor: trial of Barba Pierre Griot by Inquisitor Jean de Roma", Editions Edisud, 1979.

father. The defeat of Lothar, the legitimate heir, and the treaty of Verdun in 843, forced him to cede parts of his country to his brothers. Louis II[209] received what would become known as Germany. Germany would soon become influenced by Thrace and Bulgaria, as the Bulgarian Prince Boris allied himself with Louis against the Byzantine Empire. The goal of this alliance was apparently to stop the spread of Orthodoxy in Thrace and Macedonia. Still, the Bulgarian people, and specifically the nobility, were already very much taken by the Manichean heresy, preached in the region by the Paulicians.

King Boris then, had to renounce the alliance with Louis II, after intimidations by the Byzantine Emperor, Michael II. But as these threats did not materialise, Boris re-established his alliance with Germany, as the Bulgarian sovereign could not allow Orthodoxy to settle itself within his country, not the least because because his people were both pagan and Manichean. Still, the alliance between Germany and Bulgaria would not last. The Byzantine Empire would repeatedly question it, seeing it as a desire to maintain a religious independence within that nation, which they translated as a specific sectarian allegiance: to Bogomilism, i.e. Manicheism, but with a local (Bulgarian) flavour.

But there was a link between the two countries and it would continue throughout the Middle Ages. According to Professor Dimitar Angelov, the Manichean and Penitent cults used Bulgaria as a retreat and a base from which they could spread their cult in Italy, as well as Germany and Saxony. It meant that the Manicheans used the alliance to infiltrate the German Empire with their heresy.

Certain scientists, such as Anne Brenon[210], have pondered the question of how Catharism spread in Europe, arguing that *"an event must have oc-*

---

209   *It should also be known that St. Benedict of Anagni became the personal friend and counsel of Louis II, and that in 815, Louis II appointed Benedict as General Inspector and reformer of the German Empire's monastic communities. Under Louis II and subsequent emperors' protection, the Order of Saint Benedict thus became a full-fledged imperial institution, the monastic backbone of the German Holy Roman Empire. This fact should be viewed in light of some Benedictine monks' subsequent deep involvement whith the penitents, of which John Oldrado di Meda, who was the Prior (head) of the Humiliati Brotherhood located in Milan, Italy, is not exactly the least example. John Meda joined the Humiliati as early as 1134.*
210   *Anne Brenon, « Le Vrai Visage du Catharisme » ("The True Face of Catharism"), Ed. Loubatières, Toulouse, 1988 (re-edition). Also by the same author: « Les femmes cathares » ("Cathar Women"). Paris, Perrin, 1992 (re-edition). Anne Brenon is a paleographist, holds a degree in Religious Science from the Ecole Pratique des Hautes Etudes in Paris, and is chief conservator in the French state's heritage preservation administration.*

curred at the same time, towards the year 1000, in the Champagne region, Aquitania, Occitania and Northern Italy." This enigma could have a simple answer: the expansion of the German Empire.

When we talk about the distribution of this heresy across Europe, we come up with "pockets" of heresies, such as Flanders, Lombardy, Cologne, Champagne, Germany, Italy. Otto I the Great was the son of Henry I the Fowler, king of the Germans, and Matilda of Ringelheim. He was Duke of the Saxons, King of the Germans and arguably the first Holy Roman Emperor, for he tried to expand Germany towards the East, pushing the German frontier back to the rivers Neisse and Oder. It was the start of an expansion which would see consecutive German Emperors expand their country into Lombardy, central Italy, the kingdom of Bourgogne, Flanders, Alsace, Champagne... countries which would soon all have a Cathar presence, which had ridden in on the wave of German expansion throughout Europe.

The expansion of the new faith was not the work of the ordinary German people, who were not contaminated by this heresy, at least not in the same proportions as that of Central Italy or Lombardy. In Germany, the imperial family were the political promoters of the heresy in Europe. They protected the Manicheans and supported the foundation of their monastic orders.

The Investiture Controversy was the most significant conflict between secular and religious powers in medieval Europe. It began as a dispute in the 11th century between the Holy Roman Emperor and the Gregorian Papacy concerning who would control appointments of church officials (investiture). It was in the 11th century that the Church wanted to address the Manichean heresy, which began to menace the power structure of the Church.

Prior to the Investiture Controversy, the appointment of church officials, while theoretically a task of the Church, was in practice performed by secular authorities. Since a substantial amount of wealth and land was usually associated with the office of bishop or abbot, the sale of Church offices (a practice known as simony) was an important source of income for secular leaders; and since bishops and abbots were themselves usually part of the secular governments, due to their literacy and administrative resources, it was beneficial for a secular ruler to appoint (or sell the office to) someone who would be loyal. In addition, the Holy Roman Emperor had the special ability to appoint the pope, and the pope in turn would appoint and crown the next Holy Roman Emperor; thus the cycle of secular investiture of Church offices ensured their perpetuation from the top down indefinitely. It was a dangerous practice, which the Church, faced with the heresy, realised could soon escalate out of control – their control – and into the hands of the heresy.

The crisis began when a group within the church, members of the Gregorian Reform, decided to address the sin of simony by restoring the power of investiture to the Church. The Gregorian reformers knew this would not be possible so long as the emperor maintained the ability to appoint the pope, so the first step was to liberate the papacy from the control of the emperor. An opportunity came in 1056 when Henry IV became emperor at a young age. The reformers seized the chance to free the papacy while he was still a child and could not react. In 1059, a church council in Rome declared secular leaders would play no part in the election of popes, and created the College of Cardinals, made up entirely of church officials and it is this College of Cardinals that remains to this day the agency used to elect popes. Once Rome gained control of the election of the pope, it was now ready to attack the practice of secular investiture on a broad front.

According to Canon Law, simony is a "crime, sanctioned by major excommunication[211] and the obligation to restore to the Church the amount illegally received". The guilty party was indeed seen as a heretic, his crime being "embezzlement". Simony became ingrained in the Holy Empire as the bishop had to install, in each parish, a tribunal which had to enquire into the manners of its fellow citizens. Anyone condemned by this tribunal was forced to do penance, either by receiving the whip or spending time in prison. However, the guilty person had the right, while confessing his sins, to do penance by paying money to the Church authority. And by 1000 AD, these tribunals became largely an economic power: the "libri poenitentiales" allowed those who were condemned, to wipe out their sins by donating money[212]. Three collections stood out: the Disciplinis Ecclesiasticis, the Causis Synodalibus and the Volumen Decretorum. They were institutionalised between 907 and 1020, the first two in Trèves and the latter in Worms, both towns in Germany. These laws stated that the penalties

---

211   *The severest sanction available under Canon Law, which carries with it total rupture from the Catholic Church and eternal damnation.*

212   *Edmund Hamer Broadbent, "The Pilgrim Church", first published by Pickering & Inglis Ltd., London, 1931. Refer specifically to Section 9: "The lay world. The penitences", for the source material. Note: the source material used here was drawn from the French edition of Broadbent's book, entitled "Le douloureux pèlerinage de l'église à travers les âges" ("The painful pilgrimage of the Church through the ages"), and first published in Yverdon (Switzerland) in 1939.*

could be exchanged for money, with the amount fixed according to the wealth of the guilty party. If the guilty party's health was fragile, it was in his interest to pay quickly, as otherwise he could have to recite the psalms twenty times or, more worryingly, receive up to 15,000 lashes of the whip.

The flagellations, of course, were executed within the framework of the Penitent congregations. It meant that simony became linked with the Cult of the Dead, which was already notorious for receiving money for "mortal repentance". It allowed for a bizarre mixture, which muddied the waters, but in which the heretics reinforced their position. So, in 1056, the Church could wedge its foot in the door, making sure that things would not escalate out of control, specifically, preventing it being from taken over by the heretics. Thus, in 1056, the papacy was saved from the hands of the German Emperor; and it seems it was needed; Voltaire wrote that when the German Emperor Otto IV *"died [...] in 1218 as a penitent. [For] He would [ask that] his kitchen servants trample him beneath their feet, and he would also receive floggings from resident monks."*[213]

Although never formally instituted, in 1075, Pope Gregory VII asserted in the "Dictatus Papae" that as the Roman church was founded by God alone, the papal power was the sole universal power, and that the pope alone could appoint or depose churchmen or move them from (Episcopal) see to see. This move eliminated the practice of secularly-appointed investiture. By this time, Henry IV of Germany was no longer a child, and he reacted to this declaration by sending Gregory VII a letter in which he rescinded his imperial support of Gregory as pope in no uncertain terms: the letter was headed "Henry, king not through usurpation but through the holy ordination of God, to Hildebrand, at present not pope but false monk". It called for the election of a new pope and the letter ends: *"I, Henry, king by the grace of God, with all of my Bishops, say to you, come down, come down, and be damned throughout the ages."*

In 1076, Gregory responded to the letter by excommunicating the king, removing him from the Church and deposing him as king of Germany and Holy Roman Emperor. This was the first time a king of his stature had been deposed since the 4th century. There was, of course, some irony for – in effect – the pope and the emperor each claimed to have removed the other from office. So enforcing these declarations was a different mat-

---

213   Voltaire, « *Essai sur l'histoire générale, les mœurs et l'esprit des nations depuis Charlemagne jusqu'à nos jours* » (*"An Essay on Universal History, the Manners and Spirit of Nations from the reign of Charlemagne to the Age of Louis XIV"*), (1756), Chap. 41.

ter, but fate was on the side of Gregory VII. The German aristocracy was happy to hear of their king's deposal. They used the cover of religion as an excuse for a continuation of the rebellion started at the First Battle of Langensalza in 1075 and the seizure of royal powers. Henry IV had no choice but to back down, needing time to marshal his forces to fight the rebellion. In 1077, he travelled to Canossa in northern Italy to meet the pope and apologize in person. As penance for his sins, he dramatised the situation by wearing a hair-shirt and standing barefoot in the snow in the middle of winter in what has become known as "the Walk to Canossa"[214]. Gregory lifted the excommunication.

But not everything was what it appeared to be. In 1081, Henry IV invaded Rome with the intent of forcibly removing Gregory VII and installing a friendlier pope. But Gregory VII called on his allies the Normans, who were in southern Italy, and they rescued him from the Germans in 1085. The Normans managed to sack Rome in the process, and when the citizens of Rome rose up against Gregory, he was forced to flee south with the Normans and died there soon after.

The Investiture Controversy would continue on for several decades as each succeeding pope tried to fight the investiture by stirring up revolt in Germany. Henry IV was succeeded upon his death in 1106 by his son Henry V, who was also unwilling to give up the investiture rights. Frederic I Barbarossa and Frederic II also fought the Church and openly supported the Manichean heresy. To quote Anne Brenon[215]: *"as long as the stature of Frederic II dominated, the Cathars in the cities had hardly any cause to fear the Catholic Church, except the antipathy of the great clerics and the scandalmongering of their treatises."* She adds: *"the only political power which was able to sustain [the Cathar church] was evidently the urban oligarchy, which remained on the side of the Emperor [...]: the Ghibellines."* Indeed: the Manicheans in Italy would actually go as far as to recognise Frederic II of Hohenstaufen as a Messiah who would herald a new age: the rule of the "Holy Ghost", the advent of which would begin with the "destruction of the corrupted Roman Church" and the victory of the German Empire over the rebellious clergy.

---

214   Refer to Voltaire, « Essai sur l'histoire générale, les mœurs et l'esprit des nations depuis Charlemagne jusqu'à nos jours » ("An Essay on Universal History, the Manners and Spirit of Nations from the reign of Charlemagne to the Age of Louis XIV") (1756).
215   Anne Brenon, « Le Vrai Visage du Catharisme » ("The True Face of Catharism"), Ed. Loubatières, Toulouse, 1988 (re-edition). Also by the same author: « Les femmes cathares » ("Cathar Women"). Paris, Perrin, 1992 (re-edition).

The origins of this policy of the German Empire and the true ambitions of Frederic II of Hohenstaufen have been purposefully ignored by several historians. But in more recent times, it is slowly becoming accepted that this emperor was indeed on the side of the heretics and that his ancestors were largely situated in their camp too. As such, an article in the German magazine *Morgenstern*, based on the research of Eberhard Horst[216], a biographer of Frederic II, confirmed that the emperor was an Oriental heretic. The author notes that the accusations made by Pope Gregory IX to the emperor were based in truth.

Horst explains how in 1781, when the tomb of Frederic II was opened by the Royal Administration of Antiquities, the body of the Emperor was found to be wound inside a very peculiar Flagellant Penitent's tunic. It was made out of silk, *"embroidered with imperial eagles"*, and doubled by an *"underwear in covered flax covered with Coufic[217] characters that paid homage to Frederic as Sultan"*. *"His sword rested in a Saracen sleeve and on his sides rested, on cushions [...], his crown as well as the globe of the world, [...] without the cross [...] [which is however] always represented on the Imperial seals."* Eberhard Horst thus concluded that the mortuary dress of this emperor was definitely not the result of a haphazard decision. For Horst, Frederic II was a Shiite penitent, but it seems more likely that Frederic was instead a Manichean penitent. It is true that both orders use flagellation, but, as Voltaire observed, "the Pope never really accused the Emperor of being a Muslim. He merely affirmed in his circular letter of 1st July 1239, that Frederic had said to anyone who wanted to listen that *"the Universe has been misled by three impostors, Moses, Jesus Christ and Mohammed."*[218] But after this rather harsh statement at the door of the three largest institutionalised religions, the Emperor obviously made his peace with the Muslims as in some of his battles, he would soon begin to use Saracen archers,

---

216   Eberhard Horst, „Der Sultan von Lucera. Friedrich II und der Islam" (The Sultan of Lucera. Frederick II and Islam), Freiburg. Basel. Wien. 1997, published by Herder/ Spektrum, Bd. 4453. This work was quoted and commented upon, by Ustad Tarik T. Knapp in Morgenstern magazine, in the following articles: „War der deutsche Kaiser Friedrich II. von Hohenstaufen ein Muslim?" ("Was the German Emperor Frederick II Hohenstaufen a Muslim?"), in Morgenstern magazine no. 2, 1996. „Ein neues Indiz – Nachlese" ("A new clue – a reading review") in Morgenstern magazine no. 3, 1997.
217   "Coufic" writing is the technical name for Arabic calligraphied writing.
218   Voltaire, « Essai sur l'histoire générale, les mœurs et l'esprit des nations depuis Charlemagne jusqu'à nos jours » ("An Essay on Universal History, the Manners and Spirit of Nations from the reign of Charlemagnw to the Age of Louis XIV") (1756).
Refer to Chapitre LII, « De l'empereur Frédéric II ; de ses querelles avec les Papes. Des accusations contre Frédéric II » ("On Emperor Frederick II; about his Quarrels with Popes. About the Accusations against Frederick II") for the exact source of the quote.

received as the result of his alliance with the Sultan Salaheddin[219].

We should add that the Manicheans always lived in perfect harmony with Muslims. In Bulgaria[220], for example, when the country was overrun by the Turks, they had no qualms whatsoever in converting to Islam… but then they had no problem with converting to Christianity either…

However, it is advisable to wonder whether their interpretation of the Bible, and of Christianity altogether, was truly Christian. There is a very real possibility that their goal was to further infiltrate Christianity. One needs to look no further than the methods the Inquisition used to integrate full-fledged Cathars inside the monastic orders and even as inquisitors, by inciting them to – supposedly – "atone for their sins" by "doing penance", i.e. by whipping themselves, thereby actually reinforcing them in their convictions.

The Investiture Controversy could thus be seen as attempt of the Manichean Cult, through the political powers of the German Empire, to try to take control of the Church. The master stroke would have been the possibility of influencing the election of the Pope, through which the Church would thus have been reformed from within, from the top, according to a mutual Manichean-German agenda, in which both the heresy and the German policy would come out the winner. There were but few chances for the Church to try to break this attempted grab for power and, though it was successful, the fight lasted several decades before the Empire realised that its claim to the Papal throne was likely to be doomed. But by focussing – having to focus – so strongly on this war, it seems clear that the Manichean heresy was able to penetrate through the backdoor. Indeed, while it was not supported by the German people, it was supported by the Lombardians and Italians, and thus the heresy was a movement that would build itself up from the ground within the Church's heartland.

After the death of Frederic II of Hohenstaufen, the Empire, weakened by excommunications and the sting of Christendom, would break down into smaller, autonomous regions and the modern map of Europe slowly rose to the fore. But although it might be seen as a defeat of the cause, in truth, the Empire had served the Manicheans' purpose.

---

219   When Frederick II fought battles in the States of the Church, he used Muslims in his army, most probably as a form of provocation.
220   It should be noted that Bulgaria at that time was the headquarters of the Manichean heresy for Eastern Europe, hence the name of "Bulgarians" given to the Cathars and Weavers.

The Priory of Sion?

Originally from Lombardy[221], the Humiliati were taken to Germany by the Emperor Henry V, after the problems in Northern Italy with the Ghibelins. They humbly submitted their allegiance to the sovereign, upon which Henry V let them depart and they returned to Lombardy. There, they settled within the monasteries in the region of Milan and the confraternities began to become involved with both simony[222] and the cult of the dead, and would eventually be declared heretics.

The Order of the "Penitent Monks", known as the Premonstratensians, were also founded under the auspices of Henry V. Saint Norbert of Xanten (circa 1080 – 6th June 1134) was born at Gennep on the Maas but grew up at Xanten, on the left bank of the Rhine, near Wesel. His father, Heribert, Count of Gennep, was related to the imperial house of Germany[223] and the house of Lorraine.

He was however notorious for his dissolute lifestyle and his "passions for the pleasures of the senses" and at the age of 33, he decided to do penitence and "disavow" his past. He was ordained a priest and began to preach in

---

221   *Their deeper roots are to be traced back to Bulgaria and the Paulicians who had become entrenched there since at least the 4th century AD. Paulicians derive their name not from the Apostle Paul but most likely from either Paul, one of the four first disciples of Mani, or Paul of Samosata (260–272 AD), a heretic bishop of Antioch who indulged in simony (see the following note) and denied the Holy Trinity. The Paulicians were actually Manicheans, who would later thrive and expand under the name of "Bogomils" in the 12th century, consistently threatening the Byzantine Empire through systematic alliances with its ennemies. They are thought to be among the earliest precursors of the Cathars.*

222   *"Simony", although usually defined as the mere activity of selling Church offices (or holy relics) to the highest bidder, comes from the name of "Simon Magus", hence its connection with the cult of the dead practiced by the Chaldean Magi, since such lucrative illegal trade could well constitute a means to pay for Chaldean mortuary rituals.*
Simon Magus, also known as "Simon the Sorcerer" and Simon of Gitta, tried to offer money to the Apostles in exchange for miraculous abilities, and his request was categorically rejected. (see Acts of the Apostles, chapter VIII, verses 9-24.) The apocryphal Acts of Peter report an interesting story about Simon Magus' death, which was also reported in the writings of several Fathers of the Church. One day, as Simon was performing magic on the forum, he managed to fly up in the air. Witnessing the scene, the Apostles Peter and Paul prayed to God to stop this levitation, and Simon fell and broke his legs. The crowd, furious at the false prophet, killed him. The opinions of Simon Magus about himself – that he was God in human form – were later furthered by a Gnostic sect from the 2nd century called the "Simonians", according to Hegesippus, St. Irenaeus of Lyon and St. Epiphanius of Salamis. Simon Magus was thought of as the cultural equivalent of Merlin the Wizard during the Middle Ages.

223   *i.e. to the rulers of the Holy Roman Empire, which, as Voltaire famous quipped in his "Essay on the Manners and Spirit of the Nations" (1756) was an "agglomerate" that was "neither Holy, nor Roman, nor an Empire."*

the streets, asking the people to do penitence, by practicing self-flagellation and mortification of the body. Ordained as subdeacon, Norbert was appointed to a canonry at Xanten. Soon after, he was summoned to the court of Frederick of Cologne and later to that of Henry V, Holy Roman Emperor, whose almoner he became.

He was dressed only in a hood and a frock, when he demanded an audience with Pope Calixtus II. Norbert stated that the clergy and the people of his native town persecuted him and did not allow him to preach. There had been two assassination attempts on his life. Of course, this was the outcome of the people and the clergy having identified him as a heretic, but the Pope, prodded by the German Emperor, could do but one thing only: allow Norbert to preach.

In 1119, Pope Calixtus II requested[224] that Norbert found a religious order in the Diocese of Laon. Norbert chose a valley in the Forest of Coucy, about 10 miles from Laon, named Prémontré. Hugh of Fosses, Evermode of Ratzeburg, Antony of Nivelles, seven students of the celebrated school of Anselm, and Ralph of Laon were his first disciples. At first the young community lived in huts of wood and clay, arranged like a camp around the chapel of Saint John the Baptist, but they soon built a larger church and a monastery for the religious who joined them in increasing numbers. Going to Cologne to obtain relics for their church, Norbert is said to have discovered, through a vision, the spot where those of Saint Ursula and her companions, of Saint Gereon, and other martyrs lay hidden.

Norbert[225] gained adherents in Germany, France, Belgium and Transylvania, and houses of his order were founded in Floreffe, Viviers, St-Josse, Ardenne, Cuissy, Laon, Liège, Antwerp, Varlar, Kappenberg, Grosswardein (Oradea/Nagyvarad) and elsewhere, and he was appointed archbishop of Magdeburg by Pope Honorius II, in 1126. In Norbert's last years, he was chancellor and adviser to Lothar II, Holy Roman Emperor.

He was not alone. Godfrey of Bouillon (circa 1060, Baisy-Thy, near Brussels, Belgium – 18th July 1100, Jerusalem) was either the eldest or the second son of Eustace II, Count of Boulogne, and Ida, daughter of Godfrey III, Duke of Lower Lorraine[226]. His uncle, Godfrey the Hunchback,

---

224 *At the Council of Rheims, France.*
225 *Interestingly, Norbert of Xanten was one of the chief architects of his time in the task of codifying monastic life, for the completion of which he made a collaboration pact with Bernard of Clairvaux.*
226 *The fact that Charlemagne (Charles the Great) was his ancestor also made of him a relative of the rulers of the Holy Roman Empire, like Norbert of Xanten was.*

designated him as his successor in Lower Lorraine, but in 1076 Emperor Henry IV gave him only the Mark of Antwerp, and took back the fiefdom of Lower Lorraine, as his uncle had neither direct descendants nor male heirs. Nevertheless, Godfrey of Bouillon fought for Henry both on the Elster and in the siege of Rome, and in 1082 was finally given the duchy of Lower Lorraine.

This is where the first bizarre event of his life happens: although he had remained loyal to Henry IV in the conflict with Pope Gregory VII[227], Godfrey literally sold almost all that he had and joined the crusade preached by Gregory's successor Urban II at the Council of Clermont in 1095. Along with his brothers Eustace and Baldwin of Boulogne (the future Baldwin I of Jerusalem) he started off, in August 1096, at the head of an army from Lorraine, some 40,000 strong. He arrived in Constantinople in November, where his group of crusaders was the second to arrive (after Hugh of Vermandois) and he was the first to arrive at the siege of Nicaea, and was in the main contingent of the crusade after they split, possibly for foraging reasons, after Nicaea.

In 1099, after the capture of Antioch following a long siege, the crusaders were divided over their next course of action. Most of the foot soldiers wanted to continue south to Jerusalem, but Raymond of St. Gilles (also known as Raymond of Toulouse), by this time the most powerful of the princes, hesitated to continue the march. After months of waiting, the common people on the crusade forced Raymond to march on to Jerusalem, and Godfrey quickly joined him.

Godfrey was active in the siege of Jerusalem, and on 15th July he was one of the first to enter the city, which was the scene of a general massacre of Muslim and Jewish residents. On 22nd July, when Raymond refused to be named ruler of Jerusalem, Godfrey was elected in his place; nevertheless, he refused to be crowned "king". It is widely claimed that he took the title Advocatus Sancti Sepulchri, "advocate" or "defender" of the Holy Sepulchre, but this title is only used in a letter which was not written by the Duke. Instead, Godfrey himself seems to have used the more ambiguous term "Princeps". But was the person identifying Godfrey as "defender of the Holy Sepulchre" perhaps closer to the mark as to why Godfrey had embarked on this voyage?[228]

---

227 *When Henry IV was accused of simony by the Pope (refer to the note 223 about Simon Magus. Simony is a means to finance the Cult of the Dead.).*

228 *As Henry IV was very grateful to Godfrey for his support in the conflict against Pope Gregory VII (he and Godfrey belonged to the same family), he gave the Duchy of Lower Lorraine back to Godfrey in 1089, and asked him to closely supervise the First Crusade in order*

The Holy Sepulchre was, at the time, a site that was a hotbed for flagellants. Many penitents came to the city and the site to mortify themselves. They did not come here because they saw it as the "Sepulchre of Christ", but because they saw it as a place of death, a place of pain, a place of suffering and of extreme sorrows. When we read the commentaries of Saint Bernard[229] as to what was happening here, it is indeed far removed from a confrontation with the life and resurrection of Christ[230].

Another of Godfrey's flagellant preferences can be seen in his efforts to organise a religious community to guard over the site. A militia of twenty flagellant monks, united by Godfrey in chapters, was apparently placed under the rule of Saint Augustine. By 1118, another local confraternity of penitents, and former crusaders as well, had joined the militia, thereby becoming, as a whole, "the Order of the Penitents of Sion", which diversified into several branches, one of which would be the "Order of the Holy Sepulchre"[231]. The loss of Jerusalem by the crusaders ended the Order of the Holy Sepulchre, but it survived and eventually found itself in Italy, where it was housed by Franciscan Penitents, and in Orval as well[232]. In 1333, the Pope gave the guardianship of the Holy Sepulchre and the "Church of Flagellation"[233] to the penitent brothers of St. Francis... the Franciscans[234].

Michael Baigent, Richard Leigh and Henry Lincoln have mentioned this order in their bestselling book *Holy Blood, Holy Grail*[235]. In it, they specu-

---

to, if possible, become the official protector of the Holy Sepulchre (a sort of "double agent" acting on behalf of the German Emperor to wrestle power away from the Church). This plan was designed so that the German Emperor could fulfil his dream of becoming King of Jerusalem, a dream which eventually came true a hundred and forty years later, in 1229, when Frederick II Hohenstaufen was crowned King of Jerusalem, thereby achieving total control of the Holy Sepulchre for the German Empire.

229   *St. Bernard of Clairvaux, "Liber ad Milites Templi de Laude Novae Militiae", "In Praise of the New Militia", also known as "In Praise of the New Knighthood".*

230   *They were only interested in death and self-mortification.*

231   *Refer to « Mémento du Chevalier de l'Ordre du Saint Sépulcre de Jérusalem », published by "Mémoire et Documents" (the publishing house of the French Lieutenantship of the Order of the Holy Sepulchre), in Versailles, in 2003. This book was written under the supervision of André Damien (Lieutenant of the Order of the Holy Sepulchre for France), as well as Bernard Berthod and Joël Bouessée, both Knights of the Order.*

232   *Orval is a town located in modern Belgium, in the Luxemburg province (not to be confused with the nearby state of Luxemburg).*

233   *Now known as the "Church of Condemnation and Flagellation", where the Column of Flagellation was and is still worshipped as a holy relic.*

234   *These Franciscans monks seized on the occasion to rename themselves "Order of the Penitents of Mount Sion", and remained known as "Major Franciscan Custoy of the Holy Land".*

235   *Baigent, Leigh and Lincoln, "Holy Blood, Holy Grail", first published by Bantam Dell,*

late whether this order[236] was the original "Priory of Sion", a mythical organisation that they made famous and whose fame has been augmented in its own right by Dan Brown's novel *The Da Vinci Code*[237]. In reality, the Priory of Sion was the creation of a handful of Frenchmen, led by Pierre Plantard, who claimed to "know" the secret of Rennes-le-Château – which they linked with a secret genealogy of the Merovingian Dynasty that once ruled France. It is a bizarre twist of fate that the "Order of Sion", in the 12th century, could indeed be linked with Saunière; not in any direct manner, but because they shared a common religious framework[238].

The birth of the inquisition

Profiting from the extreme weakness of the Church following the invasion of German troops in Italy, the Flagellants decided to turn the situation to their advantage. Two orders were created: the Franciscans in 1209 and the Dominicans in 1215. The precise circumstances of this official recognition remain unclear. Perhaps the German Emperor pushed the Pope into approving these orders; perhaps it was a genuine desire of the Church to integrate heretics within its confines. Whatever scenario lay at its origins, the fact remained that the Church was powerless to fight the heretics. All it could do was to recognise the statutes of this organisation, for the heretics had become as powerful as the Church and could use such rejection as a powerful tool with which to beat it. As such, the Church's best course of action was to act as if it had taken initiative and as if it were in control: which is exactly what the ratification of the order amounted to, as it would still have remained in existence without the papal approval it sought, but did not need, for its survival.

Previously, we argued that the Inquisition, created by these two orders, was a tool of the heretics. Indeed, this was the very institution that had been formed to stamp out any "religious deviations" from the "Righteous Path". But such basic assumptions, whereby history is created as an account composed of two opposing stories, is seldom correct.

First, let us note that the penitents desired to be tortured, mutilated, flagellated; the cult of the dead and suffering were for them joyous inspira-

---

New York, in 1982.

236   *The Order of the Holy Sepulchre.*

237   *Dan Brown, "The Da Vinci Code", published by Doubleday Books, 2003.*

238   *i.e. a belief in the necessity of Chaldean mortuary rituals as a condition for, in their words, "salvation" (not under the form of resurrection in Heaven, but of a process of reincarnation on Earth).*

tions. Hence, from the heretic's perspective, torture was not "torture", but a welcome experience; it was penitence. And this is where the Inquisition, even if it was there to wipe out the heresy, failed: for its modus operandi – torture and bodily punishment – was exactly what the heretics craved. Worse: there was nothing more enjoyable than a public flogging... even if it ended in death. So, at best, the Inquisition should be considered as extremely stupid and totally unaware of the character of the heresy. At worst, it was indeed acting in complete awareness of the penitent framework, and provided these heretics with what they desired: pain.

That was only one part of the problem: the Inquisition also requested that those heretics who "changed their ways" were then admitted into the religious orders, to become monks. But these converts felt they were required to continue to do penitence for their crimes, so the flagellations and mortifications continued, not in the streets, but within the walls of the monasteries.

In summary, the Inquisition was a tool to "weed out the heresy"... but by bringing them into the fold of the Church, they had become the enemy within. Philipp Schaff in *History of the Christian Church*[239] actually argues that St. Francis was probably inspired by the Humiliati's structure when he created his order, as the two orders functioned on the same principle. The same opinion is expressed by Father Richard Weber[240], a Dominican himself. He tried to understand the origins of his order and remarked that its origins *"can be found in this lay reform movement, among the Penitents. […] All the reform groups of the later Middle Ages will have some connection with this movement. The Franciscan and Dominican movements will have a close relation with it. Out of this group as well will come all the heretics of the 13th century. There is thus an extraordinarily complex relation here, one that must be examined."* Powerful words, but there is more: *"One type of relation is exemplified in the group called the Humiliati. These lay people had dressed in a kind of "habit"; most importantly, they insisted upon their right to preach. In 1184 they were excommunicated for heresy. […] The lay Humiliati are the first group to be described as a 'Third Order'"*, which is exactly

---

239 Schaff, Philipp, "History of the Christian Church", Oak Harbor, Washington State, Logos Reseach Systems, Inc., 1997, electronic edition based on the first published version by Charles Scribner's sons, 1907, enhanced with corrections by The Electronic Bible Society, Dallas, Texas, 1998.

240 Fr. Richard Weber, O.P., "History of the Dominican Laity, Part 1". An eye-opening confession on the true origins of the Dominicans by the Dominicans themselves, published on the official website of the Dominican Order for the Province of St. Albert the Great (Chicago): http://www.domcentral.org/oplaity/layhistory.htm

how the Franciscans and Dominicans would become known, which was emphasized by Weber as well.

It is therefore clear that several historians are fully aware of the controversial and heretical origins of these two orders, but try to play down this aspect. Indeed, the orders were "inspired" and "constructed" on the model of the Manichean cults. But the conclusion that these historians should draw is that this was largely because they were Manichean cults, which had adopted the habit of the clergy. Georges Jehel[241] has made that connection, writing: *"Largely inspired by Manicheism, [...] [the heresy] was propagated under diverse forms from the Balkans to Spain, via Italy, Provence and the Languedoc. Humiliati, [...] Cathars, framed by laymen [...] or clerics such as Hugo Speroni of Piacenza, Pietro Lombardo of Orvieto and later, in the 12th century, by Anthony of Padua [a Franciscan], John of Vicenza and the Calabrian Joachim of Fiore [...] spread through the towns and rural areas the principle of a reform that was based on common ownership[242]. [...] The birth of the Mendicant Orders [the Franciscans and Dominicans] with whom they were linked, suffices to confirm this. This was no doubt more true for Franciscanism, which was to lead to the establishment of the Fraticelli [a heretical order][243] than for the Dominicans."*

The Franciscan order originated in Italy in 1207, in Assisi, in the states occupied by the troops of the Hohenstaufen. According to Professor Francesco Santucci[244], a local historian, in the 14th century, there were still two

---

241   Georges Jehel, « Les villes d'Italie, XII ème – XIV ème siècles : sociétés, pouvoirs, économies, cultures » *("The Cities of Italy from the 12th to the 14th century: societies, powers, economics, cultures"), Editions du Temps, Nantes, 2004.*

242   *i.e a system, which could be thought of as the ideological precursor of communism.*

243   *In Italian, "Little Brothers", or "Little Monks" (from "frati", "friars" or "brothers" in Italian), the Fraticelli are also known under the name of "Spiritual Franciscans" or "Spirituals", for short. When the Order of St. Francis split at the end of the 13th century, because of heresy scandals amongst its members, the most radical penitent group born in the process were the Fraticelli, who allied themselves with the Observant Franciscans, the strict branch of the Order.*

244   *Refer to Francesco Santucci, "Gli Statuti in volgare trecentesco della Confraternita dei Disciplinati di S. Lorenzo in Assisi" ("The Statutes of the Confraternity of the Disciplinati of San Lorenzo in Assisi in the Fourteenth Century"), published in "Risultati e prospettive della ricerca sul Movimento dei Disciplinati. Convegno internazionale di studio: Perugia, 5-7 dicembre 1969" ("Results and Prospects of the Research on the Movement of the Disciplinati. International Symposium of Studies: Perugia, 5th – 7th December 1969") by the Centro di ricerca e di studio sul Movimento dei Disciplinati (Center of Research and Studies on the Disciplinati Movement), collection "Quaderni del Centro, Prima serie", Assisi (1972). Also "Le fraternite medievali di Assisi. Linee storiche e testi statutari, a cura di Ugolino Nicolini, Enrico Menestò, Francesco Santucci" (same publisher, same collection, Assisi, 1989).*

fraternities of "Disciplinati" or "Battuti", who were Italian flagellants[245]. The area in which the Franciscan order was established was a den of heresy. Francis, after having led a "loose life", chose poverty and escaped from his family's bonds (he disavowed his father) to espouse a religious life, replete with mortification. Bonaventure[246], the General Minister of the Franciscan Order at the time of the death of St Francis, wrote that *"the Supreme Lord had lowered his eyes to this man who was truly poor and penitent"* and that he *"chose him to announce the penitence"*. Francis, he added, called upon *"people to cry, to groan, to shave their heads, to gird themselves with a cord"* and to *"mark themselves with the sign of penitence"*. Let us note that the shaving of the head was largely forbidden, based on a reading of Leviticus[247], and the wearing of a cord was of course a typical mortification practiced by the heretics.

Francis soon attracted followers and when they too had abandoned everything and dressed like him, he took charge of their education and exposed them to his doctrine. One day, *"he gathered his children [his followers] around him and spoke to them for a long time [...] about contempt for the world, the renouncement of their will and the mortification of the body [...] and the groans of penitence."* It leaves little doubt that Francis was indeed a flagellant himself, in the purest sense of the word. Furthermore, Bonaventure adds[248] that the *saint "continuously invented new types of abstinence"* and *"always found some method through which he could harm his flesh"*. St. Francis made self-mutilation the core of his doctrine[249]. Ac-

---

245 *The name of the "Disciplinati" comes from the whip they used, which was called "discipline", a cattail whip made of light chains with small spikes or hooks on the end. It is still in use today during prayer in some monastic communities, especially among the Carmelite monks and nuns. The name of the "Battuti" means "the Battered Ones" in Italian, which is quite a graphic reminder of their penitential customs.*

246 *« Œuvres Spirituelles de Saint Bonaventure, de l'Ordre des Frères Mineurs, Cardinal Evêque d'Albane, traduit par M. l'abbé Berthaumier, curé de Saint Pallais, Paris » ("Spiritual Works of Saint Bonaventure, of the Order of the Minor Friars, Cardinal Bishop of Albana, translated by abbé Berthaumier, priest of Saint Pallais, Paris"), published by Louis Viviès, publisher and bookkeeper, rue Cassette, 23, Beaugency, printed by Gasnier, 1854. Refer specifically to the chapter « Saint François Pénitent » ("Saint Francis, Penitent") for the source of all the subsequent quotes from St. Bonaventure.*

247 *The Book of Leviticus specifically condemns the shaving of the head, as well as the practice of making incisions or other marks on the skin, as a form of "mutilation for the dead". This means that the tonsure, the shaving of the head that until recently was universally practiced among monastic orders since their origins, can actually be related to morbid, un-Christian customs.*

248 *Refer to chapter V « De l'austérité de la vie du Saint » ("On the Austerity of the Saint's Life") of the above quoted book, for the source of this quote.*

249 *This is in direct contradiction with the Bible: see note 254 for further details.*

cording to Bonaventure and also Jacobus de Voragine[250], *"during his stay in the desert of Sartiano"*, St. Francis heard the devil speak to him, saying *"that there was not a sinner in the world whom God would not pardon, if he converted. But whoever died as the result of too severe a penitence, would never obtain mercy."*

"At once, Francis removed his clothing", took a cord and hit his body frenetically. He even insulted his body by calling it *"brother ass"*, and told it *"not to stir up too much"*. Worse was to come: full of joy, he placed the cord around his neck, removed all of his clothes and had himself dragged across the ground *"on a stone where the criminals that had to be tormented were normally placed."* Francis loved pain; for him, it was his doctrine of salvation and the only true sacrament[251]. For him, it was a method of removing demons. Indeed, one day, he is known to have said: *"I tell you, demons, to do unto my body anything that you are permitted to do. I am prepared to withstand everything, for having no greater enemy than my body, you will avenge me from my adversary."*[252]

From the above, it is clear that "Saint" Francis of Assisi was a heretic, a Penitent, because he put all his faith in flagellation and self-mutilation, so that each and every one of his acts was in full contradiction with the Scriptures, who stricly forbid such mortifications[253].

On a political level, it should be noted that the father of the Franciscan Order was a social revolutionary as well. In the modern Hachette Encyclopedia, it states that St. Francis "contested as much the social order based on privileges, as the Church itself, overwhelmed by political ambition." The same source adds about his Order that "at first, the ecclesiastical authorities were suspicious of this group of penitents, who reminded them of former movements in rupture with the clergy and condemned for heresy." (Source: Données encyclopédiques, 2001, Hachette Multimédia.) Therefore, stemming from the "Penitent Brothers of Assisi" (the brotherhood founded by St. Francis), a gang of sadistic penitents with dubious morals, the heretical origins of the Order of the Friars Minor (i.e the Order of St. Francis) is well-established.

250   *According to the "The Golden Legend" of Jacobus de Voragine, pages 154-155. Jacobus de Voragine was born en 1228 in Vorago, now Varazze, a little town not far from Genoa, Italy. In 1244, at 16, he joins the Dominican Order. It was to be the start of a career which would lead him to become a professor in theology. His predications were very successful, especially in Lombardy.*

251   *It turns out that according to St. Bonaventure, Francis also enjoyed moral suffering, since whenever he would come in front of a sympathetic audience who would "laud him for the merits of his life", he was known to have one of his fellow Franciscan penitents shout "mortifying words" at his ear, telling him he was a good-for-nothing, a miserable, a cheap parasite, and so on.*

252   *According to Jacobus de Voragine, "The Golden Legend".*

253   *This is in direct contradiction with the Bible: the Book of Leviticus is clear about the prohibition of such practices. Leviticus, chapter XXI:*

21:1 "The Lord said also to Moses: Speak to the priests the sons of Aaron, and thou shalt say

One of St. Francis' friends and admirers was St. Dominic, founder of the Dominican Order. They were in fact inseparable, brothers[254]. Jacobus de Voragine wrote that St. Dominic had a dream in which the Virgin presented him to Jesus Christ, accompanied by St. Francis. In this vision, Dominic received the same praises as his friend and he could not leave his sight. *"The following morning, having found him in the church, without ever having seen him, nor without the help of a person to point him out, he recognised him from his dream. He threw himself into his arms, he embraced him piously and said: 'You are my companion; you run the same path as me; let us remain united, and no adversary will triumph.' St. Francis told him that he had had exactly the same vision: and from that moment onwards, there was nothing more in them than one heart and one soul; a union which they recommended for their descendants to observe for eternity."*

The bond between the two orders was therefore "for eternity" and came from the two founders themselves[255]. Furthermore, Dominic did not hide his predisposition towards flagellation, for in the *Life of the Blessed Margaret of Metola*[256], we note how he recommends the whip and mortifications. The work argues that the Dominican rule prescribed *"three privileges: study, prayer and penitence"*. But, it continues, penitence was a great honour and was imposed on all, *"whether they be from the first, second or third order"*, i.e. male clergy, female nuns or laymen. The blessed Margaret of Metola thus subjected herself to several mortifications, as prescribed by

---

for them: Let not a priest incur an uncleanness at the death of his citizens.
[...] 21:4 But not even for the prince of his people shall he do any thing that may make him unclean. 21:5 Neither shall they shave their head, nor their beard, nor make incisions in their flesh. [...] 21:11 Nor shall he go in at all to any dead person: not even for his father, or his mother, shall he be defiled."
Is it a coincidence that the penitents did all these anti-Biblical things? Certainly not, since these customs were forbidden in the Mosaic Law and the entire Old Testament is based on the witnessing of Egyptian and Chaldean customs by the Jews. This is further confirmation of the connection between Chaldean Magi and penitents.
254   *Refer to: "The Golden Legend", Jacobus de Voragine, T. II, p. 114. The Golden Legend was a very popular hagiographic book (of saints' lives). It was written between 1260 and 1275 by Jacobus de Voragine.*
255   *This close relationship between the two Mendicant Orders will obviously reach its climax with the creation of the Inquisition.*
256   *« Vie de la Bienheureuse Marguerite de Métola », an electronic French edition by Christian C. and www.JESUSMARIE.com of the following book:*
« Une petite sainte de rien du tout » by William R. Bonniwell, O.P. Translated from American English into French by E. Aimont, Paris, printed by Maison de la Bonne Presse (5, rue Bayard, Paris – 8th district), 1953.
Original English version of the book: William R. Bonniwell (O.P.), "The story of Margaret of Metola", Kennedy, New York [1952].

the rule, there apparently to induce a state of dehydration, as well as sleep deprivation, public humiliation, fasts and deprivations of water.

In order for us to get a glimpse of the kind of example the life of Dominic de Guzman was to Margaret of Metola, we can find in "*The Libellus of Jordan of Saxony*"[257], an early work about the life of St. Dominic penned down by one of his contemporaries[258], a quite graphic description of the strange way in which he abused of his body:

"Using an iron chain, he [Dominic] administered the discipline upon himself three times every night; one was for himself, the second for sinners still living in the world, and the third for the souls suffering in Purgatory."

Margaret would soon die from trying to imitate Dominic in her self-imposed physical mutilations, and when her fellow Mantellate nuns[259] prepared her body, they were frightened to see how it was covered in raised scars and other scar tissue.

Lest anyone is still ambivalent as to the extent of the propensities of this saint, George Bernanos[260] notes that during his nightly whipping sessions, Dominic de Guzman was *"shouting out this very loud death rattle, the echo of which reverberated off to reach [even] the remotest cells of the friars who were listening, terrified. Then, covered in blood, he would wrap himself in his cope, and lay himself down on a bench or on a table."*

This was the man who stood at the cradle of the Inquisition…

---

257   See "*Saint Dominic – Biographical Documents*", with an introduction by Francis C. Lehner, O.P., and foreword by Most Reverend Aniceto Fernandez, O.P. Master General of the Order of Preachers. Nihil obstat: Reverend A. D. Lee, O.P. Censor Deputatus, Approved by: Patrick A. O'Boyle, Archbishop of Washington. Published by The Thomist Press, Washington, D.C., April 29, 1964., specifically "Chapter 1: Blessed Jordan – The Libellus of Jordan of Saxony", under the sections "His Vigils".

258   As Jordan of Saxony was St. Dominic's immediate successor as Master General of the Order, his testimony is that of a first-hand witness. Therefore his Libellus, which was written between 1231 and 1234, is not only the earliest of all the documents related to the life of St. Dominic, but it is universally considered to be the most authentic.

259   « Vie de la Bienheureuse Marguerite de Métola » (see note 257 for the full reference of this text) provides us with a definition of "Mantellate": "Mantellate — this word is particular to Italy — was the name of the lay women who belonged to the Order of Penance of St. Dominic, an organisation which, afterwards, will become the actual Third Order of St. Dominic." Margaret of Metola was a Mantellate nun.

260   Georges Bernanos, « Saint Dominique » ("Saint Dominic"), in his book « Les Prédestinés » ("The Predestined"), published by Points Sagesses (1983), p. 75-77. "The Predestined" is actually a compilation of three books by Bernanos: « Saint Dominique » (1926), « Jeanne relapse et sainte » ("Joan of Arc, Lapsed and Saint") (1934), and « Frère Martin » ("Brother Martin") (1943).

The fold

These orders were born out of heresy and it might be suggested that it would take time for a heretic to adapt himself the new life required of him and her by the Catholic doctrine. Indeed, even if that were the case, it is clear that St. Francis and St. Dominic did not help them on that path. While the Dominicans did indeed seem to be brought into the fold of the Catholic doctrine, we should wonder whether this was purely in appearance. The same could definitely not be said for the Franciscan Order.

St. Francis died on 3rd October 1226 and left the order in the care of Brother Elias of Cortona. In fear that his organisation would drift into sectarianism, Elias hid the rule of the order, as well as its founding principles. This occurred not only because he wanted to save the order from further prosecution, but apparently also to stem the flagellant tendencies of the Brothers, a move which was not appreciated by his penitent brethren. They furiously attacked him for not following the desires of St. Francis and told him that he was guilty of being corrupted by the Catholic clergy!

Anthony of Padua also spoke out against the Minister of the Order and engaged actively with the cabal that was mounted against him. Elias of Cortona was soon deposed from the leadership. In 1227, under the direction of Pope Gregory IX, who had been one of the friends of St. Francis, the General Chapter voted Jean Parenti into the position; he was a Franciscan visibly much closer to the original course of the Order. But the situation was very unstable, for Elias did not want to renounce his leadership and plotted in secret.

In 1232, after several months in exile, he managed to depose Jean Parenti and took firm action against the rebels: exclusion of the most reticent members from the order, blacklisting and destruction of certain books that were judged to be "diabolical". Furthermore, his worst enemies were spied upon, so that he knew every move they made. A second revolution within the order arose and Pope Gregory IX once again showed his hand… and took charge of it. Elias was once again deposed, and excommunicated. The poor leader thus found himself isolated and died in 1253, alone and abandoned by all, for having attempted to bring the Franciscans back to a semblance of Christian practice[261].

The new leader was John of Parma and he made sure that his congregation had smooth sailing, which included being able to express their Manichean

---

261 *Or rather, to a less ostentatious practice of penitence. Let us not forget that Elias of Cortona was not, after all, really against the Franciscans, being a Simoniac himself.*

ideology openly. The book by Gerardo di Borgo San Donino[262], published in Paris in 1254, thus spoke out against the Catholic Church and attacked its doctrine. He stated that a mysterious gospel would "soon" replace the four gospels of the New Testament and that the "Law of God" would thereby be abolished. He noted that the Church was corrupt and that the penitent monks had to replace the priests and the whole secular clergy, in order to establish the "Kingdom of the Holy Ghost". This kingdom would mark the beginning of a New Age, and it would be the result of terrible events. For soon, there would be great upheavals, earthquakes and signs in the heavens. Acccording to Gerardo di Borgo, many would die during this period of turmoil, and a demonic Pope and enemy of St. Francis would fight against another pope, as well as an "admirable" Emperor – no doubt a reference to Frederic II of Hohenstaufen. But the final victory would be achieved by the Franciscans, the Church would be cut down and would be replaced by a religion that had no masses, no "books of masses", no church, no temple to pray in, whereby everyone would live in common owner-ship[263] and would be dressed as penitents.

As soon as the book was available, Christianity was in shock and turmoil, crying "heresy" in the direction of the Dominicans and the Franciscans. Guillaume of Saint Amour, rector of the University of Paris, believed as much and cried scandal. Meanwhile, it seems that Gerardo di Borgo San Donino was perplexed about the impact his work had created and decided to portray himself as a martyr, which did not stop him from being severe-ly condemned. Pretending to have acted out of stupidity or worse, out of good faith, he would be despised by the people, and end his days in prison; the Pope burnt his writings and in 1256, declared that he and his work were heretical. His friend and confidante, John of Parma, superior of the Franciscan Order, was arrested and forced to convene a General Chapter in Rome in 1257, to announce his retirement[264].

---

262   Gerardo di Borgo San Donino, "Introductoris in Evangelium Aeternum" ("Introduc-tion to the Eternal Gospel"), Paris 1254. This book was condemned by Pope Alexander IV in 1255. Gerardo di Borgo San Donino was a Spiritual Franciscan (i.e a kind of Fraticelli) of Lombardian origin.

263   A precursory form of communism. Communism largely stems from Manichean sects that had emigrated to Russia.

264   With regard to the struggle between the various branches inside the Franciscan Order, see Nachman Falbel, « La lutte des Spirituels Franciscains et sa contribution pour la refor-mulation de la théorie traditionnelle concernant la puissance Papale » ("The Struggle of the Spiritual Franciscans, and its Contribution to the Redefinition of the Traditionnal Theory Concerning Papal Power"), Tesena Facultés de Philosophie, Sciences et Lettres de USP, Bul-

His successor, Saint Bonaventure, who was elected on that same year, had a difficult task: to cleanse the order of the heretics and make the true rule disappear, in fact rewriting it[265]. The task seemed impossible, as the leaders of the order continued to support the viewpoints expressed by Gerardo di Borgo. Amongst these were Brothers Hugo of Digne, Michael of Cesena, Corrado of Offida[266], Thomas of Celano, Angelo Clareno and Pietro of Macerata. They became known as the "Spiritual Franciscans", or the "Fraticelli", sometimes also known as "Zelanti" – Zealots.

It is here that Bonaventure was forced to write a "major legend", a biography of St. Francis[267], as well as a new rule for the Order, which resulted in the destruction of the two previous "Vitae" – biographies of the founder – which had served before as a model for the community to emulate. It deprived the Fraticelli of references to the life of the founding father of the Order. But, no doubt realising what was in store, they had hidden the "Vita" that had been written by Thomas of Celano and which they continued to consult, despite the interdiction from their leader.

Although Bonaventure thus made sure that the Fraticelli were put to one side, hiding of destroying every element that could be used by the heretics to teach new members about who the Real St. Francis was, no doubt in the hope that, in time, they would die out and the new conscripts would follow the new rule, it is equally clear that he was not reassured; like Elias of Cortona before him, he had his major opponents followed and spied upon. Some were even arrested and were deported to houses that did not belong to the Order. They might have been seen as "out", but they were not "down".

The Investiture Controversy, which was ongoing at that time, had resulted in a stand-off between Rome and the Emperor. A compromise was reached, in which Pietro del Morrone was elected as pope, taking the name of Celestine V. He was a hermit, an ascetic and a penitent. When he took up office, he moved about the town of Rome in "great humility", sitting

letin no. 3 Saint-Paul, 1978, p. 82. Nachman Falbel holds a degree in History and Philosophy from the Bar Ilan University, Israel (1964), a Masters' degree in History of the Religions from the University of São Paulo, Brazil (1969), and a doctorate in Social History from the University of São Paulo (1972). He is now a Professor Titular at the University of São Paulo.
265   The original rule of the Franciscan Order, i.e the one written by St. Francis, was the one who most incited the members of the Order to indulge in "deviant behaviour".
266   Also called Conrad of Offida.
267   Transcript of the course given by Pr. Pauline Leclercq-Lhermite (profession: historian), entitled « L'Église et la vie religieuse au Moyen-Âge » ("The Church and Religious Life during the Middle Ages"), Paris-IV University, 1997-1998.

upon a mule, passing himself off as a miserable and poor beggar. But this was but a smokescreen, for underneath was a monk with dark thoughts. He made a pact with the Ghibellines and caused great damage to Christianity, claiming he was ignorant, the poor victim of absences of consciousness, if not an idiot. But, wonders of all wonders, his reign would include the recognition of the Franciscan Order, i.e something which cannot be ascribed to an "absence of consciousness". Worse, in league with Pietro of Macerata and Angelo Clareno, the leaders of the Fraticelli (i.e the Spiritual Franciscans), he allowed this group to claim that they, more than all others, were the true followers of St. Francis of Assisi. Empowered by the support of Celestine V, the Fraticelli proceeded to challenge the Order and its leadership continuously.

Celestine's rule was short. Cardinal Benedetto Caetani, the future Boniface VIII, had been manoeuvring in the shadows for several months. Boniface convinced Celestine V that no person on Earth could go through life without sin. Therefore, Celestine V left and Boniface VIII (1294-1303) took his place as pope. One of his first acts as pontiff was to imprison his predecessor in the Castle of Fumone in Ferentino, where he died at the age of 81, attended by two monks of his order. We can only wonder what rite these monks performed upon his death...

Despite this loss of papal protection, the Fraticelli survived. And they had a hard time doing so: Boniface VIII condemned them[268], there was the papal bull "Ad Augmentum" of November 1295, then Pope John XXII and the bull "Super Cathedram"[269]. The latter accused them of witchcraft and had the leaders of the movement arrested for claiming that "all the sacraments of the Church are in vain". Four of them would be burnt alive in Marseilles.

Several Franciscans would equally be accused of heresy, amongst them Pierre-Jean Olieu[270] (1248-1298), loyal disciple of Bonaventure, whose writings would be burned during the General Chapter of Lyon, as well as Ubertino of Casale (1259-1330), a Spiritual Franciscan who was a professor of

---

268   Llorca, Garcia, Villoslada, Montalban, Histoire de l'Église Catholique, Madrid : Bac. 1963, vol. II, p. 562.

269   « Les principales erreurs des Spirituels Franciscains condamnées par Jean XXII » in Denzinger, 484-490. Heinrich DENZINGER, « Symboles et définitions de la foi catholique », ("Symbols and Definition of the Catholic Faith"), under the supervision of Peter HÜNERMANN for the original edition and of Joseph HOFFMANN for the French edition, Paris, Éd. du Cerf, 1996, LII.

270   Also called Peter John Olivi in English.

the Holy Cross of Florence, and the author of "Arbor Vitae Crucifixae Jesu Christi", which forced his excommunication[271] by John XXII.

Many things can be said about the Franciscans, but being in the fold of the Catholic Church is definitely not something that typified them. And it is our hope that by providing this overview, we have made it clear that a person like Saunière was not an isolated case; that he was not unique. Imagine for a moment, difficult as this may be, that there is no mystery of Rennes-le-Château. For many, it would appear as if there is just "one" church. In truth, there was a struggle going on for the Church, an enemy within, in which powerful factions fought and followed a doctrine that was anathema to the official doctrine: The Cult of the Dead. Now reinsert Saunière into this framework, and all of a sudden, we are not confronted with an anomaly of a priest in a small Southern French village, but with one person amongst thousands, found across Europe at the end of the 19th century, if not beyond – an adept of the Cult of the Dead.

---

271   *Transcript of the course given by Pr. Pauline Leclercq-Lhermite (profession: historian),* « *L'Église et la vie religieuse au Moyen Âge* » *("The Church and Religious Life during the Middle Ages"), Paris-IV University, 1997-1998.*

Chapter 8

The Penitents of Rennes-le-Château

The Franciscan and Dominican heretics settled in various parts of Western Europe, including the area around Rennes-le-Château. In this country, two areas stand out: the first is Limoux, 20 kilometres north from Saunière's village; the second is Prouilhe, 43 kilometres north-west of the same village[272].

In Limoux, the presence of Franciscan monks dates back to the reign of Saint Louis, or 1270 AD, at the latest. The historian Gérard Jean[273] notes that in July 1292, Philippe le Bel[274] assembled his companions in *the "cloister of the convent of the Brothers Minor of Limoux"*[275] (another name for the Franciscans). The Brothers of Limoux were originally based in Assisi, Italy, and so were amongst the first of their denomination to settle in France. Thus it seems likely that the men who settled in Limoux came from the immediate circle of the founder of the order, St. Francis. This, of course, is not without importance. Furthermore, it is likely that in this first community were some Fraticelli, the branch of the Order that was the most heretical and most inclined to simony[276].

Two orders

It seems that these Franciscans had little financial means. The convent was not of significant size and, still according to Gérard Jean[277], was situated

---

272   *The town of Limoux is located on the very road which goes from Rennes-le-Château to the monastery of Prouilhe, to where Saunière was sent by his bishop in 1910 (Mgr. de Beauséjour), and ordered to do penitence for 10 days.*

273   *All of the information and quotes with regard to the Monastery of the Franciscans of Limoux are extracted from the research of historian Gérard Jean, as well as the works of the historical society « Mémoire Historique de Limoux » ("Historical Memory of Limoux"), of which he is the president. Gérard Jean is also the Secretary General of the Académie des Arts et des Sciences de Carcassonne (Arts and Science Academy of Carcassonne), and a prominent member of the knowledgeable Société d'Etudes Scientifiques de l'Aude (SESA: Society for Scientific Studies of the Aude region).*

274   *King Philip IV of France, also known as "Philip the Fair" in English.*

275   *Archives départementales de l'Aude (Archives of the Aude Department), Chart Register no. 4E206/AA1, f° XXXII, r°.*

276   *Refer to note 223 concerning Simon Magus. Simony is a means of financing the Cult of the Dead.*

277   *Refer to Gérard Jean's research report entitled « Une chronique de Gérard Jean - Rue des Cordeliers, L'ordre mendiant des Frères mineurs » ("A chronicle by Gérard Jean – Street of the Cordeliers, The Mendicant Order of the Friars Minor"), which is on display on his personal website: http://perso.orange.fr/limoux/rue73.htm (text in French) This text is the*

"outside of the protection of the feeble defensive walls [of the city], near the Aude [the river that runs through the city], very likely on what is now the 'Esplanade François Mitterrand'."

Hence, the English troops under the command of Edward Woodstock did not spare the house of this religious community during the capture of Limoux. In November 1355, Edward *"crossed the river to the North of Carcassonne"*, marched to the *"Monastery of Prouilhe"* and attacked *"several cities in the regions"*. He sacked Limoux[278], as its defenses were insufficient to keep him at bay for any length of time, and burned *"more than 4,000 houses"*[279]. The monastery disappeared and for a period of time, not a single trace of its existence is found in the various remaining archives of the region.

But the Franciscan monastery was not "lost" and would re-enter history, in several stages. After the sack of the town by Edward Woodstock, the council demanded financial and material aid from the Count of Armagnac. This was the signal for the Franciscans to reconstruct their community and to equip it with a *"new infrastructure"*; to use the words of Gérard Jean once again: *"Like the myth of the Phoenix, Limoux was reborn from its ashes*[280]. *[...] The Franciscan Brothers decided to rebuild their convent inside the walls, occupying the location that would remain theirs until the 14th century; this was the triangle formed, today, by the streets 'Maurice Lacroix', 'Gaston Prat', and 'des Cordeliers'. The essential part of the construction seemed to have been well under away by 21st November 1360, for the Archbishop of Narbonne visited to bless the Saint-Jacques hospital, and received a protest letter from the perpetual vicar of the parish of Saint Martin, who complained about some of the actions of the 'Confraters', the Franciscans*[281]. *On 20th December 1369, the church is known to have been in existence, since those who wished to be buried inside it were then allowed to do so in exchange for a money transaction*[282].

exact source for all of the quotes used here.

278   *Letter of the Duke of Normandy, 17th October 1359, in: Fonds-Lamothe, L.-H. « Notices historiques sur la ville de Limoux » ("Historical Notices on the Town of Limoux") (1838), p. 142.*

279   *Froissart, J., « Chroniques » ("Chronicles"), Editions Kervyn de Lettenhove, Bruxelles, 1867-1877.*

280   *Letters of the Count of Armagnac, 5th February 1356, 25th October 1356, in: Fonds-Lamothe, L.-H. « Notices historiques sur la ville de Limoux » ("Historical Notices on the Town of Limoux") (1838), p. 141.*

281   *Most likely, these dealings involved tomb desecrations, or quarrels over the price asked in exchange for the mortuary rituals...*

282   *« Brevet et répertoire des titres, papiers et documents contenus dans les archives du royal monastère de Prouille » ("Register of the Titles, Papers and Documents contained in the Archives of the Royal Monastery of Prouille"), volume III, 1788, located in the Archives*

[...] The monastery consists of a church, a chapel, a cloister, a refectory, annex buildings and gardens. The sanctuary, which is ostentatiously orientated north-south [rather than the more conventional east-west], is quite spacious: in length it is longer than that of the Saint-Etienne Cathedral, in Toulouse, but not as wide. The great nave, alone, is built in a style that is unique to the buildings constructed by the Mendicant Orders[283] and has, along its sides, ten chapels. The heptagonal southern end, which is the extension of a disproportionate choir, houses the raised main altar. The building is entered through an open door in the north, on the current Place Alcantara. The bell-tower, almost square, prolonged by a small eight-faced building capped with an eight-faced dome, is still there to remind visitors astonished by its rather Oriental look, of the presence, for more than five centuries, of Franciscan brothers within the walls of Limoux."

As to the other order, that of the Dominicans, they settled in the region under the direction of their founding father, Dominic de Guzman[284], later to be worshipped as Saint Dominic. Indeed, Dominic founded his first monastery in this area[285], the Monastery of Prouilhe, as well as running into St. Francis for the second time, in a place known as "Le Soler", near Perpignan.

After having worked with Mgr. Diego d'Azevedo, Dominic was sent on a mission to Denmark by King Alfonso IX of Castille, in 1201. The trip was long and dangerous and its purpose was to bring the daughter of the Danish king to Spain. She was to marry the son of Alfonso IX, which would thus create a strong alliance between the two kingdoms. It was during this journey that Dominic crossed the Razès[286], a countryside with which, it seems, he fell in love; and it was in Toulouse where he was lodged one night by a Cathar, that the Saint wondered about his "religious mission in life". Full of pity, he converted the Cathar Penitent. When crossing the

départementales de l'Aude (Archives of the Aude Department), no. H514, f° 51 à 55.

283   "Mendicant Orders" is the generic name usually given to all Dominican and Franciscan Orders.

284   All information on the life of Dominic of Guzman and the history of the Monastery of Prouilhe is extracted from the Archives Royales du Monastère de Prouilhe (Royal Archives of the Monastery of Prouilhe), and from the official press dossier entitled « Projet de Prouilhe » ("The Prouilhe Project") published by the monastery.

285   The area in which Dominic settled was almost entirely populated by Cathars at that time.

286   The "Razès" ("Rhedaesium" in Latin) is the region of Rennes-le-Château. Interestingly, "Razès" sounds very much like "Rhagès", a town located in Media (modern Iran) and where Tobias, accompanied by the Archangel Raphael, goes to fetch the money left in the house of Gabael by his father Tobit for his burial, the price that was to be paid for the mortuary rituals.

area around Rennes-le-Château, he had a desire to return there later and help these "heretics that misunderstand Christ". So, upon his return from Denmark, Dominic demanded the help of Diego d'Azevedo to intervene with Pope Innocent III, to give him the authorisation to preach penitence to these Cathar heretics, a mandate he received in December 1206. His mission could begin.

From that moment onwards, the impetuous Dominic went in search of a location in the Razès where he could found a community. The region was full of heretics, so he knew that it was an area where he could fulfil his mission. In March 1207, he participated in the "Dispute of Montréal", where certain theologians had invited the Cathars to a theological debate, in the vain hope to make them see the error of their ways. Two weeks later, he left Montréal and settled in Fanjeaux. In 1214, he became its local priest, but he did not feel that his mission was succeeding. Dominic wanted to build a bridge towards the heretics and was not content with teaching merely from the pulpit of his church, which was a place that no heretic ever entered. He therefore quit his position in Fanjeaux and moved to Prouilhe, where he would live "according to the Penitence", that is to say that he would wear penitent's clothing and live in extreme poverty.

The location he chose was not picked at random but was quite specific. In 1206, Dominic had already seen a "sphere of fire" hanging over the abandoned hamlet, which had been devastated by feudal wars. The luminous phenomenon was witnessed during several consecutive nights and the saint interpreted it as a "divine signal" (though some interpreted it as demonic), which foreshadowed the glorious destiny of his work. For many years if not centuries, the site, a hill also known as "Seignadou", had been known as the location of several "apparitions". It was also the destination of a pilgrimage in honour of the Black Virgin, whose statue, a small representation with strange looks, was displayed there in a small chapel. In 1206, he asked Bishop Foulques of Toulouse for the concession of the chapel, with "33 steps" of pastures around it.

Dominic built a most basic building on it, the floor of which was nothing more than sand. Some years later, he *made the site into a religious community, where he placed several sisters who had been converted from Catharism*. The Royal Archives of the Monastery of Prouilhe note that *to these women who, in their heresy, lived a quasi-religious life, penitence and austerity*, Dominic offered *a similar way of life according to the Catholic tradition*. While it might seem that these women had become "sisters", in truth they had not changed anything at all about their heretical practices. Indeed, the sisters of Prouilhe continued to practice "penitence" as well as mortifications.

The Monastery of Prouilhe[287] thus became a closed community of women who had received the religious habit of Saint Dominic, but who were, in essence, still as heretical as they were before their "conversion" to the Catholic faith. To this, Dominic added a male community, who were charged with performing the more menial tasks, as well as ensuring the protection of the sisters. Saint Dominic himself remained in the area for a further ten years and made Prouilhe into the premier female monastery of the region. In 1217, he used the Monastery for a reunion where the "Rule" of the Order was discussed and it was from Prouilhe that he would later send his preachers out to evangelise the heretics. Prouilhe was thus at once the centre of the pseudo-attack on the Cathar heretics, as well as a centre of the heresy itself.

The scandal of the Cult of the Dead in Limoux

The Dominicans of Prouilhe and the Franciscans of Limoux were two monastic powerbases that are, for many, but two communities the members of which practice a monastic lifestyle behind closed doors, islands of "religious devotion" within the noisy life of a busy market town – at least in the case of Limoux. But behind this façade – the walls of the monastery – we find an implantation of heretical thinking, hermetically-sealed and preserved by those very walls. In truth, what went on inside had in no way changed from the old heretical lifestyle; and it was populated by heretics who continued to practice their own rites… the cult of the dead.

It is the very fact that both groups fought for the rights of burial in Limoux that exposes much of their true allegiance. Geographically, Limoux and Prouilhe are situated close to each other (approximately 23 kilometres). This meant that both religious communities tried to grasp control of these practices within the city, and soon this rivalry ended in quarrels and lawsuits.

Prouilhe and the Franciscan monastery of Limoux were both, to use the

---

287   *The information on the history of the Monastery of Prouilhe is extracted from the Archives Royales du Monastère de Prouilhe (Royal Archives of the Monastery of Prouilhe), and from the official press dossier entitled « Projet de Prouilhe » ("The Prouilhe Project") published by the monastery.*

words of Philipp Schaff[288] and Georges Jehel[289], communities which were - in reality - heirs of the Humiliati penitent sect. This means that they practiced the Cult of the Dead. It means that they were able to provide a service for those who wanted to make use of it: in return for money, the body and the soul of the deceased would be looked after.

Both the Franciscans and the Dominicans offered this service to the citizens of Limoux, the town itself a former hotbed of Catharism, and thus no doubt predisposed to welcome (and feel a religious need for) such services. The city had a large elderly population, many of whom had only outwardly embraced Christianity[290]. Even so, bearing in mind the usual cost of securing the Mortuary Rite[291], it seems unlikely that the rather poor people of Limoux would be an ideal target. However, the fact that no single community held the monopoly of these practices, meant that prices went down... and it meant that there were numerous legal proceedings between both organisations, evidence of which has been preserved by the Archaeological Association of the city. Gérard Jean[292] thus writes that *"the titles, papers and documents that are preserved in the Archives of the Royal Monastery of Prouilhe inform us, in detail, of the customs and habits through which the exclusivity of the 'burial of the dead' was given to a certain Order. But more than that, they inform us of the [surprisingly] irrational conflict that existed in Limoux, for more than three centuries, between the clergy of the church of Saint Martin, directed by the community of Dominican nuns of Prouilhe and its priors, and the Franciscan brothers."*

After consulting the Dominican archives, we discovered – with some horror – the extent of the disputes that reigned over the bodies of the de-

---

288   Schaff, Philipp, "History of the Christian Church", Oak Harbor, Washington State, Logos Reseach Systems, Inc., 1997, electronic edition based on the first published version by Charles Scribner's sons, 1907, enhanced with corrections by The Electronic Bible Society, Dallas, Texas, 1998.

289   Georges Jehel, « Les villes d'Italie, XII ème – XIV ème siècles : sociétés, pouvoirs, économies, cultures » ("The Cities of Italy from the 12th to the 14th century: societies, powers, economics, cultures"), Editions du Temps, Nantes, 2004.

290   It means that the population of Limoux retained and observed certain customs and superstitions which are unique to heretics.

291   The price asked by the penitents was determined based on the personal fortune of the deceased, or else the wealth of his family. The price could reach as much as half the dead person's fortune, which was bound to make the penitent brotherhoods and monastic orders incredibly rich, considering that apart from monks, mostly noble families and kings requested such rites.

292   The information on the Monastery of the Franciscans of Limoux is extracted from the research of historian Gérard Jean, as well as the works of the historical society « Mémoire Historique de Limoux » ("Historical Memory of Limoux"), of which he is the president.

ceased. This fight had taken on unusual proportions, to the extent that it could no longer be settled between the two communities but had to be referred to higher authorities for resolution.

It was thus the "Provincial of Provence" that heard the arguments of both parties, after which the "Court of the Tribunal of Toulouse" and, finally, the Archbishop of Narbonne was required to render a verdict. But litigation lasted for more than three centuries and was, in fact, never satisfactorily adjudicated, with the result that the remains of various deceased were often subjected to acts of brutality while the debate between the two parties raged on. Each wanted to take possession of the dead bodies for their own purpose, bury them in their own cemetery, and pocket the money that went with this service.

The following chronology emerges from the work of local historian Gérard Jean and the documents located in Prouilhe[293], revealing the extent of the quarrel, which extended from 1271 to the XVth century[294]. Towards the end of the 13th century, after terrible disputes, the prior of the order of the Franciscans addresses the claims of the Monastery of Prouilhe and proposes to cease the hostilities, at least temporarily. He agrees to leave certain bodies to the Dominicans, but intends to recover those of the little children *"whose family already elected to be buried in the cemetery of their fellow brothers[295]."* The people of the city and the affected families do not seem to be against this proposal. Still, on 10th October 1336, the Vicar of the church of Saint Martin (reporting to the Monastery of Prouilhe), with the support of the archbishop of Narbonne, issues an injunction to the Franciscans, forbidding them to touch the remains of any child. Their remains become the sole property of the Dominicans and, by extension, that of the parish of Saint Martin, in Limoux.

The deliberations commence and, in 1337, the Franciscans are sentenced to repay the money that they have received "illegally". Mortal remains are also exhumed and transferred, at least if they are still in a fit state to do so. The sanction is nevertheless not prohibitive enough to prevent the Fran-

---

293   *These documents have now been relocated in the Archives Départementales de l'Aude (Archives of the Department of Aude) for the most part.*

294   *« Brevet et répertoire des titres, papiers et documents contenus dans les archives du royal monastère de Prouille » ("Register of the Titles, Papers and Documents contained in the Archives of the Royal Monastery of Prouille"), volume III, 1788, located in the Archives départementales de l'Aude (Archives of the Aude Department), no. H514, f° 51 à 55.*

295   *i.e the fellow brothers of the Franciscans, in the cemetery of the Franciscans themselves.*

ciscans from rebelling. In fact, it seems that they pay little notice to the judgment and remain convinced that they are within their rights, and thus continue to take ownership of dead children.

In 1341, the quarrels intensify and Prouilhe takes the case before the Official of Razès. The verdict is clear: the Franciscans are no longer allowed to bury the remains without the specific agreement of the Vicar of the Church of Saint Martin and Prouilhe. Furthermore, the Franciscans are obliged to return all money, as well as all the rights received. The original texts speak of "burial rights" and it is of course how, within a more modern organised society, the "Cult of the Dead" had become known. On 20th December 1369, tariffs are placed on what the Franciscans must pay to the Dominicans, and these prices are high[296].

The Franciscans soon found a loophole in the new arrangement. The ingenious idea took the form of inviting people who are close to death to join the Franciscan community, offering them the Rite as well as a burial within the cemetery. Gérard Jean states that on 30th November 1367, the Vicar of the church Saint Martin, by order of the Monastery of Prouilhe, *"delivers an act to the Guardian of the Franciscans of Limoux, accusing him of having buried, on his own authority and without any right, the corpse of Pierre de Calmon"*, draper of Limoux and *"parishioner of Saint Martin's church, of the same city"*. The vicar protests and the superior of the Franciscans answers quite simply that *"Pierre de Calmon was a brother of the Order of which he had taken the habit some time before his death"*.

The case turns into a scandal once again and on 15th February 1482, the Parliament of Toulouse hands down a judgment, confirming that the Monastery of Prouilhe is authorised *"to take the dead bodies of those who have chosen to be buried with the Franciscans, into the parish church of Saint Martin, to celebrate the mass there, to exonerate them, to receive offerings and, only then, to carry them to the door of the church of the Franciscans to be buried there"*. Let it be said that this, once again, is not the end of the problem and that the quarrels continue.

Of course, the "offerings" were nothing more or less than the money

---

296 *Actually, "eight pounds of wax which are to be paid each year, forever, according to the following instructions: 2 pounds at Christmas, 2 at Easter, 2 at the summer equinox, and 2 on the feast of St. Michael." Furthermore, two additional pounds of wax had to be given to the Vicar of the church of Saint Martin for each corpse buried in the cemetery of the Franciscans. This arrangement was specifically designed by the Dominicans to force the Franciscans to only bury their own members in their cemetery – thereby acquiring a monopoly for themselves on the burials of lay people. It should be noted that wax – the currency of exchange in this arrangement – was extremely expensive at that time.*

that the friends and family were willing to pay for the Mortuary Rite. And it was this Rite that was the main reason for which people like Pierre de Calmon entered the Franciscan Order at the end of their life, to ensure receiving it. The excuse being used was that this would enable them to be buried in their cemetery and it was neatly circumvented by the court's verdict, which essentially gave the profits to the Dominicans, and the burden and cost of the burial to the Franciscans.

The Hautpoul family

Any profitable organisation, by definition, became of interest to the local landlords. In Orléans, the Saint-Mesmin family offered considerable sums to the local Monastery of the Franciscans and, in return, hoped that the members of the family could benefit from their special final farewell. This soon led to abuse, for the brothers felt that one of the lords did not give them enough, so they unearthed the body of his deceased wife and declared it "damned"[297]. It is therefore necessary to regard, at least in daily practice, the Cult of the Dead as a financial means through which pressure could be applied on the more fortunate ones, i.e. the nobility. Of course, for this to succeed, it is required that the affected person is someone who wants to see the Mortuary Rite performed on himself or his dearest. Of course, if the local noble family was Cathar in origin, then it is to be expected that they would frequent Penitent circles and piously keep their allegiance with these organisations.

Who is the noble family whose rule held sway over the Franciscans and Dominicans in Limoux? The answer is the Hautpoul family – and they ruled from Rennes-le-Château. The family was Cathar in origin, and, most importantly, it is the tomb of the last descendant of this family, Marie de Nègre d'Ables, the widow of the last Lord of Hautpoul, whose grave has been identified as "key" in the mystery of Saunière. It would seem, then,

---

297   « *Seigneur de Saint-Mesmin contre Pères Cordeliers Pénitents d'Orléans* » (*Trial of Lord of Saint-Mesmin against the Franciscan Penitents of Orléans) 1534, a manuscript housed in the Bibliothèque du roi de France (Library of the King of France), n°1770. The ruthless way in which the Dominican nuns and Franciscan friars of Limoux each lay claim to ownership of the corpses evokes this quote from the article entitled "Vision" in Voltaire's "Philosophical Dictionary": "These good Franciscans took it upon themselves to unearth the deceased lady, so as to force the widower lord to have his wife buried again, in exchange for a higher payment to them." The most efficient way for these heretics to force believers to pay the desired amount of money is obviously to have the deceased buried in their own cemetery. The burial rights, i.e. the prices charged for the burials, and therefore the "offerings" derive from this. Money is indeed acquired through blackmail if necessary, and notably by threatening to exhume the corpse.*

that we have come almost full-circle.

Historically, the area which was the native land of the Hautpoul family was situated under the Cathar bishopric of Carcassonne. This feudal territory was under Cathar domination and recognised its religious leadership. We have evidence that supports this, from the enumeration of castles, strongholds and fiefdoms that was listed at the time of the Council of Saint Félix en Lauragais[298]. This Council was held in 1167, in Saint Félix en Lauragais, situated between Carcassonne and Toulouse and very close to the home grounds of the Hautpoul family. We should add that Noël Corbu, the man who bought Saunière's villa from Marie Denarnaud, sold this estate later in life and then bought the castle of Saint Félix en Lauragais, where the Council had been held. Intriguingly, Noël Corbu died shortly afterwards in a car accident in front of the monastery of Prouilhe[299].

---

298   Also called "Cathar Council of Saint Félix de Caraman". The castle in which the Cathar elite held their Council is known as "Saint Félix de Caraman" or as "Saint Félix en Lauragais". For more information on this Council, see Antoine Dondaine, « Les Actes du Concile Albigeois de Saint Félix de Caraman. Essai de critique d'authenticité d'un document medieval » ("The Acts of the Albigensian Council of Saint Félix de Caraman. An Attempt at a Critical Study of a Medieval Document's Authenticity"), Miscelanea Giovanni Mercati, Roma, 1946, pp. 324-355.

299   Noël Corbu (1912-1968) was a manufacturer from Perpignan, who worked in the sugar industry. As he was losing money during the Second World War, he relocated to the region of Rennes-le-Château (the Razès) in 1942 to start anew. Interestingly, he first settled in the village of Bugarach, south-east from Rennes-le-Château. There he learned from the villagers about an estate that was for sale nearby, in Rennes-le-Château, and about a mysterious "inheritance". The heir, Marie Denarnaud, was 74 at that time, and was more than a little suspicious of impromptu visitors. In spite of Corbu's insistence, she apparently never told her secret to him. Corbu did become good friends with her, and finally convinced her to sell Saunière's estate to him in exchange for annuities paid to her until her death. Under this arrangement, Corbu was able to move into the Villa Bethania with his wife and children, while Marie Denarnaud continued to live in the presbytery. Then, the Corbu family transformed the Villa Bethania into a hotel, "Hôtel La Tour" (Hotel of the Tower), in reference to the Tour Magdala. Noël Corbu owned Saunière's estate from 1947 to 1965, at which date he sold the estate to Henri Buthion. Corbu did some research into the story of Saunière's treasure, and used it largely as a means to promote his hotel business. Nevertheless, he invited local journalists and the ensuing publicity worked so well, that soon the "Hôtel La Tour" received bookings from those deeply interested in what they called the "curé aux milliards" ("The Billionnaire Priest"). Noël Corbu must have encountered more strange or dangerous people in the process than is usually known, as the somewhat intriguing circumstances of his death (or perhaps murder, as some argue), in 1968 leave some with question marks. Factor in what we now know about Saunière's unorthodox religious beliefs and the Cathar (Manichean) past of the region, and it becomes simply inconceivable that Noël Corbu could have bought the Castle in the village of Saint Félix en Lauragais (which he did shortly after having sold Saunière's estate to Henri Buthion) just by accident.

Dignitaries from the Manichean Churches of Lombardy, Bulgaria, even Anatolia, appeared at this Cathar Council, the first of its kind in France. It shows the level of cross-border organisation that existed within the Cathar community. Amongst the members who attended was the Bogomil Pope Niceta, Robert d'Epernon (the Cathar Bishop of France), Siccard Cellerier (the representative of the Cathar church of Albi), Giraud Mercier (the Cathar bishop of Carcassonne), Bernard Raimond (Cathar bishop of Toulouse), Raimond de Casals (Cathar bishop of Agen), and finally Marc of Lombardy (the bishop of the Cathar church of Italy). In short, the "crème de la crème", the elite of the Manichean religion.

The Council had but one mission, namely, to organise the local Church and to make it into a European power. The Bogomil Pope thus used the Council to consecrate certain bishops and assign them to certain dioceses. The Council had previously defined the borders and territories of each diocese and it is here that we see that the territory of the Hautpouls is of primary strategic importance for the Cathars[300]. The document states that *"the territory of the [Cathar] bishopric of Carcassonne extends [...] starting from Saint Pons, [...] between the castle of Cabaret, and that of Hautpoul, [...] between Montréal d'Aude and Fanjeaux"*.

As such, the castle of the lords of Hautpoul became a stronghold for the Cathar bishopric of Carcassonne. Other sources intimate that ancestors of this family were previously directly implicated in militant Catharism, and were considered to be dangerous activists. A certain Isarn Bonzhom d'Hautpoul had been listed as a heretic in the register of the Inquisition of Toulouse. Jean Duvernoy[301], commenting on this source material, states that in the period 1273-1280, amongst the Cathars of this region, *"one finds the Roqueville, the Hunaud de Lanta, the Roquefort, the Puylaurens-Montesquieu, the Saissac, Isarn Bonzhom d'Hautpoul, the Corneilles, the Palajac."* In fact, when we leaf through the history of this heresy, it is clear that there are repeated references to the Hautpoul family, several members of which were identified as apostates and sectarians.

At the same time, we note that not all branches of the Hautpoul family

---

300 Guillaume Besse, « Histoire des Ducs de Narbonne » ("History of the Counts of Narbonne"), 1660.

301 « Registre de l'Inquisition de Toulouse (1273-1280) » ("Records of the Inquisition in Toulouse: 1273-1280"), Ranulphe de Plassac, Pons de Parnac, Pierre Arsieu, Hugues Amiel, Hugues de Bouniols. Ms Fonds Doat, T. XXV et XXVI, Bibliothèque nationale de Paris. A text published, translated and commented upon by Jean Duvernoy, 1993.

were descended from these Cathar ancestors. As René Descadeillas[302] noted: *"at the beginning of the 18th century, [the Hautpoul family] was divided in three branches:*

1. the Rennes-le-Château branch descended directly from the adversaries of Simon de Montfort [the leader of the Cathar Crusade], Isarn d'Hautpoul, via Pierre Raymond, who married in 1422 with Blanche de Marquefaves de Rennes.
2. the Félines branch founded by Auger d'Hautpoul, second son of Guillaume Pierre and of Hermeninde de Poudens, born circa 1380.
3. the Salettes branch born of the principal branch by Pierre, second son of Georges and Izalguier de Clermont, born circa 1525."

From these three branches, that of the Hautpoul of Rennes-le-Château is generally considered to be the most direct line of descent… and also the most heretical in nature. And it is therefore to be expected that, in Limoux, they would want to receive the Mortuary Rite, whether it was administered by the Dominicans or the Franciscans.

As Anne Brenon writes in *Historia*[303], the Cathars often presented themselves *"in the heart of the villages as penitent communities and guarantors of a good death, very often counting among them members of the local aristocracy, which did not go unnoticed, and specifically the local ladies – in Laurac, in Fanjeaux, or in Mas-Saintes-Puelles, in Lanta, Tarabel, Ségreville or Caraman, in Hautpoul, Puylaurens, Lautrec or Rabastens."* Here we have, before us, the ingredients that will be thrown into the "soup" that will become the "mystery" of Rennes-le-Château.

Just before the Cathar Crusade and the fall of the Cathar bishoprics in the region, the Hautpoul family, like so many other noble families with similar allegiances, or those who were just afraid of what the Crusade would do even to the innocent, moved. The Barons of the North had not only plotted the repression of the heresy, but had already drawn up new maps of the Languedoc, in which the former estates were "realigned" and "reassigned"

---

302   *René Descadeillas was a journalist for the "Dépêche du Midi" newspaper, the president of the Société des Etudes Scientifiques de l'Aude (SESA), as well as the author of the book « Mythologie du Trésor de Rennes » ("A Mythology of the Treasure of Rennes-le-Château") (1972). See note 56 for more biographical details about this distinguished researcher.*
303   *Anne Brenon, "Le Nord royal contre le Sud cathare", ("Royal North versus Cathar South"), an article published in the 2006 issue of the Revue Historia Thématique (Historia Thematic Magazine) entitled « Les hérétiques » ("The Heretics"), under the section « Les ingérences politiques » ("Political Meddling").*

conform to their desires.

Of course, these Cathar-supporting families were not unaware that their strongholds were the prizes that these northern lords were really after. Let us explain: the Cathar nobles anticipated the crusade that would soon be waged against them. They preferred the shadows rather than become Icarus-like victims. Thus they stopped voicing their Cathar opinions and changed their appearance into that of "Penitent Catholics". According to the Dominican Richard Weber[304], these "Penitent Catholics", "women first", should not be considered any less heretical than the Cathars – and we should wonder whether this "move" was exactly the trick that Dominic performed with the foundation of Prouilhe, as its founding members were nine "converted" Cathar women, including several nobles, who adopted a penitent lifestyle. And amongst these nobles that "evolved" were the Hautpoul family, specifically the female members.

The mystery of Rennes-le-Château

French researcher Franck Daffos, in his book *Le Secret Dérobé*[305], highlighted that various financial transfers were made by Mgr. Billard, bishop of Carcassonne, in the days leading up to his death. Similar events can be seen with certain members of the Hautpoul family, where it is clearly known that the receivers of the money were the Franciscans of Limoux, as well as the clergy of the church of Saint Martin. For Daffos, the conclusion was straightforward: the Hautpoul family had discovered the treasure of Rennes-le-Château and Mgr. Billard had taken over this discovery, using Saunière to launder the money discreetly. Saunière was, therefore, a money launderer and received, in that capacity, "commissions" from Billard, even as late as a few days before the bishop's death.

From our perspective, things are not quite that simple. Furthermore, the types of transfers, in the days leading up to an individual's death, and - specifically - to the Franciscans and Dominicans, have all the signs of being payment for the Mortuary Rite. On the surface, it may seem like money laundering, but when one is familiar with the religious background, it becomes clear that this was not the case: rather than purely financial transactions, Billard was involved with the Cult of the Dead, thus adding further

---

304   Fr. Richard Weber, O.P., "History of the Dominican Laity, Part 1". An eye-opening confession on the true origins of the Dominicans by the Dominicans themselves, published on the official website of the Dominican Order for the Province of St. Albert the Great (Chicago): http://www.domcentral.org/oplaity/layhistory.htm

305   Franck Daffos, "Le Secret Dérobé" (The Robbed Secret), published by Editions Oeil du Sphinx, collection Le Serpent Rouge no. 3.

substance to the allegations that he was running a "church within a church", the allegation levelled against him shortly after his death[306].

From Gérard de Sède, the author who started it all, via Henry Lincoln and Noël Corbu to Franck Daffos, even René Descadeillas, all agree unanimously that, at its bottom-line, the mystery of Saunière is linked to a secret. For some, it was Saunière's accidental discovery of one or more parchments in the altar column of his church, for others it was a secret that involved the tomb of Marie de Nègre d'Ables de Blanchefort, located in his cemetery. Gérard de Sède stated that from the moment he was assigned to his posting, the priest of Rennes-le-Château suffered tremendous "destitution", he as well as his maid, Marie Denarnaud. In Corbu's manuscript[307], we can read how Saunière spent the first seven years of his posting *"living the life of a completely impoverished rural priest"*[308]. In his archives and in his accounting books[309], we read, on the date of 1st February 1892: *"I need to give Léontine 0 Franc 40"* and *"I need to give Alphonsine 1 Franc 65"* and the money at his disposal, to which he refers to as his "secret funds", consists of no more than 80.65 Francs.

His church was in a dilapidated state and the altar, so old it almost beggared belief, was dressed with a stone which was more than likely ruined

---

306   All these charges are noted in the « Notice Laborde » (the "Laborde Note" in English), named after a priest who, after Mgr. Billard's death, denounced the former bishop's actions during his episcopate as related to Simony (see notes 222-223) and payment for burials, i.e to Mortuary Rites and the Cult of the Dead. The "Notice Laborde" ("Laborde Note") is a crucial and revealing document about Monseigneur Billard and much of his priests who where his "partners in crime", possibly including Saunière himself, although he is not named in the document (Simony is a crime according to Canon Law, and the Canonic Dictionary of abbé J.P. Migne). The Notice Laborde (Laborde Note) was first discovered and published by French researcher Pierre Jarnac in his book « Les archives de Rennes-le-Château » ("The Rennes-le-Château Archives"), Editions Bélisane (1988), pp. 456 et al. The "Notice Laborde" was first published on the Internet by French researcher Laurent Buchholtzer, on his website: http://www.octonovo.org/RlC/Fr/docu/Billard02.htm (text in French)

307   The Corbu manuscript was written by Noël Corbu, the then-owner of Saunière's estate, during the 1960s. Although historical analysis has since discarded some of the opinions that are voiced by Corbu about the source of Saunière's wealth, this document is still very valuable as it contains one of the very few first-hand accounts of the life of Bérenger Saunière, coming from somebody who discovered Rennes-le-Château as early as 1942, and knew Marie Denarnaud.

308   Saunière was appointed as priest of Rennes-le-Château by Mgr. Leuillieux in 1885, so his "poverty period" is 1885-1892.

309   As published by Pierre Jarnac in « Les archives de Rennes-le-Château » ("The Rennes-le-Château Archives"), Editions Bélisane (1988) for Saunière's correspondence, and by Laurent Buchholtzer on his website, with regard to Saunière's accounting books: http://www.octonovo.org/RlC/Fr/carnets/compta/compta01.htm

and could, so to speak, collapse each time he rested the chalice on it. In 1888, the priest received a donation of 600 francs, from the legacy of his predecessor abbé Pons, with which he was able to carry out the most urgent repairs. In 1891, the municipal council lent him about 1,400 francs. Saunière hired some help in order to commence work on the altar. The verdict: it was considered impossible to restore. Gérard de Sède[310] says that on this occasion, he *"removed the heavy flagstone"*, and was surprised to discover that one of the pillars of the altar *"was hollow"*, *"stuffed with dried ferns"*. Amongst this dusty vegetation, they (Saunière and his helpers) found *"three sealed wooden tubes"*, which, upon opening, the priest realised that they contained parchments. In *Holy Blood, Holy Grail*[311], by Michael Baigent, Richard Leigh and Henry Lincoln, the authors stipulate that these documents are three legal documents: genealogies, one dated 1244, a second dated 1644 by François-Pierre d'Hautpoul and the third dated 24th April 1694, by Henri d'Hautpoul. Gérard de Sède, himself, never offered any suggestion as to the nature of the parchments and, instead, decided to concentrate on one document, which should henceforth be called the "fourth document", as this document was a series of passages from the Bible, apparently containing a code, at least, that is the opinion of some authors.

Entering the territory of cyphers is as dangerous as entering a swamp, so we will not tread there. Instead, let us focus on the opinions of René Descadeillas[312], one of the most competent observers of the mystery, who wrote that *"the Hautpouls of Rennes, who represented the elder branch, were favoured when it came to the division of the family possessions. Their archives have disappeared, probably in the fire of 1212 which devastated their residence. However, one can still, at the end of the 18th century, retrace far*

---

310   Gérard de Sède, « Le Trésor Maudit de Rennes-le-Château », J'ai Lu éditions (1972). *For an English translation, refer to "The Accursed Treasure of Rennes-le-Chateau", DEK Publishing, 2001, translated by Bill Kersey.*
311   *Baigent, Leigh and Lincoln, "Holy Blood, Holy Grail", first published by Bantam Dell, New York, in 1982.*
312   *René Descadeillas, « Notice sur Rennes-le-Château et l'abbé Saunière » (« Notice on Rennes-le-Château and abbé Saunière ») (1962). This famous writing was subjected to several modifications before being finally included in « Mythologie du trésor de Rennes »: René Descadeillas, « Mythologie du Trésor de Rennes: Histoire Véritable de l'abbé Saunière, Curé de Rennes-le-Château » ("Mythology of the Treasure of Rennes-le-Château: the Real Story of Abbé Saunière, priest of Rennes-le-Château"), in « Mémoires de la Société des Arts et des Sciences de Carcassonne » (Research Bulletin of the Arts and Science Society of Carcassonne), 1971-1972 years, 4th series, volume VII, 2nd part; published in 1974. See note 56 for more biographical details about this distinguished researcher.*

enough back into time to substantiate their ownership of various tracts of land since the 11th century. At the time, there was a vital document that es-tablished the genealogy of the Hautpouls: the will of François-Pierre, baron of Hautpoul and Rennes, husband of Marguerite de Saint-Jean de Pontis, daughter of François and Catherine de Voisins."

For Descadeillas, the entire mystery is quite simple: the parchments do not mention a treasure at all: the genealogy of the Hautpouls of Rennes had partially disappeared, as a result of the fire of 1212. Under a monarchic system, ownership of land was linked with genealogical records, or at least acceptance by the monarch of one's claims of certain territories, if no hard evidence could be produced. Logic dictates, as the researcher and journalist Philip Coppens noted, that the "parchments" are therefore not mysterious documents, but three genealogical titles, i.e. documents that are extremely important in order to identify a family's possession. The first, dated 1244 and ratified by the monarch, thus validated their possessions up to that date. The second established the continuation of the first document, up to 1644 and Francois-Pierre d'Hautpoul, and also contained his will. Finally, the third, dated 24th April 1695, was the will of Henri d'Hautpoul.

The documents were indeed extremely important to the Hautpoul fam-ily. Placing them inside a hollow pillar in the church that was once the chapel of their castle may have been an excellent method of safeguarding them, – or at least guaranteeing their survival - more than in any other hiding place. But for anyone else, the value of the three parchments is lim-ited in scope, especially for a man like Saunière. Indeed, the documents may establish the chain of possession of certain properties by the Hautpoul family, but the French Revolution of 1789 abolished the privileges of the nobility and it is hard to see how the priest could have derived any profit from them. As such, the genealogies had lost all of their financial value, even for the Hautpouls, for which they were nothing more than a souve-nir, a memory of better days. In short, they could not be used to cash in on anything, nor be used to blackmail anyone. Perhaps Saunière could sell them to the Hautpoul family, as a memorabilia of more fortunate days now gone. It might help him in restoring a church window if he could sell it, but it would definitely not explain the source of his wealth.

We need therefore to put some question marks next to the statement of de Sède[313], who states that Saunière carefully preserved the parchments and,

---

313   *Gérard de Sède, « Le Trésor Maudit de Rennes-le-Château », J'ai Lu editions (1972). For an English translation, refer to "The Accursed Treasure of Rennes-le-Chateau", DEK*

"in early 1893", showed them to his bishop, Mgr. Billard. According to the author, the bishop *"examined the documents carefully"*, after which *"as soon as he returned home*[314], *our priest recommenced the works, helped by several people"* and destroyed numerous tombs.

If the above sequence is largely correct, how do we explain the strange interest of Mgr. Billard in these papers and the strange effect they will have on the life of Saunière? The solution may be, once again, more simple than most have made it. We note that, apart from genealogies, the documents also contained two wills: that of François-Pierre d'Hautpoul, dated 23rd November 1644 and Henri d'Hautpoul, dated 24th April 1695. These two documents themselves should be more than enough to excite our curiosity, since they were both said to be secret in their time and hence seem to have contained some secret that was important within the ranks of the Hautpoul family, and one that they tried to maintain.

De Sède[315] wrote that in *"1644, François-Pierre d'Hautpoul, Baron of Rennes, made his will. [...] The document was registered on 23rd November with Captier, notary at Esperaza"*. Everything so far seems normal, but once the Baron dies, the document disappears. No-one shows it to the heirs and they are therefore ignorant of its contents. We do not know who has the document, though it seems that something in it is classified as "dangerous knowledge".

Whatever the will stipulated, Rennes-le-Château was given to Blaise I d'Hautpoul, the son of François-Pierre. He maintained his noble title and possession of the stronghold by "sovereign judgment" of M. de Bezons. Apparently, he married Marie-Lucrèce du Vivier de Lansac on 10th July 1644, and had, according to René Descadeillas, ten children, two daughters and eight sons[316]. Whether the result of a bad education or conceited minds, five of his offspring were delighted to leave their family, and take

---

Publishing, 2001, translated by Bill Kersey.

314   *Some authors think that Saunière traveled to Paris to show the so-called coded parchments to a priest of Saint-Sulpice in order to "decipher" them. However, as of this day, this journey to Paris has never been corroborated.*

315   *Gérard de Sède, « Le Trésor Maudit de Rennes-le-Château », J'ai Lu editions (1972). For an English translation, refer to "The Accursed Treasure of Rennes-le-Chateau", DEK Publishing, 2001, translated by Bill Kersey.*

316   *René Descadeillas, « Mythologie du Trésor de Rennes: Histoire Véritable de l'abbé Saunière, Curé de Rennes-le-Château » ("Mythology of the Treasure of Rennes-le-Château : the Real Story of Abbé Saunière, priest of Rennes-le-Château"), in « Mémoires de la Société des Arts et des Sciences de Carcassonne » (Research Bulletin of the Arts and Science Society of Carcassonne), 1971-1972 years, 4th series, volume VII, 2nd part; published in 1974. See note 56 for more biographical details about this distinguished researcher.*

part in the "wars of Louis XIV", where they got killed.

The wills, consequently, are numerous but they are, nevertheless, shown discreetly. We make a particular note of that of Antoine d'Hautpoul, concerning which some strange remarks have been made, and that of the elder son, Henri d'Hautpoul, Baron of Rennes, written down in 1695. The son of Henri, François, lived in Rennes-le-Château. Following the strange custom that seemed to run in his family, he too refused to show copies of his father's will and we should add he was very obstinate about this. Finally, in December 1780, the entire batch of archives and testaments were given to the notary Siau and, according to de Sède, Siau gave them to Marie de Nègre d'Ables, widow of François d'Hautpoul de Blanchefort. She apparently transferred the documents secretly to her confessor, Antoine Bigou, the then resident priest of Rennes. And it was a century later that one of his successors, Bérenger Saunière, discovered the parchments that Bigou had hidden in one of the pillars of the altar… or so the story goes.

In the end, as remarked by Gérard de Sède, *so many disappearing wills, so many mysteries and litigations are enough to make one ponder as to whether there was indeed some secret […] within the Hautpoul family*. De Sède added that this secret could be *of great consequence. […] In any case, if such a secret existed, its last legitimate agents could only be Marie de Nègre d'Ables, her husband François d'Hautpoul de Blanchefort and their chaplain Antoine Bigou.* Which of course begs the question: what was in these documents – in these wills – that was of such importance that it could not be divulged?

A family secret

We directed our research towards trying to find answers to the questions as to what the subject matter of these testaments was, who their authors were and what secrets they could potentially contain.

The testament of Henri d'Hautpoul was reputedly "lost", which is not of much help to us. That of his brother Antoine could be of some interest or help. First, we needed to make sure that he was indeed related to the Hautpoul family, for this man is hardly known to historians and only rarely makes an appearance in their genealogical records. Still, we assumed that he was indeed Henri's brother. We also relied on Paul Saussez, a specialist on the Hautpoul family and their tombs. After he had consulted his archives, he confirmed to us[317] that Antoine d'Hautpoul had indeed existed, but did not appear in the genealogy of the Hautpoul family un-

---

317   *In a message dated Sunday 22nd January 2006.*

der that name. The man we were looking for was, more than likely "Jean-Antoine"[318], who died in 1676 and was the son Blaise and Marie-Lucrèce du Vivier de Lansac, and therefore a brother to Henri and the uncle of François d'Hautpoul. Saussez thus confirmed our initial impressions, namely that Antoine – or Jean Antoine – was indeed relevant to this story. We had also found references to him in the work *Histoire du Pèlerinage de Notre-Dame de Marceille*. According to its author, Lasserre[319], (Jean-)Antoine had rewritten his will in 1674, or two years before his death. Again according to Lasserre, Antoine's testament insisted forcefully that his body had to be buried in the church of the Franciscans in Limoux, yet his heart had to be placed in the basilica of Notre-Dame de Marceille, on the outskirts of Limoux[320]. So that this would be accomplished, Antoine donated 2,000 pounds to the Franciscans and the basilica – a large sum of money for only two masses per week. In fact, it is a curious will, with various secret clauses. And we will eventually understand why it was felt prudent that not too many people got sight of it!

For one, let us not forget the various judiciary pronouncements, like the one from the Tribunal of Toulouse, dated 15th February 1482, which forbade the Franciscans to bury corpses in their cemetery. The judgment spoke in favour of the Monastery of Prouilhe and its annex, the church of Saint Martin de Limoux. As a result, lay people were buried – or should be buried – exclusively in the Dominican cemetery, as well as "offering" the money to them. But Jean-Antoine d'Hautpoul's testament makes it clear that he "demands" to be buried with the Franciscans, which goes against the judgment. And it is immediately clear that there have to be profound reasons why Antoine insists on this. What could he seek there that he is so forceful about this request? What un-avowable reason pushes him into the arms of the Franciscans and their subsidiary in Notre-Dame de Limoux? Why willingly tell your children and executors that they need to break the law?

---

318   *There was definitely a risk of confusion, since as Paul Saussez told us, "there are two 'Jean-Antoine' in the Félines branch of the Hautpoul family, the first one (around 1661) and his grandson, born in 1694." However, the "Antoine d'Hautpoul" we were looking for belonged to the Rennes-le-Château branch of the family and not the Félines branch, which therefore eliminates all possibilities of him not being the "Jean-Antoine, brother of Henri d'Hautpoul" who died in 1676.*

319   *Joseph-Théodore Lasserre, « Histoire du Pèlerinage de Notre-Dame de Marceille » ("History of the Pilgrimage of Notre-Dame de Marceille"), 1891. Duplicated in fac-simile: Impr. C. Lacour, published by RediViva, Nîmes, 1998.*

320   *On page 41 of Lasserre's book, see previous note for the full reference.*

There is one simple answer: could it be that Antoine d'Hautpoul had doubts that, should he be buried with the Dominicans, he would not receive a proper Mortuary Rite? That he, therefore, demanded that his heirs break the law, for his spiritual welfare, and ensure that he was buried with the Franciscans, so that a proper rite would be his? Let us note that if this were the case, he was definitely not the only person who preferred the Franciscans over the Dominicans, as we have already seen in the case of Pierre de Calmon, who became a penitent so that he would receive a burial within the Franciscan cemetery.

The episode underlines the lengths to which adherents of the Cult of the Dead would go, so that their soul would be saved. After all, in their eyes, there was nothing more important in life than a proper death and people like Antoine d'Hautpoul did not seem willing to take any chances. After all, if the Mortuary Rite was not properly administered, the cycle of incarnations would be terminated and one would face eternal imprisonment and torture in the underworld.

No wonder therefore that Antoine "demanded" to be buried with the Franciscans in his will.

Antoine's secretiveness about his will is now explained. What about his brother Henri? If Antoine was an adherent of the Cult of the Dead, it wouldn't surprise anyone to find that his brother was too. But as his testament has disappeared, it is impossible to know what he wanted. Still, we note that one researcher, Alain Féral, was able to recover an extract from this will which, even though it is not the complete text, could at least resolve part of the puzzle. In the excerpt, we read how *"in the year 1695, the 24th of April, before noon, in the castle of Rennes, in the diocese of Alet"*, "Henry d'Hautpoul", the local lord, ill for a very long time, but still with a clear memory, decided to write down his final wishes, for he says that *"he needs to die"* and *"as the hour is uncertain"*… As such, as death often creeps brutally up on someone and that his last wishes may otherwise not be followed up correctly, Henri therefore decides to write everything down "as follows":

"I desire that after my death my body is buried in the parish church of the aforesaid Rennes, in the tomb of my predecessors, and that the funeral honours are made to me according to the will of Lady Marie Dupuy my wife [...] I desire that during the year after my death, God is requested for the rest of my soul, and that to this effect requiem masses are celebrated, namely one year in the church of the Capuchin Fathers [a branch of Franciscans] of Limoux, two years in the parish church of Rennes by the appointed priest of the place, a half-year in the aforementioned church by Deydiès, priest [...]."

It then adds that the will was made personally by Henry d'Hautpoul, the rightful heir of his father Blaise d'Hautpoul. Present were: *"Master Jean Vernat, priest of Rennes, Messrs Sebastien Michel, vice-chancellor of Saint-Just, Antoine Saunière, master apothecary, Gabriel Captier, master surgeon of Espéraza, Messrs André Deydiès, priest living in Rennes, etc."*

Of course, we would have hoped that in this testament, Henri d'Hautpoul would have been more specific about his intentions, and perhaps even give sordid details about the Cult of the Dead the rite of which he may have hoped to receive upon his passing. And indeed, such information may well be found in the other, missing pages.

But it is clear that though there is some detail about the masses that needed to be said, there is no mention of the money set aside for this. Still, we know that in his brother's testament[321], such details were clearly identified, as of course if they were not, the contract between the deceased and the friars would have been null and void, and family members would inevitably dispute the correct amount of money that should go to them and what should go to some religious order – with the religious order no doubt losing out. Hence there existed a strong motivation for the will-makers, for example in the case of Henri's testament, for hiding such documents from the scrutiny of the rest of the family, so as to avoid some embarrassing questions about the disappearance of a large portion of the inheritance. Hence there was also a powerful incentive for the religious congregation involved to officially describe such donations as merely intended for "pious works".

Logically, it would have been Henri d'Hautpoul's entire testament that Saunière would have recovered and not just those pieces that found their way into the hands of Alain Féral. Still, though not complete, the little information we have is not without value. For one, it reveals that the local lords kept the local priests employed and paid them money to say masses for their souls. We also learn that Henri wants to be buried in the church of Rennes itself[322], in the "tomb of his predecessors". As many have stated, including the architectural analysis of Paul Saussez[323], this is further evi-

---

321   *i.e Antoine d'Hautpoul's testament.*
322   *i.e. the Eglise Sainte Marie-Madeleine (Church of Saint Mary Magdalene) of Rennes-le-Château, where Saunière would later serve as a priest.*
323   *Paul J. Saussez, « Le Tombeau des Seigneurs » ("The Tomb of the Lords"), published*

dence of the existence of a crypt underneath the church – although a crypt which apparently no-one now knows how to enter.

However, in Henri d'Hautpoul's time, when its entrance was still accessible, such a crypt would have posed no difficulties for performing mortuary rites in the framework of the Cult of the Dead. On the contrary, the place was well hidden; the corpses incurred no risk of being discovered, so the Franciscans would have had lee-way to indulge in their favourite mortuary rites without being disturbed...

Henri's will is further confirmation that the Hautpoul family was devoted specifically to the Franciscans of Limoux. In his will, he, too, asks for requiem masses to be said by this congregation for a period of one year. He adds that these are to ensure the rest of his soul, but somewhat curiously does not add here the total amount that he bequeaths to them. It means that such detail will be found in another part of the document, or another document altogether, though this latter option is less likely as it would not have formed part of the will and would thus come without the legal power a will can execute.

Stranger still is the fact that Henri mentions two other types of masses that need to be said in his favour: both are celebrated in the church of Rennes, the first by the priest of the village, Jean Varnat, and the other mass by a priest residing in the village, by the name of Deydiès. It means that in 1695, there were at least two priests present in this miniscule village. This is truly remarkable, given its small size and the near ruinous state of the church. The village only had about 300 souls to cater for (nevertheless, almost ten times the present population!) and it is clear that few people from neighbouring villages would feel any need to climb the hill (and definitely not in winter!) to celebrate mass in a ruined church. So there must have been another reason why two priests were resident there. One possibility is that there were so many mortuary masses to be said that the task could not possibly be accomplished by only one priest – which is something of an echo of the life of Saunière himself, who also said that, on occasion, he received so many mortuary masses that he had to involve other priests in fulfilling the requests.

There is another possibility, which may seem odd to suggest, but which we will nevertheless offer: what if the Franciscans of Limoux had displaced

by Editions Arkeos, 2003. Refer also to the exclusive interview given by Paul Saussez about his book, and published by the staff of the RennesleChâteau.com website: « Paul Saussez Présente 'Le Tombeau des Seigneurs' » ("Paul Saussez Presents: The Tomb of the Lords"). Location: http://www.renneslechateau.com/francais/saussez1.htm

the cemetery they cherished so much to Rennes-le-Château? In Limoux, all profits of the burial rights went to the Dominicans and no-one was allowed to be buried in the Franciscans' cemetery. So why not change the location of their cemetery, away from the prying eyes of the Dominicans? It is at least a possibility and it could explain – although there is no evidence for this suggestion as yet – why the Hautpoul family wanted, no matter what, to have the Franciscans taking care of their souls. Furthermore, it would mean that the local lords of Rennes would not even have to displace themselves (or their mortal remains) to receive the Mortuary Rite. When we consult Voltaire, he notes that, in the case of the Lords of St. Mesmin and the penitent Franciscans of Orleans[324], there is no specific requirement that the Rite needs to be performed on the premises of the monastery.

Let us scroll forward in time, to François d'Hautpoul, husband of Marie de Nègre d'Ables, who died in 1753 and who desired that his body be buried in the Franciscan monastery of Limoux. It cannot be stated for certain, but it seems quite clear that the Dominicans would have objected to this. Still, to quote Paul Saussez, it is known what happens next: François d'Hautpoul paid the Dominicans and was then buried on their premises, in the church of Saint Martin de Limoux, in a secret chapel dedicated to Saint Sebastian. A "secret chapel" indeed, for according to Saussez, there is no such chapel in the church of Saint Martin, though he adds that this may be located *"under the lane which skirts the church on the left, where some think that there are still remains."*

Anyway, we are certain that the Hautpouls did have a very clear preference for the Franciscan Cult of the Dead over its Dominican version. They did resort to the services of the Dominicans for their rites, yet only did so when they had no other choice, at a very late time (1753), and probably because by then their tomb in Rennes-le-Château (the "Tomb of the Lords") was already blocked[325]. Therefore, nothing forbids us to think that the Hautpouls could have continued to receive their favourite Mortuary Rites in secret, underneath the church of Rennes-le-Château, in a crypt built and prepared long before, for which need they would have displaced their dear Franciscan friars from Limoux to Rennes. However, such a scheme

---

324   « *Seigneur de Saint-Mesmin contre Pères Cordeliers Pénitents d'Orléans* » ("*Trial of the Lord of Saint-Mesmin versus the Franciscan Penitents of Orleans*") 1534, a manuscript housed in the Bibliothèque du roi de France (Library of the King of France), n°1770. This precious document is commented upon by Voltaire in his Philosophical Dictionary [1764], in the article entitled "Vision".
325   See the following note.

could only have lasted until 1740 at the latest[326], that is to say, not long before the French Revolution[327], when the Monastery of the Friars Minor of Limoux was destroyed.

But back in time: re-reading Henri d'Hautpoul's testament, one name that is mentioned retains our interest: Saunière. When the act was written, on 24th April 1695, the notary made sure that a sufficient number of witnesses were present, so that any chance that the will might be contested was less likely. This list includes one "Mr. Antoine Saunière, master apothecary". Is this an ancestor of Bérenger Saunière? We think so, for amongst the other witnesses, we also find a "Gabriel Captier", and a descendant of his becomes embroiled in the story of the discovery of parchments at the end of the 19th century – the discovery that is identified as the beginning of the mystery of Rennes-le-Château and the wealth of the priest.

If this were the case, then the story of the mystery of Rennes-le-Château did not originate from out of nowhere at the end of the 19th century, but had its roots within the Hautpoul family, and was "resurrected" by Saunière two centuries later. Also, we note that Henri himself expected to receive the Mortuary Rite and, for this purpose, transferred money to the Franciscans. At that time, both the Hautpoul family and the locals knew about the existence of the crypt underneath the church of Rennes, and that this crypt served as the resting place of the family. Over the course of two centuries, knowledge or a rumour could have made its way through the Saunière family – and the Captier family – before Bérenger Saunière either stumbled upon it by accident, or solved the mystery – and in the process, created one of his own.

Once Saunière had found the parchments, he had in his possession the 1644 testament of François-Pierre d'Hautpoul, of which we unfortunately do not have a copy, as well as the 1696 testament of Henri d'Hautpoul. In our opinion, the most probable possibility implies that Henri's testament not only contained a "public" act (the transcript of which we have provided), but a "private" act as well. This second act would thus have had the purpose of specifying the rates of the "offerings" given to the Franciscans, of mentioning the nature of the rites performed, as well as the necessary

---

326   According to Paul Saussez, 1740 is the most probable date for the blocking of the Tomb of the Lords' entrance (i.e the entrance of the crypt located underneath the church of Rennes-le-Château) to have occurred.
327   The French Revolution began in 1789, and lasted until 1799, when Napoléon Bonaparte took power.

invocations[328] that were to be said.

In short, these two testaments (Henri's and François') would not have been of any monetary value to Saunière, but may have contained key details about the Mortuary Rite and specifically the organisation of the Cult of the Dead… and certain practices occurring in nearby Limoux, practices which, two centuries after Henri's death, may still have been in operation in that town. Did Saunière see in these documents a possibility to step into the footsteps of his predecessors and become a priest of the Cult of the Dead?

After the discovery of the parchments, Saunière's first act was, according to Gérard de Sède[329], to *"move […] the stone placed at the foot of the altar"*. According to de Sède, *"one side of the stone was sculpted, and represented two knights"*. This apparently encouraged Saunière to think that he was on the right track, as he, still according to de Sède, ordered *"that an opening was made that was one meter deep"* and then told his people *"it was time for lunch, and remained alone in the church"*. For de Sède, when the opening had been made, Saunière found two Merovingian skeletons. But in our opinion, what Saunière found was the entrance to the crypt – or at least, "an" entrance to the crypt. That entrance was probably blocked by a tomb containing two skeletons buried according to the ritual, the purpose of which was to indicate the nature of the place.

Saunière thus gained access to the tombs of the Hautpoul family and may have discovered an alien world, unlike anything that we would expect to find within a purely Christian setting, but which would have been common for human remains that had been subjected to the mortuary rite[330]. Even de Sède, in his conclusion that Saunière had found Merovingian skeletons, states that the bodies showed the characteristics of a ritual trepana-

---

328 *This is only logical: the intensity and scope of the inner wars opposing the Dominican nuns of Prouilhe to the Franciscan monks of Limoux about "burial rights" and "burial money" (300 years of uninterrupted, unmitigated conflict) suffices to prove the specifically religious importance that "mortuary offerings" had in the eyes of those penitents. Competition must have been all the fiercer, in the present case, since lords don't die everyday…Therefore, the corpses of these "distinguished customers" were very much sought after: 2,000 pounds (such is the rate of the offering that Antoine d'Hautpoul, the brother of Henri, had ascribed in his will to the Franciscans of Limoux and of Notre-Dame de Marceille so as to have himself buried in their church) is no small amount of money! Let us add that such a rate was most certainly not chosen at random: it must have been, without a doubt, the price asked by the Franciscans themselves in exchange for their so-called "salvation of the soul".*

329 *Gérard de Sède, « Le Trésor Maudit de Rennes-le-Château », J'ai Lu editions (1972). For an English translation, refer to "The Accursed Treasure of Rennes-le-Chateau", DEK Publishing, 2001, translated by Bill Kersey.*

330 *We are specifically referring to mortuary rites in the tradition of the rituals performed by the Chaldeans (especially by the Magi) on the corpses of the deceased.*

tion. Their skull was opened with an instrument, so that their soul could escape. Such practice is of course part of a cult of the dead, particularly the Arian[331] rites.

Such discoveries, as strange as they appear to us, are nevertheless not unique, for Father Ancé and the archaeologist Bertrand Louis Polla have found similar tombs elsewhere in the region, in Limoux, to be specific. These tombs also showed the signs of an unknown mortuary rite. André Douzet has compiled the writings of these two researchers and notes that the terrain in which their discoveries were made was situated between Notre-Dame de Marceille and the Franciscans' monastery. It involved the discovery of several "human skeletons", some of which were "almost complete". But the curious aspect of this discovery was that each skull was intact, except for the trepanation performed on them. Such consistency obviously betrays a ritual aspect of this practice. Father Ancé's notes additionally mention that the few weapons unearthed there were all strangely set down on the ground outside of the burial pits, that is to say that they were lying down against the graves...[332]

---

331 "Arians", the disciples of the heretical priest Arius of Alexandria (256-336 BC) who denied the sanctity of marriage, negated the Holy Trinity and the divinity of Jesus. "Arians" was the most common name given to the Manicheans during Antiquity, and it was sometimes still used during the Middle Ages in some regions to refer to the Cathars and other heretics, for the same reasons. Eusebius of Nicomedia, who baptised Constantine after his death, and savagely assassinated all the Christians in the Emperor's family, was an Arian. Meanwhile, the Visigoths all became Arians too, after their mass conversion by Goth and Arian Bishop Wulfila (311-383), and their subsequent migrations hugely contributed to entrench the dualistic heresy across Europe.

332 We are probably in the presence of the type of mortuary ritual that was described on the strangely written text of the epitaph engraved on Marie de Negre d'Ables de Blanchefort's stele. Indeed, a series of peculiarities (small letters, obvious orthographical mistakes that would not have been tolerated if they were not intentional) allowed some researchers of the Rennes-le-Château enigma to discover the following phrase: "MORTÉPÉE" hidden inside Marie's epitaph. At first some believed it was a contraction of « Morte Épée » ("Dead Sword" in French), which did not really make sense. However, it now appears that « Mortépée » was merely the juxtaposition of « Mort » + « épée » ("Corpse" + "Sword"). The presence of this hidden message on Marie de Negre d'Ables' tombstone would thus serve as a powerful reminder to indicate that her corpse had received the Arian (i.e Chaldean-Manichean) mortuary rites! However, though it is certainly true that Marie de Nègre d'Ables received the Mortuary Rites, it was probably not from Bigou, as we will see, since he had to flee Rennes-le-Château to escape the anti-clerical fury of the French Revolution. Being part of the attempt at covering-up Saunière's activities and distracting attention away from him, such allegations about "coded" tombstones are quite recent, and have no basis whatsoever in history. Furthermore, Marie de Nègre d'Ables' original stele, and therefore epitaph, was probably not the same as the version that later surfaced in Eugene Stublein's book "Pierres

When Saunière entered the crypt of Rennes, he was thus confronted with hard evidence of the mortuary rite. He had the testaments in his possession. He saw first-hand how the mortuary rite had been performed on the former lords of his village. He realised that there was a powerful connection with the convent of the Franciscans in Limoux. He knew that this type of rite was expensive. If he did not yet know already, he would soon find out that the cult of the dead was not dead at all, but still practiced, both locally and elsewhere.

Saunière most likely informed his superior, Mgr. Billard, about his discovery – or perhaps Billard had even asked Saunière to commence his search[333]. Billard had already tried and succeeded in taking possession of the sanctuary of Notre-Dame de Marceille, an exercise that involved a circle of people that Saunière knew, either directly or indirectly, via abbé Boudet, priest of neighbouring Rennes-les-Bains.

There are a few possible scenarios, but all revolve around one core fact, which is that with the discovery of the crypt of the Hautpoul, Saunière entered, or was fully accepted, within the group of priests inside the bishopric of Carcassonne that were involved with the Cult of the Dead. And Saunière became a mortuary magician, following in the footsteps of Tobit.

Gravées du Languedoc", *a book which has never been shown to exist. Yet these allegations are useful here insofar as they reveal how the modern manipulators (notably Philippe de Chérisey) had their attention firmly fixed on Limoux and the Cult of the Dead. The fact that these words ("Mortépée": "Corpse" + "Sword") also seem to appear in two other parchments allegedly discovered by Saunière (though such a discovery has never been proven) and which contain a montage of several Biblical passages mentioning Mary Magdalene (i.e the patron saint of all penitents) and her "burial ointments", thus hardly seems coincidental. Although these particular parchments are certainly part of the "additional layer" spread on Saunière's mystery in recent times (mostly during the 1960s), we have to acknowledge that this feature (the use of the phrase Mortépée) nevertheless does not make them less valuable sources of clues about the cult of the dead itself and its hijacking of the meaning of certain Biblical texts. These fabricated parchments also provide us with indications about who practiced the cult of the dead, with the exception that they were part of an effort to "clean up" Saunière's reputation, to transform him into a suitable character for use in subsequent media campaigns.*
* *Gérard de Sède, « L'Or de Rennes, ou la vie insolite de Béranger Saunière curé de Rennes-le-Château », Editions Julliard, Paris, 1967.*
** *Pierre Jarnac, « Histoire du trésor de Rennes-le-Château » (The Story of the Rennes-le-Château Treasure), Editions Bélisane, Nice, 1985.*
*** *Jean Markale, « Rennes-le-Château et l'énigme de l'or maudit », 1985 (pp. 108 and following).*
333 *As we will see, His Eminence Monseigneur Billard was, after all, an expert in Simony, which is a means to finance the Cult of the Dead (see notes 222-223 on Simon Magus and Simony), so that he simply could not ignore the importance of the mortuary cult material that Saunière had found.*

Chapter 9

A golden cemetery

Once Saunière had made his discovery[334], his life changed quickly – and so did his conduct, in the worst sense of the word. The first thing Saunière did was to attack one particular tomb. As Gérard de Sède[335] wrote, there were two tombstones placed against the church wall, *"marking the sepulchre of Marie de Nègre d'Ables, wife of François d'Hautpoul, Marquis of Blanchefort, Lord of Rennes"*. The priest attacked the tomb, erasing the inscription and the epitaph, apparently relocating the stone and even removing the mortal remains of its occupant. However, this is only one opinion as to what Saunière actually did. Paul Saussez believes that Saunière did not relocate it, but merely removed any means of identifying Marie de Nègre d'Ables's tomb, and that he also removed another tombstone, that of Marie's son, Joseph d'Hautpoul, who died in 1739, "about whom we do know that his tomb was located in the parish cemetery, right next to the large cross."

Such actions – removing or altering tombstones – reveal that Saunière had indeed discovered something of interest involving the Hautpoul family and the most likely source is the infamous testaments. Let us not forget that Marie de Nègre d'Ables was the wife of François d'Hautpoul, who could be buried neither with the Franciscans, nor in the crypt of the church of Rennes (which had been blocked in 1740, according to Paul Saussez). He

---

334   *According to René Descadeillas in his « Notice sur Rennes-le-Château et l'abbé Saunière » ("Note about Rennes-le-Château and abbé Saunière"), 1962, at that time Saunière chose to "let people say that he had found a treasure". The implication here is that it wasn't true, at least in the traditional monetary sense, and we share his opinion. On the other hand, from a theological point of view, saints' relics are traditionally called a "treasure" by the priest of the church to which they are entrusted, and relics (i.e body parts or bones of sometimes strange, often penitent "saints") happen to also be used as tools in the mortuary rites of the Cult of the Dead…*

335   *Gérard de Sède, « L'Or de Rennes / Le trésor maudit de Rennes-le-Château ou la vie insolite de Bérenger Saunière, Curé de Rennes-le-Château » (The Gold of Rennes / The Accursed Treasure of Rennes-le-Château or the Strange Life of Bérenger Saunière, Priest of Rennes-le-Château):*
1) Julliard, 4ᵗʰ trimester of 1967, 215 pages,
2) Le Cercle du Nouveau Livre d'Histoire (New History Book's Society), 17ᵗʰ January 1968, 181 pages [limited edition, each copy is numbered],
3) J'ai lu, collection « L'Aventure Mystérieuse » (The Mysterious Adventure), 1968, 178 pages. For the English translation, refer to "The Accursed Treasure of Rennes-le-Chateau", DEK Publishing, 2001, translated by Bill Kersey.

thus had to pay the "mortuary offering" to the Dominicans of the church of Saint Martin, who then placed his mortal coil in an enigmatic subterranean chapel. Apparently, his widow refused to be buried with the Dominicans, and thus there remained only one option: a burial in the cemetery of Rennes-le-Château.

Just before the French Revolution, her confessor, Antoine Bigou, deposited the testaments in the column of the altar. Fearing that he would never return (he didn't) and deciding, like his archbishop, to flee to Spain, he would no doubt have left some indication for potential successors that the church had a crypt and perhaps even that Marie de Nègre d'Ables wanted to be buried there. Such a scenario, of course, relies on the existence of a friendly priest who, first of all, would have to find the testaments and Bigou's instructions to give the body of Marie de Nègre d'Ables the proper burial. In this scenario, a specific sum of money would have been set aside – hidden – so that the mortuary rite could be administered and as such, it is not so astonishing to find that Saunière had the body of Marie de Nègre d'Ables and her son, Joseph, moved to an unknown location[336].

According to the accounts, it seems that in the effort to accomplish this task, Saunière destroyed the tombstone. Many interpret this "destruction" as Saunière removing certain important elements that, to him, were the key to his wealth – suggesting he had removed any clues that would enable others to stumble upon "the treasure" themselves. Indeed, the inscriptions on this tombstone have led to numerous interpretations, including some that argue that it contains geographical information on the whereabouts of "the treasure". But this seems unlikely for several reasons. For one, many attest that Bigou coded this tombstone, but Paul Saussez states that the inscription on the tombstone largely post-dated the death of Marie de Nègre d'Ables in 1781. Of course, the key question is by how many years, for Bigou only left the area in 1792. If later, who worked on this tombstone?

Saussez implies that it is much more recent than 1781. Indeed, what if certain inscriptions date from Saunière's time, and what if they are by his own hand? Rather than destroying a tombstone, did he create another? Did he create the one that appeared in the *Bulletin of the Société des Études Scientifiques de l'Aude*[337], dated 1905? Rather than destroy it, Saunière may

---

336   *See note 333 for more details. It appears that if Marie de Nègre d'Ables did indeed receive the mortuary rites she longed for, they were more likely to have been performed by Saunière than by Bigou, since Bigou had to flee to Spain to escape the anti-religious claws of the French Revolution.*

337   *This « Bulletin de la Société d'Etudes Scientifiques de l'Aude » (SESA), volume XVII,*

merely have altered or changed one tombstone with another, and few people would have been the wiser.

René Descadeillas[338] notes that on 21st June 1891, during the celebration of the First Communion, Saunière *"had a statue of the Virgin erected, which he called Notre-Dame de Lourdes, on a piece of land that belonged to the council, located in front of his church's door, and [that] he blessed it"*.

This constituted a clever trick on Saunière's part, who immediately took advantage of the situation by asking *"the town council to allow him to utilize this piece of land, to have it enclosed at his expense and to erect religious monuments there."*[339] The triangular area became a meeting place for those worshippers to gather before and after services. But the location is also strategically located, for it acted as a key location through which Saunière could control access to the cemetery.

From the Mayor's perspective, he was not particularly appreciative of Saunière's initiative. For example, as early as 15th February 1891, the town council refused to cede ownership of the site and questioned the priest's intentions. But as the site was already an enclosed area, the mayor did not have too many options left, and only stated that the priest was indeed allowed to refurbish the area, but that he was not allowed to construct any buildings there. He also told Saunière that he required a copy of the key, for *"it is not tolerable for us not to be able to enter this public space"*.

Despite such conditions, Saunière had what he had aimed for, because the land in front of the church would function as his rampart. Indeed,

---

was written by M. Elie Tisseyre and published in 1906 under the following title: « Excursion du 25 juin 1905 à Rennes-Le-Château » ("Excursion to Rennes-le-Château on 25th June 1905"). However the authenticity of his particular "SESA" account is highly controversial and debated. When we contacted the SESA so as to have more details about this crucial document, and possibly even get a copy of the original, we were told that they did not have it in their records, nor did they remember having it at any moment. To put it mildly, this fact does not exactly lend credence to Elie Tysseire or whomever really wrote it (since it may well be yet another modern fabrication), let alone the contents of the bulletin itself.

338 René Descadeillas, « Notice sur Rennes-le-Château et l'abbé Saunière » (Notice on Rennes-le-Château and abbé Saunière) (1962). This famous book was subjected to several modifications before being finally included in his master work « Mythologie du trésor de Rennes », the full reference of which is: René Descadeillas, « Mythologie du Trésor de Rennes: Histoire Véritable de l'abbé Saunière, Curé de Rennes-le-Château » ("Mythology of the Treasure of Rennes-le-Château : the Real Story of Abbé Saunière, priest of Rennes-le-Château"), in « Mémoires de la Société des Arts et des Sciences de Carcassonne » (Research Bulletin of the Arts and Science Society of Carcassonne), 1971-1972 years, 4th series, volume VII, 2nd part; published in 1974. See note 56 for more biographical details about this distinguished researcher.

339 To quote again from René Descadeillas.

while the municipality may have had a key, in reality, once Saunière locked the door at night, he had the area all to himself. We also note that the iron gate that currently locks the entrance to the cemetery was another installation by Saunière; in short, two gates, both locked, stood between the village and the cemetery. And Saunière had both keys. It meant that he could do as he pleased during the night, without anyone being any the wiser. The wall we see around the modern cemetery was yet another of Saunière's additions, meaning that he was fencing off the few remaining sides from which anyone could potentially spy on his activities.

There will, of course, be those who believe we have read too much into the efforts of Saunière and that he merely used money (of whatever origin) to upgrade the cemetery and village for the welfare of the villagers. But it is on record, according to René Descadeillas[340], that the mayor, annoyed by Saunière's persistence, finally agreed to his request that the cemetery would only be open to the public *"on Sundays and holy days"* and this *"from sunrise to sunset"*. It means that for six days per week, the cemetery was Saunière's private property, locked to anyone but himself. And shortly afterwards, he began to desecrate some of the tombs, for which the villagers soon began to make official complaints against him[341].

But it was something else that really upset the authorities. Saunière, against the express desire of the council, constructed, in a corner of the public land in front of the church and next to the gate to the cemetery, a small building. At first, the mayor did not react and Saunière took advantage of his silence to install his library and his office inside. Several researchers have pointed out that this building sits in a strategic location: right next to the cemetery's entrance. Why did Saunière not place his library and office inside the presbytery where he lived? Why did he install it so far away? Indeed, from its windows, he could see the garden... and also the cemetery's gate and anyone who entered. Like a guard dog lying in wait at the door, Saunière sat in wait at the cemetery's door.

But this was not the main problem, which was that Saunière refused to give a copy of the small building's key to the mayor. And the mayor had a specific interest in this building. On the other hand, the building must

---

340 *Refer to the Archives départementales de l'Aude (Archives of the Aude Department), "O" series, "Rennes" section, for the source of the document quoted by René Descadeillas. René Descadeillas, « Notice sur Rennes-le-Château et l'abbé Saunière » (Notice on Rennes-le-Château and abbé Saunière) (1962).*
341 *To our knowledge, at least two of these complaints were lodged before the Rennes-le-Château town council, on 12th March and 14th March 1895, respectively.*

have also had another use for Saunière than simply a guard post, since as we can note today, it is slightly elevated, requiring a climb up some steps to get in. This is because there is a large cavity underneath it, containing a cistern full of water. And the mayor had an interest in this water cistern, because if there was a fire in the village, he might need to have access to its water. And this is exactly what happened on 14th July 1895, when two or three buildings near the church caught fire and the villagers needed to get to the cistern. The fire brigade arrived but Saunière was not at home, so they broke into the building to gain access to it.

Upon his return, Saunière was apparently furious, even making an official complaint, even though it was he who should have left a key with the mayor, specifically for such emergencies. Still, it is clear that the fire brigade did not appear to have found anything out of the ordinary inside the library, or with the cistern: it seems that there was no secret passage, or tunnel, just a cistern filled with water.

But that, in and of itself, may be the crux of the matter. The Cult of the Dead required the presence of water, for the bodies of the deceased were to be plunged in water as a part of the "baptism of the dead". Did Saunière use the cistern for this purpose? Perhaps the reason why he did not want anyone to touch it, why he was so upset when he discovered that the fire brigade had broken into it, was that the water may have been "blessed"? That perhaps, he had "charged" the water with certain heretical, or pagan rituals, and the mundane intervention of the fire brigade had destroyed its "aura".

Saunière definitely was greatly upset when he discovered that the fire brigade had broken into his library. As soon as 15th July 1895, i.e on the very day after the fire, he filed a complaint for "violation of the home", which he deposited with the gendarmes. This angered the mayor, who retaliated soon after. The municipal council decided, in a statement dated 20th July 1895, that the priest's interest in the cemetery was for "nefarious" purposes. So they ordered Saunière to relinquish the keys to the cistern, as well as to the area in front of the church. From that moment onwards, Saunière was no longer the sole ruler over the cemetery and could rightly fear that his night-time activities would one day – soon – be discovered.

But he was an intelligent man and decided to bide his time. He gave in to the desires of the council and cleaned up the area around the church. He then spent 20,000 francs to restore the presbytery and the church, and the latter, of course, won him great credit points with the local villagers. By 1897, his relationship with the villagers and the council was much improved… and once again he turned his attentions to the cemetery. At that time that he was finally in a position to build the surrounding wall and the ossuary, as René Descadeillas tells us.

Meanwhile, Saunière was taking advantage of his newfound popularity to dislodge all of the graves, and a vast amount of the deceased's bones simply vanished in the process. Saunière obviously wanted to make room in his cemetery, and at that time he was no longer shy about it. He continuously lobbied for a petition to be brought before the town council, as Descadeillas[342] puts it, *"considering all the embellishments he had made in the church and the presbytery"*. Such a move had no other purpose than to authorise him to modify the distribution of the cemetery's grave allotments as he pleased, to build new funerary monuments, and to free up as much space as possible there…

Records of the town council's deliberations from 24th July 1899 and 1st and 19th April 1900 make it clear that Saunière had but one goal: to appropriate the cemetery for his sole use… and to reserve certain plots to himself.

The above named documents, of which Laurent Buchholtzer kindly sent us copies, hardly leave any doubt as to what Saunière intended to do with the cemetery. In these town council records, we discovered that the mayor gave to *"M. Saunière Bérenger, priest of Rennes-le-Château, a perpetual concession of 6 m² of terrain in the cemetery of the community."* [343] The location, it specifies, is there to receive the tomb of the priest and those of his potential successors. However, it seems that this was merely a pretext for Saunière to gain a foothold in the cemetery. In step two, the priest requests and obtains indeed that *"the entire surface area of the cemetery [be] divided into two main sections: one, which will comprise [approximately] a quarter of the total area, will be used exclusively for special tomb burials […] and will be located in the* western *part of the cemetery. The other section, which will contain the three remaining quarters of the cemetery's total surface area, and which will be located in the* eastern *part of the said cemetery, will be reserved for ordinary burials."* [344]

Through this ploy, Saunière was able to gain control over a quarter of the cemetery. Furthermore, it should be noted that these "special tomb

---

342 René Descadeillas, « Notice sur Rennes-le-Château et l'abbé Saunière » (Notice on Rennes-le-Château and abbé Saunière) (1962).

343 Records of the Rennes-le-Château town council. These particular deliberations are dated 24th July 1899.

344 Records of the Rennes-le-Château town council. These particular deliberations are dated 1st April 1900.

burials" mentioned in the document were related to specific concessions, reserved for 15 years, 30 years or eternity. The first ones costed 6 francs per meter, the second 12 francs and the latter 25 francs. No wonder therefore that the mayor remarked that there is no-one in the village who can afford such sums and hence *"not a single request for any [type of] concession other than this one [other than the free concessions asked for by the villagers] has ever been made. [That is the reason why] a tariff for concessions has never been established and [why] there is no use in creating one now."* [345]

This enigmatic proposal has received scant attention from other researchers who, while they may certainly see a ploy in Saunière's approach… fail to ask "for what purpose?" The answer is simple. Indeed, one quarter of the cemetery would no longer be for the villagers, but for rich people, from elsewhere, whom he would be able to bury there… and for whom he would perform the Cult of the Dead. Their "Mortuary Offering" would more than adequately cover the price of the concession and the remainder of the money was listed in Saunière's accounts as "money for masses".

There is one final intriguing detail in the correspondence between Saunière and the mayor. When addressing the tombs in this quarter of the cemetery, the mayor stipulates on behalf of the town council that *"funerary monuments may be erected on the ceded terrain, [but only] after the inscriptions and emblems that are proposed to be engraved have been submitted for the mayor's approval."* [346]

It is almost as if the mayor expects to see certain strange engravings on these tombs. If so, was this because the mayor realised what Saunière was doing? Or had the mayor seen strange engravings appearing in the cemetery already, like the one on the tombstone of Marie de Nègre d'Ables? Indeed, it seems that while Saunière was "shuffling" the tombs in the cemetery some years previously, he left certain enigmatic signs on the tombs, which apparently eluded any interpretation that the villagers might have been able to give to them. Within this context, the mayor's request to give his approval in the matter is quite understandable.

1908, the trial and some unused documents

From 1899 onwards, Saunière extended his marketing area and contacted some religious hospitals and monasteries in Normandy, Flanders and the

---

345 *Records of the Rennes-le-Château town council. These particular deliberations are dated 1ˢᵗ April 1900.*
346 *Records of the Rennes-le-Château town council. These particular deliberations are dated 19ᵗʰ April 1900.*

North of France. There is no argument about this fact; they are all listed in his accounts. Today, not all of Saunière's accounts survive, and most are in the possession of several private parties. But René Descadeillas[347], in the early 1960s, had access to most, if not all of them, and thus noted that Saunière's donations largely came from France, but *"also from the Rhine region, from Switzerland, and from the North of Italy."* It is difficult not to interpret this as evidence that Saunière had penetrated the centuries-old network of the Cult of the Dead, which had been a prominent feature of the specific areas from which Saunière received his "offerings".

But it may come as a surprise to hear that at his trial, Saunière did not deny this, for he admitted that his fortune came largely from *"tariffed mortuary penitences"*, i.e. he had fixed prices which people could pay if they wanted him to perform a penitence for the dead. And this is also borne out by witness statements and certain details of the procedure. If this information is not largely public knowledge or well-known, it is because it has been – in our opinion – purposefully withheld, to spin certain theories that are largely absurd in scope, but which have nevertheless guaranteed the success of *The Da Vinci Code*[348], among others; one money spinner has been turned into another.

No-one denies that Saunière was rich. He was able to buy land and have a large villa built, surrounded by beautiful gardens. And it is clear that these constructions were a luxury to complement which he continually ordered best cases of fine wine and other luxury items. Our priest lived a good life, in fact, better than the one lived by his bishop. We can readily imagine how a wealthy aristocratic family might have a family member who becomes a priest, and so make him a large allowance, so that he may live in a lifestyle to which he is accustomed. But Saunière's family was not wealthy; he did not inherit money from a rich uncle, or aunt, or grandfather. People were confused as to his sources of revenue… then, as well as now. Already accused of defiling tombs, it is clear that Saunière might easily fall foul of his superiors.

When Mgr. Billard died in 1902, he was replaced by Paul-Félix Beuvain de Beauséjour, who opened the hunt in 1908. On 15th January 1909, he tried to remove Saunière to another parish. Saunière refused, stating he would

---

347 *René Descadeillas, « Notice sur Rennes-le-Château et l'abbé Saunière » (Notice on Rennes-le-Château and abbé Saunière) (1962). This famous writing was subjected to several modifications before being finally included in his master work « Mythologie du trésor de Rennes ». See note 56 for more biographical details about this distinguished researcher.*
348 *Dan Brown, "The Da Vinci Code", published by Doubleday Books, 2003.*

rather quit the priesthood than move. But de Beauséjour is somehow able to "force" Saunière to remain a priest and summoned him repeatedly to Carcassonne, to discuss the situation. Saunière was not really interested, though he was, in absentia, ordered to cease and desist from "soliciting masses". On 27th May 1910, de Beauséjour demanded that Saunière be heard in front of an ecclesiastical tribunal, but Saunière failed to attend the hearing. He was thus condemned in absentia, but then obtained that the trial be reviewed, and took Canon Huguet as his defence attorney. The bishopric wanted to see the accounts. Today, we know that these contain the list of donations that Saunière received from monasteries and other religious institutions in exchange for masses, or rather for Chaldean mortuary rituals. At the time, no-one knew where his money came from, though perhaps the bishop had his suspicions. And Saunière himself did his best to protect these accounts. He declined to attend the hearings, which meant that no-one could interview him.

Throughout the trial, Saunière behaved as obstinately as possible, on occasion presenting doctor's notes showing that he was too ill to attend a hearing (though apparently not too ill to go shopping in Limoux, with Marie Denarnaud), making sure throughout that he did not have to produce the accounts.

Some researchers have claimed that Saunière was condemned for trafficking in masses and that this is the be all and end all of the mystery. Indeed, Saunière continued to solicit masses after the interdiction[349] of

---

349 *According to a letter sent to Saunière by the Bishopric of Carcassonne and dated 18th December 1909, it appears that Saunière did not comply to Mgr. de Beauséjour's orders, and that requesting masses outside of the bishopric was the chief concern that Mgr. de Beauséjour had with him:*
"From the Bishopric of Carcassonne, 18th December, 1909.
M. l'abbé Saunière,
The Mother Superior of St. Joseph's Hospital, Pierre Larousse street no. 7, Paris, wrote to Monsignor [de Beauséjour], in order to ask him whether she could send you fees for masses in all confidence. You can easily guess which kind of answer we have given to her:
"Please abstain from continuing to make such donations, since we have no confidence whatsoever in the way that this priest fulfils requests for masses, which he obtains from wherever he can."
Monsignor is pained to see that you have carried on asking for fees for masses from outside the diocese. And still, you had promised and contended that you would no longer ask for such things except to him [the bishop], personally. This is how you keep your word.
His Highness is wondering whether his conscience doesn't make his duty to take efficient measures so as to bring an end to such deplorable behaviour.
With my sincerest salutations, H. Rodière [Vicar General]"

1909. Huguet apologised on Saunière's behalf, but stated that he had soon afterwards stopped all such solicitation and had thus complied with the bishop's order. Saunière was nevertheless condemned again, officially on charges of "trafficking in masses", "excessive spending", and "disobedience" towards his new bishop. He received a rather small punishment for these "crimes", namely a retreat of ten days, and within a certain period of time, he accepted.[350]

But the court case had revealed that Saunière had spent vast amounts of money, but had not shown how he had come by this money. The court – contrary to what the sceptics argue – did not accept that Saunière received this money from selling masses, at least not "ordinary masses" that most priests were paid to perform. Saunière tried to claim that he got the money from selling postcards, a lottery, a raffle, guided tours of the village, as well as donations through his brother Alfred. But the total sum of all those efforts still fell far short (by tens of thousands of francs) of what the court knew he had spent.

Realising the court would not relax in its demand, Saunière claimed that he had no detailed accounts (a lie, as we know now) and that the bishop should not be afraid to be faced with an insolvent parish priest, which would force the bishopric to pay out substantial amounts of money (potentially as much as 100,000 francs, if not 150,000 francs). Saunière informed the bishopric that he was solvent; he just was not a professional accountant and had not kept a log of all money he had received and had paid out.

Saunière spent approximately 200,000 francs on his buildings and refurbishments. In today's money, that is three million dollars. If we are to believe that Saunière received money from selling masses, this at a price of approximately 1 franc per mass, he would have required 200,000 people

---

350   *This condemnation was issued on 5th November 1910. The court then demanded of Saunière not only that he relinquish his accounting books to Mgr. de Beauséjour, but also that he go "to a religious retirement house so as to perform spiritual excercises there for a ten-day period". According to canon law, the choice of the location thus rested with Saunière's direct superior, i.e. Mgr. de Beauséjour, the Bishop of Carcassonne. Of all possible places, Mgr. de Beauséjour chose the Monastery of the Dominican nuns of Prouilhe as a location for Saunière's penitential retreat. His choice has to be understood in the broader context of the centuries-long power struggle between the Franciscan monks of Limoux and the Dominican nuns of Prouilhe, spawning a judicial fight that had resulted in the official recognition of a monopoly on "burial rights" in favour of the Sisters of Prouilhe, for the Rennes-le-Château region. Through his attempts to enlarge the "activity zone" of his traffic to the whole of France and beyond, Saunière had committed an offence both against the well-established Dominican monopoly on burial rights in the region, and the monastic custom which stipulates that the Cult of the Dead be an exclusively local activity.*

to send him one franc. Why people would choose to pay Saunière to say a mass for a deceased person, rather than ask a more local priest to do so, is a mystery the sceptics cannot explain. But if he was dealing in "mortuary masses", in the tradition of the Cult of the Dead, then it becomes an altogether easier case.

We know that the Mortuary Rite was very expensive. Let us suggest first that Saunière charged 1,000 francs for this service, which is actually not overly excessive. This would mean that he required only 200 donations over a period of, let's say ten years; that is twenty masses a year. If, however, Saunière charged 5,000 francs per service, he would only require forty people and only four donations per year. This is perfectly manageable... and just from a logical point of view, far more likely than 200,000 people from all over Europe giving him one franc.

Few people of course could pay 1,000 or 5,000 francs. But we know that Saunière wined and dined the "crème de la crème" of French society, a list which included counts and barons, people whose families, in previous centuries, had desired the Mortuary Rite... and may have asked Saunière to do as much for them now.

It is now quite obvious that Bérenger Saunière indulged in "trafficking in masses", though, in fact, this is merely a misnomer for what truly occurred: he was a minister in the "cult of the dead". The source of his wealth was simply the surcharge collected by him in exchange for performing Chaldean mortuary rites on the dead. This also explains why he collected much larger amounts of money than the usual price for masses of remembrance...

Saunière admitted it himself, and René Descadeillas bears witness of this confession, as in his *"Notice on Rennes-le-Château and abbé Saunière"* [351], we learn that Saunière had written "draft defence pleas" during his trial, and that these documents "were never produced" before the court. In these defence plea drafts, he mentioned several letters sympathetic to his cause, which he had received from a number of priests in the region. Most of them were advising him not only to never inform the bishopric of the source of these donations, but to never concede that he was even "receiving donations" [352]. And "donations" is the word they used. But what kind of

---

351   René Descadeillas, « Notice sur Rennes-le-Château et l'abbé Saunière » (Notice on Rennes-le-Château and abbé Saunière) (1962). This famous writing was subjected to several modifications before being finally included in his master work « Mythologie du trésor de Rennes ».

352   According to letters received by Saunière from Father Gazel, from the parish of Floure

"donations"? Descadeillas adds that during his trial, Saunière wrote in one of his drafts: *"Monsignor [the bishop] absolutely wants to know the source of all this money, which served me to construct all these buildings. [...] He cannot force me to divulge the names of my donors without wreaking trouble within certain families or households whose members have given to me, some hiding this from their husband, others from their children, or their heirs".*

Let us note immediately that such "trouble" would never have arisen if these families had paid one franc for a mass of remembrance. But, in fact, Saunière has worded this in such a way that clearly he is stating that he was taking money for Mortuary Rites: certain people being those who put money aside throughout their life, so that when they died, they would receive a specific Rite that would not only upset their family because they had set such money aside and hence was not part of the will, but also because the rite was "demonic" – pagan.

Equally, if Saunière had surrendered his accounts, the bishopric would have discovered from whence Saunière had received the money. If directly, they would have had detailed information about which families were involved in the cult of the dead. If indirectly, the trail would lead to certain religious hospitals that acted as intermediaries in testamentary transactions aimed at buying "salvation", whose local bishop could then demand to see their accounts. And whereas Saunière claimed that he was not a professional accountant, nor an institution, and hence was not required to keep detailed accounts (even though he did), there would be no such escape for religious institutions, unless their accounts might somehow be damaged by an unfortunate flood or accidental fire.

According to Gérard de Sède[353], Saunière had a private encounter with the bishop, which somehow seems to have been a confession – and admission of guilt:

"De Beauséjour: 'You live a far greater lifestyle than I do, and I desire that you give me a statement about the origins of your income, [which is] as sudden as it is abundant.'

---

and abbé Barthélémy Rouanet, priest of Bagès-les-Flots, in 1909 and 1910. Abbé Rouanet, who died in 1911, remained in constant contact with Saunière throughout his trial. See note 15 for further details.

353   Gérard de Sède, « L'Or de Rennes / Le trésor maudit de Rennes-le-Château ou la vie insolite de Bérenger Saunière, Curé de Rennes-le-Château » (The Gold of Rennes / The Accursed Treasure of Rennes-le-Château or the Strange Life of Bérenger Saunière, Priest of Rennes-le-Château).

And the priest replied: 'Unfortunately, Sir, you have asked me the single thing that I cannot reveal. Considerable sums have been given to me by great sinners whom, with the help of God, I have shown the way of Penitence. You must understand yourself that I would not like to, by giving their names, betray the secret of the confession.'

De Beauséjour: 'Agreed, I can understand your scruples. But if you have nothing to say about the origin of your income, at least enlighten me about what you did with it.'

Bérenger: 'I do not need to render an account about this, Sir. The donors have left me alone in my judgment as to what best use their money would have, for it is me personally who has been given this money, and not the Church.'"

We do not know whether this meeting ever occurred, or whether de Sède invented it, but if it did, it is clear that Saunière was not mincing words. He was saying what he did and in words that the bishop should have well understood. Whether de Beauséjour did or not, is not clear. Perhaps he was indeed totally unfamiliar with the details of the Cult of the Dead and when Saunière was speaking about "penitence", he was speaking in code, referring not to the normal, every-day sacrament, but instead to the Mortuary Rite. And yet the fact that the bishop chose to enforce the judgment of the ecclesiastical court by sending Saunière to the Monastery of Prouilhe, provides us with a hint to the contrary. It is entirely possible that he was not only perfectly aware of the gruesome mortuary rites that were the source of Saunière's wealth, but that he also knew that by practicing them, Saunière was violating the monopoly held by the Dominicans of Prouilhe on burial money in the region.

While commenting on this episode, de Sède added that "the bishop could have retorted that by inciting other people to do penitence, his visitor (Saunière) certainly had a lot of nerve." However, such an analysis squarely ignores the very real possibility that by using the word "penitence", Saunière was actually referring to the price paid for the Cult of the Dead.

Indeed, it was the Mortuary Rite, and not the normal sacrament, that was paid to the individual priest (or monastery), and not to the Church. And it is precisely this point that Saunière emphasised: the money was his, not the Church's, for the money was given for a service that he, but not the Church, could perform. And that is why people were willing to pay dearly, rather than the usual 1 franc for a mass of remembrance that the Church offered.

The Magi

The Razès has several legends, including one which tells that Alaric, a Visigothic king, had the fortune of the "Three Kings". *"Between Alaric's Mountain and Mount Alaricou, the treasure of the Three Kings is hidden."* There is a legend about an Alaric treasure, though it is mostly linked with the sack of Rome by the Visigoths, who may have removed certain precious artefacts the Romans themselves had stolen from the Holy Land, and brought them to the Razès. Driving on the A65, in the area of Carcassonne, drivers are told that on the southern side of the motorway is "Alaric's Mountain", for some researchers a "clue" to the enigma. After all, why name a mountain after Alaric? Perhaps because his treasure is hidden there? Perhaps indeed…

But regardles of what certain authors have done with the legend, the fact remains that the area had a tradition, in which people believed that there was a deposit hidden somewhere, which belonged to the "Three Kings". As a local, Saunière must have been familiar with this legend. But so what?

Gérard de Sède[354] wrote that he could consult Saunière's copy-book, and that this began in a curious manner. *"The frontispiece was covered with two drawings cut from the journal La Croix. The first shows three angels that take a child wrapped in a shroud, to heaven and is accompanied with the following explanation: 'the year 1891, carried into eternity with the fruit which is spoken about, below.' Below, one finds a drawing featuring the adoration of the Three Magi, with as explanation: 'Receive, O Lord, the gold, symbol of royalty.'*

These prints are all the more strange as the journal itself, written on the succeeding pages with a precise and steady hand, only commences in May 1901. […] But the year 1891 brought gold as fruit, and it is precisely when Saunière found the documents that would make him rich."

Though many may doubt de Sède's words, we should note that this copy-book has since been made public by Antoine Captier; in this instance, what de Sède wrote conforms to reality.

Saunière seems to single out 1891 as a specific year. We note how in the garden, he installed the statue of the Virgin Mary, underneath it adding "Mission 1891", yet another reference to 1891. And above, we can read "Penitence! Penitense!", a clear, though coded as it now seems, reference

---

354 *Gérard de Sède, « L'Or de Rennes / Le trésor maudit de Rennes-le-Château ou la vie insolite de Bérenger Saunière, Curé de Rennes-le-Château » (The Gold of Rennes / The Accursed Treasure of Rennes-le-Château or the Strange Life of Bérenger Saunière, Priest of Rennes-le-Château).*

that the discovery of 1891 started him on a mission, in which he would follow in the footsteps of Tobit and become a priest in the Cult of the Dead. And as late as 1901, he remembered this event, also linking it with gold… and the Three Magi, also known as "the Three Kings".

The Magi presented not merely gold, but also myrrh and incense. But this omission is not the most worrying aspect. Saunière has made certain modifications in the usual representation of the Epiphany, i.e. the revelation of Jesus Christ to the Three Magi, an event now celebrated on January 6th. Worryingly, the infant Jesus is dead, and covered by a shroud. This is clearly a "reinterpretation" of the story of Epiphany, where Jesus is very much alive… miraculously, for Herod allegedly wanted to have every newborn male murdered. This reinterpretation leaves us with the impression that the Magi are worshipping Jesus' shroud and his deceased body!

Rather bizarrely, Gérard de Sède[355] states that the secret cache of Rennes *"is associated with chthonic images: the gold of Rennes is the gold of the Dead".* This does not seem to be a throwaway line, for elsewhere, de Sède repeats it, when he is wondering about possible Cathar or Visigothic origins for the treasure of Rennes-le-Château. It suggests that de Sède had grasped the core of the enigma, but did not want to say as much, perhaps thinking that the morbid theme that underlined it would not make for a good read, or perhaps aware that no-one wanted to hear this morbid tale.

Next, de Sède emphasizes the parallel between Rennes-le-Château and Saunière's copy-book image, referring to Bethlehem, and the offerings of the Three Magi. He states that *"it seems that in Rennes, as in Bethlehem, the shepherds are the first to arrive at the cave".* Right now, let us note that there is some discrepancy about whether Jesus was born in a house, stable or cave… but that de Sède decides to go for a cave. He then states that, in Rennes, there was an old local legend, from the 17th century, well *"before Saunière, when [...] a shepherd had the dangerous privilege of laying his hands upon a mysterious treasure".* This shepherd was Ignace Pâris and, still according to de Sède, *"in the spring of the year 1645, Ignace Pâris, a young shepherd from Rennes, was searching for a lost ewe. Suddenly, he hears the animal bleating: it had fallen in a pit."* The shepherd descended into the opening and after walking a few metres in this "narrow tunnel", he discovered a cave, containing skeletons and tombs, which had obviously been there for several centuries. The floor of the cave was filled with offerings. It seems that the stories and landscapes described in the Bible were

355   *Ibid.*

constantly reinterpreted in Rennes-le-Château, moreover in a strange way! The cave or stable of Bethlehem, where Christ was born, had become, in the minds of the locals, a rather sinister cave, somewhere in the vicinity of Rennes-le-Château, a cave where corpses are waiting to receive presents from the shepherds...

The theme of the Three Magi appears regularly in the enigma of Saunière. Let us take as an example the case of Maurice Leblanc, a famous author who is often brought in as an ingredient of the mystery. The hero he created was Arsène Lupin. In his book *L'Aiguille Creuse* (The Hollow Needle)[356], he states that his hero arrives at the end of the quest and *was "directed towards a great triptych of Rogier de la Pasture, i.e. Van der Weyden, which represents the Three Magi. He folded open the shutter on the right-hand side and thus discovered a small door which he took by the handle."* And in this manner, his secret den, the "Hollow Needle", was entered.

We note many resemblances between this approach and the mystery of Rennes-le-Château, whereby many have pointed to enigmatic paintings as "holding the key" to unlock the mystery. We mention this incident, as it may have served as the inspiration for these stories... and because there is a connection with the Three Magi.

The story of the Three Magi originally only appeared in the Gospel of Matthew, Chapter 2, verses 1 to 12. In this account, there is no reference to their names, or to their number. The story states that a star guided them towards Bethlehem, where they learned of the birth of the Messiah. Only in the 8th century was this story enlarged and it is from that period onwards that it became both more popular and more important.

Referring to certain apocryphal books, such as the Armenian Gospel of the Youth, or the Pseudo-Matthew, their number was then fixed at three and they were given names: Bithisarea, Melchior and Gathaspa.

In the 13th century, Jacobus de Voragine[357] tried to assemble all the

---

356   Maurice Leblanc: « *L'Aiguille creuse, ou les nouvelles aventures d'Arsène Lupin* », *first published as a series of short stories in « Je Sais Tout » Magazine n° 44-52, dated 15th November 1908 to 15th May 1909, and first published as a book in June 1909.*
For an English translation, refer to "The Hollow Needle: Further adventures of Arsene Lupin" by Maurice Leblanc, translated by Alexander Teixeira De Mattos, and published by BiblioBazaar (August 1, 2006), or to the electronic text available courtesy of the Gutenberg Project: http://www.gutenberg.org/dirs/etext03/hlwnd10.txt
357   *Jacobus de Voragine, "The Golden Legend". The "Golden Legend" was a very popular hagiographic book (of saints' lives). It was written between 1260 and 1275 by Jacobus de Voragine.*

known documentation on the subject. Thus he wrote that *"the first Magus was Melchior, king of India, an old man with a long beard, who came to offer gold to Our Lord"*. The second, Gaspard, was *"lord of the Persians"*, who apparently *"had a youthful appearance"*, a red complexion and no beard, and offered incense. Finally, Balthazar, king of the Chaldeans, who had a black face, looked somber and offered myrrh. In Hebrew, their names respectively become Galgalat, Malgalat and Sarathim.

Voragine argued that the bodies of these three kings were preserved, were originally venerated in the East and then transported to Milan by bishop Eustorgus. In 1164, during the Investiture Controversy, Frederic Barbarossa invaded and sacked Milan, where he seems to have found the three skulls of the Magi. On 23rd July 1164, he mounted an escort that moved them to Cologne, Germany, where a multitude of penitents had assembled to render homage to these relics. From then onwards, Cologne became an important centre of pilgrimage, in fact, one of the most important ones in the world. The German Emperor demanded that his artisans create a reliquary the likes of which had not been seen in the Christian world, in order to house these relics. The man selected to carry out this work was Nicolas de Verdun, who used nothing but the purest and most precious materials. In 1209, Emperor Otto IV decided to have his portrait done with the skulls of the three Magi, and it is around this time that the relics were deposited in their reliquary.

Now, considering the interest that German Emperors had for Manicheism[358], we can assume that their fondness for these relics meant that such objects were of some utility to this doctrine. There is indeed a very real possibility that the tradition related to the Three Magi, which was considerably enriched with details in the 8th century, and completed with apocryphal sources, could serve as a liturgical foundation for the Chaldean Cult of the Dead.

The introduction of the Three Magi into the Christian dogma seems yet another example of the Cult of the Dead redefining Christianity. It is clear

---

358   *Let us remember that during the Investiture Controversy, the German Emperors supported the Ghibellines against the papacy. Doing so actually amounted to supporting the Cathars against the Church, according to Anne Brenon, who writes: "As long as the stature of Frederic II dominated, the Cathars in the cities had hardly any cause to fear the Catholic Church, except the antipathy of the great clerics and the scandalmongering of their treatises." She adds: "the only political power which was able to sustain [the Cathar church] was evidently the urban oligarchy, which remained on the side of the Emperor [...]: the Ghibellines." (Source: Anne Brenon, « Le Vrai Visage du Catharisme » ("The True Face of Catharism"), Ed. Loubatières, Toulouse, 1988 (re-edition).)*

that de Voragine added details which made it clear, right or wrong, that these Magi were in fact priest-kings from the Chaldean religion. Regarding Balthazar, we can wonder whether his name was derived from the Chaldaean deity Belzebuth (Baal-Zebub). He offers myrrh, which is a substance originating largely from Abyssinia (Ethiopia), and its primary purpose was to be used in the embalming of the dead. Even Jacobus de Voragine admitted that the present of King Balthazar had a strong undertone of "death" attached to it. This may explain Saunière's reinterpretation of the scene, in which he made the Infant Jesus into a dead infant Jesus.

Indeed... why did Balthazar present Jesus with myrrh? Was he expecting Jesus not to live? It is a biblical question that is not often widely discussed... or at least not widely enough. Hence, the standard explanation is that the myrrh was conserved and then – thirty-odd years later – used for the embalming of Jesus, after his death on the cross.

Long before Christianity, incense was widely used in temples. In fact, there was a belief that, once a temple was filled with incense, the spirit of the deceased could somehow attach themselves to it and render themselves visible. As to gold, that precious susbstance that continues to dominate our economy, yet which seems to have little real value as a metal, and is not particularly rare, was known as the symbol of the price that had to be paid for the Mortuary Rite. Three gifts, three vital ingredients in the Cult of the Dead!

Tradition has it that for the feast of Epiphany, a wafer of frangipane was shared. This tradition predates Christianity and has origins in both the Celtic lands and in Ancient Egypt. The broad bean, which one was supposed to discover in the wafer, was an aspect of the Cult of the Dead. For the ancient Egyptians, it symbolised the human embryo and was reputed to contain the soul of the dead. In Ancient Egypt, the "Field of broadbeans" was the site that acted as cemetery. The bodies were buried there and the broad-beans that grew there were not meant for consumption, for they contained the souls that awaited reincarnation. Pliny the Elder stressed the ancient Egyptians' devotion to this cult, and so did Pythagoras. The latter travelled to Egypt and was instructed in the local customs[359]. Afterwards, he always refused to eat broad-beans or even to cross a "field of broad-beans", for he considered it to be a profanation of the land of the dead.

---

359 *Pythagoras learned about the symbolism that the Egyptian attached to broad-beans from Oenuphis, a priest of Heliopolis.*

Within the Chaldaean religion, the Magi were astrologers. Their tasks were to observe of the heavens and to control the calendar that fixed certain religious feasts in relation to the position of stars. January 6th, as the date for Epiphany, was thus not a haphazard choice, but the outcome of a carefully planned intent, which today may no longer seem apparent. We should note that our Christian calendar was reformed by Pope Gregory XIII in 1582, and that therefore our dates are not synchronised with the Orthodox calendar. There is an 11 to 12 day difference between both calendars and so while we celebrate Christmas on December 25th, the Orthodox Church celebrates it on January 6th, i.e. Epiphany. If we extend this feature further, we end up with a correspondence between January 6th and January 17th. (See my notes. Gay)

For the Latinists, the 17th day of January was seen as nefarious. The reason for this was that 17 was written as XVII in Latin and which could consequently be read a "VIXI", which means "I have lived". This is yet another ingredient to throw in the pot of the Wagy Festival, which we have previously discussed as being an important festival for the dead.

In the Orthodox liturgy, the Adoration of the Magi, i.e. Epiphany, was not celebrated on January 6th, but instead on January 17th. We have a suspicion that January 17th was important – if only because it is the date on which Marie de Nègre d'Ables died – but could it be more important than that? Did Saunière follow the Orthodox calendar? In which case the feast of the Magi would not be celebrated on January 6th, but January 17th. And it seems that he held the Three Magi dear, judging from the frontispiece in his 1901 copy-book – and in which he transformed the usual scene into something far more ominous... morbid.

Guilty as charged

While the relationship between Bérenger Saunière and Bishop de Beauséjour was strained, his predecessor, Bishop Billard, seems to have been a trusted ally. The attitude of each towards Saunière diverges so widely that it begs several questions. Billard saw much more of Saunière's wealth on display than did de Beauséjour, and yet he did not ask a single question. The younger Saunière had numerous altercations with his parishioners during Billard's rule of the bishopric, but on each occasion, the bishop supported Saunière.

So why did Billard not react? Insights into the life of Billard come from another priest, abbé Laborde[360], who wrote a scathing document against

---

360   *All these charges are stated in the « Notice Laborde » (the "Laborde Note" in English),*

Billard – though only after the bishop's death! This "Note" is written in the format of an opening statement in a court of law: *"This December 1901 [...] the Diocese of Carcassonne has lost [....] its Bishop, His Lordship, Billard, Félix Arsène... But the Diocese was badly run... One must be allowed to be a critic and to judge [Billard] for his actions, in the name of truth and only the truth, as we say in Court."* It is of course impossible to have a dead person stand trial, but Laborde makes it clear that he is doing just that... judging Billard.

The specific charge is worded so:

"His Excellency has very much appreciated wealthy people and the entire noble hierarchy which, to perpetuate the feudal traditions, maintain with the ecclesiastic authority some relationships that are almost always detrimental to the poor priest."

Laborde illustrated how, under the guise of charitable work, noble ladies "with their charming smile" came to visit him, then opened their purses and "donated" money to the bishop. *"How could Monsignor not listen to this Noble Lady, who asked for an important post for a priest she likes?"* Indeed, we should all accept that, on occasion, a charity has to be rewarded in some way and it may seem at the moment that Laborde is slightly unwise in the ways of the world if he thinks that Billard was the only bishop who would occasionally accept a large donation but would not want to do a single favour in return for it.

Laborde also argued that Billard placed his personal friends in enviable positions. In the end, he states, those priests who deserved to be well placed always had secondary postings and did not seem able to advance in the bishopric. But worse, Laborde asks why Billard placed five vicars in Saint Vincent de Carcassonne, or three priests in Pezens, which had only a congregation of one thousand souls? Why was there sometimes the need for one or more vicars in a small parish, where one priest alone would have

---

named after a priest who, after Mgr. Billard's death, denounced the former bishop's actions during his episcopate as related to Simony (see notes 222-223) and payment for burials, i.e to Mortuary Rites and the Cult of the Dead. The « Notice Laborde » ("Laborde Note") is a crucial and revealing document about Monsignor Billard and much of his priests who where his "partners in crime", possibly including Saunière himself, although he is not named in the document (Simony is a crime according to Canon Law, and the Canonic Dictionary of abbé J.P. Migne). The « Notice Laborde » ("Laborde Note") was first discovered and published by French researcher Pierre Jarnac in his book « Les archives de Rennes-le-Château » ("The Rennes-le-Château Archives"), Editions Bélisane (1988), pp. 456 onwards. The « Notice Laborde » was first published on the Internet by French researcher Laurent Buchholtzer, on his website: http://www.octonovo.org/RlC/Fr/docu/Billard02.htm (text in French)

more than sufficed?

But that does not seem to be the only problem with Billard. Arrufat, priest of Pradelles-en-Val, *"suffered from insanity and displayed extraordinary extravagances in his parish. The mayor and other people informed Monsignor of these facts, but his Excellency always replied that he believed nothing of it."* Monsieur Arrufat, he said, was a saint. Saintly, but insane as well, it seems, for one month after the Bishop's reply, Arrufat was committed to an insane asylum in Toulouse!

Laborde lists the example of Andrieu, priest of Escales and one who, according to researcher Laurent Buchholtzer, could have been one of the priests who said some of the masses that were given to Saunière in 1898. He was another hot topic of debate, but Billard would have none of it. The Prefect, the town councillors, even the noblest families of Escales complained; Andrieu remained in his post until the day that he had to leave his position threatened by a crowd that booed him and which might have attacked him… if he had stayed any longer.

"And for Monie and Fresquet and for so many other people, the bishop has always been deaf to any sort of complaint. His Excellency, to protect his youngest members, always had answers with which to sidestep the truth and he never re-assigned them against their wishes."

All was not well in the diocese of Carcassonne under Billard's rule, it seems. Laborde makes harsh accusations, arguing that positions could be bought, and that complaints against certain priests were filed without due care and attention. But he goes further. He argues that some priests were "spies", positioned by the bishop in strategic places, where they often conspired against other priests. Billard sent several vicars and priests to small towns, while some larger towns often had no-one to celebrate mass. Laborde charged Billard with carrying on a type of "feudal tradition", in which the rich families – most often of the nobility – continued to direct the bishopric of Carcassonne. He argued that since the French Revolution, this "feudal tradition" had stopped – or should have been stopped – but not so under the rule of Billard.

In the final analysis, Billard is depicted as a dictator, who promotes whomsoever he wants to promote, leaving obviously better candidates to the side, and when his preferred priests become the subject of complaints, Billard always finds in favour of his protégés.

That, of course, is exactly what we see with Billard's treatment of Saunière. Saunière preached against the Republic and though Billard could not let this go unchallenged, he made sure that Saunière had a comfortable position for the time of his suspension. When Saunière was found to be desecrating the tombs, you would imagine that the bishop would take a strong disciplinary line with him. But Billard does not even see fit to send a courteous letter to the town council of Rennes-le-Château, arguing along the lines that he has had a word with Saunière, who has promised to rectify the situation as soon as possible.

Some in the diocese can get away with murder, it seems… Let us not forget that in 1897, in Coustaussa, a priest, abbé Gélis, was actually brutally murdered. Although it is most likely that Gélis knew his murderer, no suspect was ever caught. One can only wonder whether the police had a genuine suspect, but that someone – a bishop, for example – persuaded the police not to pursue that avenue?

Friendship, recommendations, denunciations, spying… the diocese under Billard operated under a specific set of guidelines, which are not those we should expect. Instead, they seem more at home in a secret society than a bishopric.

What was going on? Laborde has charged Billard with various crimes, but are they merely evidence of this man's despotic and corrupt nature? The Note states that Billard *"to get some money, gave the position of titular canon, for thirty thousand francs"* and *"Monsignor was a simoniac, that's all"*. Simony[361] is, of course, a mortal sin and a sacrilege, as indicated in the Migne dictionary of canon law.

But there is more: to get his hands on money, he forced priests of grand seminaries to put money into pension funds. Here is the content of article VI: *"No Seminarian will be promoted to sub-diaconate if he has not committed, in writing, to subscribe to the pension funds, immediately after his ordination."* For 19 years, Monsignor never produced any accounting as to the status of the pension funds.

According to the report of Father Saint-Marcel, the pension funds should have contained no less than 1,052,121 francs. But Monsignor, in a meeting of 27th October 1896, without stating any reason, would only acknowledge 568,000 francs, and without providing any documentary evidence. *"The accountant confessed frankly that there was nothing, which stunned all the priests attending this meeting."*

---

361   *See notes 222-223 about Simony and about Simon Magus for further information.*

With the Laborde document, we get a clear view of the atmosphere that prevailed at the Bishop's Palace in Carcassonne. Billard supervised a simoniacal network; he ran his diocese not as a bishopric, but as a money making scheme. When Laborde declares the "Bishop was a simoniac", he can't ignore the impact of these accusations. But Laborde must know more than he says when he speaks about the pension funds and connects this with simony. What could be the use of a pension fund, where more than half of the funds have disappeared at the final payment?

Is it about a sort of subsidy for the retirement home built by Bérenger Saunière, to receive priests at the end of their life? If so, the pension funds would have been a financial plan for "death insurance", aimed towards paying contributions in order to receive the Mortuary Rite. This information is confirmed later, when Laborde's document reveals – quite matter-of-factly – something extraordinary:

"Father Rauffet became priest of Devejean and said to his Bishop [Billard] that he planned to celebrate 'a funeral service for the peace of Father Olive's soul', his predecessor. 'No', answered the Bishop curtly; 'he is dead, let him stay so.' This is a monstrous answer from a Bishop; only the souls of the damned are refused prayers. Was Bishop Billard certain that Father Olive was damned?"

Laborde's declaration catches Billard red-handed on the subject of "a deceased's service". If the Bishop refuses prayers being said for the peace of Olive, it is obviously for the reason proposed in the document: Olive can't receive masses because they are refused to the souls of the damned. In this case, the soul of a faithful, a believer, a Priest, is presumed damned, although this verdict is arrived at without consultation, without any investigation or gathering of evidence?

We note how, in the above incident, there are clear references to the cult of the dead. Money – in large amounts– is involved in performing rituals that "ensure" the salvation of the deceased's soul. Without sufficient money or regular contributions, the rite is refused and the deceased is regarded as damned, without any other consideration. That seems to have been the fate of Olive... and we should ask the question whether the required pension fund was there merely so that the bishopric did not have to provide financial support for retired priests, or whether it was a mafia-type operation to make money, and/or whether there was more going on... and whether that "more" was the Cult of the Dead.

We note that the "no money, no salvation" motif is exactly what Laborde notices with regard to the activities of Mgr. Billard. After accusing him of Simony and exposing his whole diocese to this practice, he judges it as "monstrous" and pins it on the "worship of the dead" and maintains that there was no reason at all to condemn Father Olive.

A new era
With de Beauséjour's clean-up of the diocese and Saunière's death, peace returned to the bishopric of Carcassonne. The story of Saunière was picked up again in the 1950s, and completely transformed by the so-called "Priory of Sion", a group of people that had one Pierre Plantard as its nominal head. One of his closest "advisors" was an aristocratic half-Belgian actor, Philippe de Chérisey. The latter is seen as the man who created two mysterious parchments that have become the backbone of the mystery of the Priory and its knowledge of the mystery of Saunière. De Chérisey did state that he had created these parchments and wrote as much in a document, "Stone and Paper", a document he gave to journalist Jean-Luc Chaumeil with the specific request to publish it only twenty years after his death. True to his word, in 2006, Chaumeil published the document.

The document provides details about the church of Rennes-le-Château. De Chérisey writes how "the inversion of the cross of St. Peter in relation with the cross of Jesus is evoked on the funerary tombstone by the sign P.S., which serves both to invert St. Peter and to remind us of the sabbath "Second Premier" (Second-First), which is featured in [the second parchment]. The actual church of Rennes-le-Château evokes this inversion in another manner. At the foot of the altar, we find the same indication as at the bottom of the [second parchment]: 'Jesu Medela Vulnerum Spes Una Poenitentium Per Magdalenae Lacrymas Peccata Nostra Diluas'. This invocation brings the priest to the altar, underneath a great relief of Christ with his arms outstretched. Seated in the confessional, the priest sees before him the Magdalene underneath the altar, who beckons him to her. In other words, the church of Rennes-le-Château contains two churches in the same building, inviting the priest to turn, continuously, to either of its two separate functions, that of the Eucharist and that of Penitence."

Elsewhere we read how the second parchment "relates a Gospel text from John (X, II, 1-12). It is the famous story of the sinner Magdalene, using a very expensive vase of perfume on Jesus in the week of his Passion. This generous gesture infuriates the apostles, who estimate that the perfume has a value of 300 dinars, for which they could have bought many things which might have been distributed to the poor, their followers. In his capacity as treasurer, and thus receiving ten percent of the income, Judas finds himself particularly frustrated, but will recover his losses by selling Christ for thirty dinars. In this lovely parable, the evangelist John issues a warning, which the Church historians do not seem to have understood very well: the proportional value of flesh of Christ to her perfume is ten percent; His history to His legend being 30 to 300."

Elsewhere we also learn that: "Abbé Saunière learned at his expense how costly it was to exceed the fees of the wicked apostle, having died on 22nd January 1917, a few days after dipping his hands too often in the cookie jar.

Secondly, the discoverer will have to get used to the prospect of looting a necropolis where the dead dwelt for centuries in a natural state of mummification and in quite a good state of preservation.

From this angle, one might consider Magdalene the sinner in her capacity as patroness of embalmers, which would be very fitting, bearing in mind that Christ declared that she had poured out the perfume for his burial."

Could it be that de Chérisey was aware of the Cult of the Dead? Perhaps it was within that context that he and Plantard became focused on Saunière. Perhaps they understood the references to Mary Magdalene, which de Chérisey, in the above, at no point links to some notion that she somehow was the wife of Jesus, and that she ran away with His children and settled in France, as the popular myth of the Priory of Sion would have it. Perhaps de Chérisey hoped that his references to Mary Magdalene might put people on the tracks of the Cult of the Dead? If so, it is clear that such an ambition never succeeded. Instead, a far more literal, and in our opinion, incorrect, meaning was attached to the role of Mary Magdalene in the church of Rennes-le-Château.

Elsewhere in the document, we find an interview between Jean-Luc Chaumeil and de Chérisey:

"Is there a primary system with the P.S.?"

"Yes, that is it. But this is another matter altogether. In fact, we need to take [first -] that which is second. That which is secondary, needs to become primary. It is a bit like the Japanese money-boxes with their key on the inside. The beauty of the decoding resides in one of the gospels of Luke, which begins thus: 'In Sabbato Secundo Primo.' This text has been proven to be a brain-twister for secret societies. It should say 'a certain day of the Sabbath, the second first', but this is difficult to say, or translate. No-one ever heard anything like it. Therefore, it is understood as if they are walking in a grain field and they are hungry and are eating the grain, and thus it should be 'the Second

Sabbath following the first day of the unleavened bread'. It is all that they have been able to find as an interpretation. [...] In summary, 'In Sabbato Secundo Primo' [means] 'in the quality of second, Sabbasius became first'. It is amusing that the reunions of the sorcerers were labelled as 'Sabbaths', not because of the Jewish feast, but more because of Sabbasius, the god of the Phrygians. The Sabbath of the Sorcerers is in fact a god for the Eucharist, which has a quality, that of being dismembered in pieces and eaten, because he is the first bread.

[The first parchment] is a montage of three Synoptic gospels, reporting on the same event, namely Luke (I, 5), Matthew (XII, 1-8) and Mark (II, 23-28). The first sentence contains enigmas that the exegetes gave up trying to elucidate. 'Jesus in sabbato secundo primo', Jesus on the day of the Sabbath Second First, which could be the second Sabbath after the first day of the unleavened bread, or the first Sabbath following a second day? Unfortunately, there is no reference to this expression in the Biblical literature. The truth is far simpler. We need to remember that Saint Luke was Phrygian. This means he was a follower of the solar deity Sabazius, before his conversion. Jesus sabbato secundo primo, means that Luke, the author of this Gospel, venerated Jesus in his capacity as the second Sabazius who became the first. [...] At the same time, we note that the witches' Sabbath has no specific link with any particular day of the week, but rather with the Sabazies, feast days dedicated to the fallen god who had taken up diabolical aspects.'

It is clear that de Chérisey was very much aware of certain ill-known interpretations the biblical text. He was aware of the role of Osiris and similar gods, deities who have played a primary role in the Cult of the Dead. We can only ask why it is that he chose this text, to work it into the parchments. Again, it seems that those who were confronted with the parchments went off in radically different directions from those intended by its encoder, de Chérisey. And what he was talking about clearly had everything to do with penitence and "Witches' Sabbaths". Our study has shown a close link between the two and has shown furthermore that Saunière was in the thick of it. Is it really a coincidence that de Chérisey made specific use of this theme? Does it not imply that he must have known? That he knew what Saunière had been involved with? And that he used Saunière as an example in an effort to illustrate the power of the Cult of the Dead?

De Chérisey was part of the original group that promoted the story of Saunière. This group used Gérard de Sède as their writer, and it is clear, from the quotes we have reproduced, that he knew the truth: that Saunière was a practicing magician in a heretical cult. Unfortunately, it seems that specifically under the influence of *Holy Blood, Holy Grail* in the 1980s[362], and more recently *The Da Vinci Code*[363], the true story slowly eroded and became substituted for a myth. Out of the ashes, let the truth arise.

362 *Baigent, Leigh and Lincoln, "Holy Blood, Holy Grail", first published by Bantam Dell, New York, 1982.*
363 *Dan Brown, "The Da Vinci Code", published by Doubleday Books, 2003.*

APPENDIX I

The Book of Tobit

Chapter 1

Tobit of the tribe and city of Nephtali, (which is in the upper parts of Galilee above Naasson, beyond the way that leadeth to the west, having on the right hand the city of Sephet,)

When he was made captive in the days of Salmanasar king of the Assyrians, even in his captivity, forsook not the way of truth,

But every day gave all he could get to his brethren his fellow captives, that were of his kindred.

And when he was younger than any of the tribe of Nephtali, yet did he no childish thing in his work.

Moreover when all went to the golden calves which Jeroboam king of Israel had made, he alone fled the company of all,

And went to Jerusalem to the temple of the Lord, and there adored the Lord God of Israel, offering faithfully all his first fruits, and his tithes,

So that in the third year he gave all his tithes to the proselytes, and strangers.

These and such like things did he observe when but a boy according to the law of God.

But when he was a man, he took to wife Anna of his own tribe, and had a son by her, whom he called after his own name,

And from his infancy he taught him to fear God, and to abstain from all sin.

And when by the captivity he with his wife and his son and all his tribe was come to the city of Niniveh,

(When all ate of the meats of the Gentiles) he kept his soul and never was defiled with their meats.

And because he was mindful of the Lord with all his heart, God gave him favour in the sight of Salmanasar the king.

And he gave him leave to go whithersoever he would, with liberty to do whatever he had a mind.

He therefore went to all that were in captivity, and gave them wholesome admonitions.

And when he was come to Rages a city of the Medes, and had ten talents of silver of that with which he had been honoured by the king:

And when amongst a great multitude of his kindred, he saw Gabelus in want, who was one of his tribe, taking a note of his hand he gave him the aforesaid sum of money.

But after a long time, Salmanasar the king being dead, when Sennacherib his son, who reigned in his place, had a hatred for the children of Israel:

Tobit daily went among all his kindred, and comforted them, and distributed to every one as he was able, out of his goods:

He fed the hungry, and gave clothes to the naked, and was careful to bury the dead, and they that were slain.

And when king Sennacherib was come back, fleeing from Judea by reason of the slaughter that God had made about him for his blasphemy, and being angry slew many of the children of Israel, Tobit buried their bodies.

But when it was told the king, he commanded him to be slain, and took away all his substance.

But Tobit fleeing naked away with his son and with his wife, lay concealed, for many loved him.

But after forty-five days, the king was killed by his own sons.

And Tobit returned to his house, and all his substance was restored to him.

Chapter 2

But after this, when there was a festival of the Lord, and a good dinner was prepared in Tobit's house,

He said to his son: Go, and bring some of our tribe that fear God, to feast with us.

And when he had gone, returning he told him, that one of the children of Israel lay slain in the street. And he forthwith leaped up from his place at the table, and left his dinner, and came fasting to the body:

And taking it up carried it privately to his house, that after the sun was down, he might bury him cautiously.

And when he had hid the body, he ate bread with mourning and fear,

Remembering the word which the Lord spoke by Amos the prophet: Your festival days shall be turned into lamentation and mourning.

So when the sun was down, he went and buried him.

Now all his neighbours blamed him, saying: Once already commandment was given for thee to be slain because of this matter, and thou didst scarce escape the sentence of death, and dost thou again bury the dead?

But Tobit fearing God more than the king, carried off the bodies of them that were slain, and hid them in his house, and at midnight buried them.

Now it happened one day, that being wearied with burying, he came to his house, and cast himself down by the wall and slept,

And as he was sleeping, hot dung out of a swallow's nest fell upon his eyes, and he was made blind.

Now this trial the Lord therefore permitted to happen to him, that an example might be given to posterity of his patience, as also of holy Job.

For whereas he had always feared God from his infancy, and kept his commandments, he repined not against God because the evil of blindness had befallen him,

But continued immoveable in the fear of God, giving thanks to God all the days of his life.

For as the kings insulted over holy Job: so his relations and kinsmen mocked at his life, saying:

Where is thy hope, for which thou gavest alms, and buriedst the dead?

But Tobit rebuked them, saying: Speak not so:

For we are the children of the saints, and look for that life which God will give to those that never change their faith from him.

Now Anna his wife went daily to weaving work, and she brought home what she could get for their living by the labour of her hands.

Whereby it came to pass, that she received a young kid, and brought it home:

And when her husband heard it bleating, he said: Take heed, lest perhaps it be stolen: restore ye it to its owners, for it is not lawful for us either to eat or to touch any thing that cometh by theft.

At these words his wife being angry answered: It is evident thy hope is come to nothing, and thy alms now appear. And with these, and other such like words she upbraided him.

Chapter 3

Then Tobit sighed, and began to pray with tears,

Saying: Thou art just, O Lord, and all thy judgments are just, and all thy ways mercy, and truth, and judgment:

And now, O Lord, think of me, and take not revenge of my sins, neither remember my offenses, nor those of my parents.

For we have not obeyed thy commandments, therefore are we delivered to spoil and to captivity, and death, and are made a fable, and a reproach to all nations, amongst which thou hast scattered us.

And now, O Lord, great are thy judgments, because we have not done according to thy precepts, and have not walked sincerely before thee:

And now, O Lord, do with me according to thy will, and command my spirit to be received in peace: for it is better for me to die, than to live.

Now it happened on the same day, that Sara daughter of Raguel, in Rages a city of the Medes, received a reproach from one of her father's servant maids,

Because she had been given to seven husbands, and a devil named Asmodeus had killed them, at their first going in unto her.

So when she reproved the maid for her fault, she answered her, saying: May we never see son, or daughter of thee upon the earth, thou murderer of thy husbands.

Wilt thou kill me also, as thou hast already killed seven husbands? At these words she went into an upper chamber of her house: and for three days and three nights did neither eat nor drink:

But continuing in prayer with tears besought God, that he would deliver her from this reproach.

And it came to pass on the third day, when she was making an end of her prayer, blessing the Lord,

She said: Blessed is thy name, O God of our fathers: who when thou hast been angry, wilt shew mercy, and in the time of tribulation forgivest the sins of them that call upon thee.

To thee, O Lord, I turn my face, to thee I direct my eyes.

I beg, O Lord, that thou loose me from the bond of this reproach, or else take me away from the earth.

Thou knowest, O Lord, that I never coveted a husband, and have kept my soul clean from all lust.

Never have I joined myself with them that play: neither have I made myself partaker with them that walk in lightness.

But a husband I consented to take, with thy fear, not with my lust.

And either I was unworthy of them, or they perhaps were not worthy of me: because perhaps thou hast kept me for another man.

For thy counsel is not in man's power.

But this every one is sure of that worshippeth thee, that his life, if it be under trial, shall be crowned: and if it be under tribulation, it shall be delivered: and if it be under correction, it shall be allowed to come to thy mercy.

For thou art not delighted in our being lost: because after a storm thou makest a calm, and after tears and weeping thou pourest in joyfulness.

Be thy name, O God of Israel, blessed for ever.

At that time the prayers of them both were heard in the sight of the glory of the most high God:

And the holy angel of the Lord, Raphael was sent to heal them both, whose prayers at one time were rehearsed in the sight of the Lord.

Chapter 4

Therefore when Tobit thought that his prayer was heard that he might die, he called to him Tobias his son,

And said to him: Hear, my son, the words of my mouth, and lay them as a foundation in thy heart.

When God shall take my soul, thou shalt bury my body: and thou shalt honour thy mother all the days of her life:

For thou must be mindful what and how great perils she suffered for thee in her womb.

And when she also shall have ended the time of her life, bury her by me.

And all the days of thy life have God in thy mind: and take heed thou never consent to sin, nor transgress the commandments of the Lord our God.

Give alms out of thy substance, and turn not away thy face from any poor person: for so it shall come to pass that the face of the Lord shall not be turned from thee.

According to thy ability be merciful.

If thou have much give abundantly: if thou have a little, take care even so to bestow willingly a little.

For thus thou storest up to thyself a good reward for the day of necessity.

For alms deliver from all sin, and from death, and will not suffer the soul to go into darkness.

Alms shall be a great confidence before the most high God, to all them that give it.

Take heed to keep thyself, my son, from all fornication, and beside thy wife never endure to know a crime.

Never suffer pride to reign in thy mind, or in thy words: for from it all perdition took its beginning.

If any man hath done any work for thee, immediately pay him his hire, and let not the wages of thy hired servant stay with thee at all.

See thou never do to another what thou wouldst hate to have done to thee by another.

Eat thy bread with the hungry and the needy, and with thy garments cover the naked.

Lay out thy bread, and thy wine upon the burial of a just man, and do not eat and drink thereof with the wicked.

Seek counsel always of a wise man.

Bless God at all times: and desire of him to direct thy ways, and that all thy counsels may abide in him.

I tell thee also, my son, that I lent ten talents of silver, while thou wast yet a child, to Gabelus, in Rages a city of the Medes, and I have a note of his hand with me:

Now therefore inquire how thou mayst go to him, and receive of him the foresaid sum of money, and restore to him the note of his hand.

Fear not, my son: we lead indeed a poor life, but we shall have many good things if we fear God, and depart from all sin, and do that which is good.

Chapter 5

Then Tobias answered his father, and said: I will do all things, father, which thou hast commanded me.

But how I shall get this money, I cannot tell; he knoweth me not, and I know not him: what token shall I give him? nor did I ever know the way which leadeth thither.

Then his father answered him, and said: I have a note of his hand with me, which when thou shalt shew him, he will presently pay it.

But go now, and seek thee out some faithful man, to go with thee for his hire: that thou mayst receive it, while I yet live.

Then Tobias going forth, found a beautiful young man, standing girded, and as it were ready to walk.

And not knowing that he was an angel of God, he saluted him, and said: From whence art thou, good young man?

But he answered: Of the children of Israel. And Tobias said to him: Knowest thou the way that leadeth to the country of the Medes?

And he answered: I know it: and I have often walked through all the ways thereof, and I have abode with Gabelus our brother, who dwelleth at Rages a city of the Medes, which is situated in the mount of Ecbatana.

And Tobias said to him: Stay for me, I beseech thee, till I tell these same things to my father.

Then Tobias going in told all these things to his father. Upon which his father being in admiration, desired that he would come in unto him.

So going in he saluted him, and said: Joy be to thee always.

And Tobit said: What manner of joy shall be to me, who sit in darkness, and see not the light of heaven?

And the young man said to him: Be of good courage, thy cure from God is at hand.

And Tobit said to him: Canst thou conduct my son to Gabelus at Rages, a city of the Medes? and when thou shalt return, I will pay thee thy hire.

And the angel said to him: I will conduct him thither, and bring him back to thee.

And Tobit said to him: I pray thee, tell me, of what family, or what tribe art thou?

And Raphael the angel answered: Dost thou seek the family of him thou hirest, or the hired servant himself to go with thy son?

But lest I should make thee uneasy, I am Azarias the son of the great Ananias.

And Tobit answered: Thou art of a great family. But I pray thee be not angry that I desired to know thy family.

And the angel said to him: I will lead thy son safe, and bring him to thee again safe.

And Tobit answering, said: May you have a good journey, and God be with you in your way, and his angel accompany you.

Then all things being ready, that were to be carried in their journey, Tobias bade his father and his mother farewell, and they set out both together.

And when they were departed, his mother began to weep, and to say: Thou hast taken the staff of our old age, and sent him away from us.

I wish the money for which thou hast sent him, had never been.

For poverty was sufficient for us, that we might account it as riches, that we saw our son.

And Tobit said to her: Weep not, our son will arrive thither safe, and will return safe to us, and thy eyes shall see him.

For I believe that the good angel of God doth accompany him, and doth order all *things well that are done about him, so that he shall return to us with joy.*

At these words his mother ceased weeping, and held her peace.

Chapter 6

And Tobias went forward, and the dog followed him, and he lodged the first night by the river of Tigris.

And he went out to wash his feet, and behold a monstrous fish came up to devour him.

And Tobias being afraid of him, cried out with a loud voice, saying: Sir, he cometh upon me.

And the angel said to him: Take him by the gill, and draw him to thee. And when he had done so, he drew him out upon the land, and he began to pant before his feet.

Then the angel said to him: Take out the entrails of the fish, and lay up his heart, and his gall, and his liver for thee: for these are necessary for useful medicines.

And when he had done so, he roasted the flesh thereof, and they took it with them in the way: the rest they salted as much as might serve them, till they came to Rages the city of the Medes.

Then Tobias asked the angel, and said to him: I beseech thee, brother Azarias, tell me what remedies are these things good for, which thou hast bid me keep of the fish?

And the angel, answering, said to him: If thou put a little piece of its heart upon coals, the smoke thereof driveth away all kind of devils, either from man or from woman, so that they come no more to them.

And the gall is good for anointing the eyes, in which there is a white speck, and they shall be cured.

And Tobias said to him: Where wilt thou that we lodge?

And the angel answering, said: Here is one whose name is Raguel, a near kinsman of thy tribe, and he hath a daughter named Sara, but he hath no son nor any other daughter beside her.

All his substance is due to thee, and thou must take her to wife.

Ask her therefore of her father, and he will give her thee to wife.

Then Tobias answered, and said: I hear that she hath been given to seven husbands, and they all died: moreover I have heard, that a devil killed them.

Now I am afraid, lest the same thing should happen to me also: and whereas I am the only child of my parents, I should bring down their old age with sorrow to hell.

Then the angel Raphael said to him: Hear me, and I will shew thee who they are, over whom the devil can prevail.

For they who in such manner receive matrimony, as to shut out God from themselves, and from their mind, and to give themselves to their lust, as the horse and mule, which have not understanding, over them the devil hath power.

But thou when thou shalt take her, go into the chamber, and for three days keep thyself continent from her, and give thyself to nothing else but to prayers with her.

And on that night lay the liver of the fish on the fire, and the devil shall be driven away.

But the second night thou shalt be admitted into the society of the holy Patriarchs.

And the third night thou shalt obtain a blessing that sound children may be born of you.

And when the third night is past, thou shalt take the virgin with the fear of the Lord, moved rather for love of children than for lust, that in the seed of Abraham thou mayst obtain a blessing in children.

Chapter 7

And they went in to Raguel, and Raguel received them with joy.

And Raguel looking upon Tobias, said to Edna his wife: How like is this young man to my cousin?

And when he had spoken these words, he said: Whence are ye young men our brethren?

But they said: We are of the tribe of Nephtali, who are captive in Niniveh.

And Raguel said to them: Do you know Tobit my brother? And they said: We know him.

And when he was speaking many good things of him, the angel said to Raguel: Tobit concerning whom thou inquirest is this young man's father.

And Raguel went to him, and kissed him with tears, and weeping upon his neck, said: A blessing be upon thee, my son, because thou art the son of a good and most virtuous man.

And Edna his wife, and Sara their daughter wept.

And after they had spoken, Raguel commanded a sheep to be killed, and a feast to be prepared. And when he desired them to sit down to dinner,

Tobias said: I will not eat nor drink here this day, unless thou first grant me my petition, and promise to give me Sara thy daughter.

Now when Raguel heard this he was afraid, knowing what had happened to those seven husbands, that went in unto her: and he began to fear lest it might happen to him also in like manner: and as he was in suspense, and gave no answer to his petition,

The angel said to him: Be not afraid to give her to this man, for to him who feareth God is thy daughter due to be his wife: therefore another could not have her.

Then Raguel said: I doubt not but God hath regarded my prayers and tears in his sight.

And I believe he hath therefore made you come to me, that this maid might be married to one of her own kindred, according to the law of Moses: and now doubt not but I will give her to thee.

And taking the right hand of his daughter, he gave it into the right hand of Tobias, saying: The God of Abraham, and the God of Isaac, and the God of Jacob be with you, and may he join you together, and fulfil his blessing in you.

And taking paper they made a writing of the marriage.

And afterwards they made merry, blessing God.

And Raguel called to him Edna his wife, and bade her prepare another chamber.

And she brought Sara her daughter in thither, and she wept.

And she said to her: Be of good cheer, my daughter: the Lord of heaven give thee joy for the trouble thou hast undergone.

Chapter 8

And after they had supped, they brought in the young man to her.

And Tobias remembering the angel's word, took out of his bag part of the liver, and laid it upon burning coals.

Then the angel Raphael took the devil, and bound him in the desert of upper Egypt.

Then Tobias exhorted the virgin, and said to her: Sara, arise, and let us pray to God to day, and to morrow, and the next day: because for these three nights we are joined to God: and when the third night is over, we will be in our own wedlock.

For we are the children of saints, and we must not be joined together like heathens that know not God.

So they both arose, and prayed earnestly both together that health might be given them,

And Tobias said: Lord God of our father, may the heavens and the earth, and the sea, and the fountains, and the rivers, and all thy creatures that are in them, bless thee.

Thou madest Adam of the slime of the earth, and gavest him Eve for a helper.

And now, Lord, thou knowest, that not for fleshly lust do I take my sister to wife, but only for the love of posterity, in which thy name may be blessed for ever and ever.

Sara also said: Have mercy on us, O Lord, have mercy on us, and let us grow old both together in health.

And it came to pass about the cockcrowing, Raguel ordered his servants to be called for, and they went with him together to dig a grave.

For he said: Lest perhaps it may have happened to him, in like manner as it did to the other seven husbands, that went in unto her.

And when they had prepared the pit, Raguel went back to his wife, and said to her:

Send one of thy maids, and let her see if he be dead, that I may bury him before it be day.

So she sent one of her maidservants, who went into the chamber, and found them safe and sound, sleeping both together.

And returning she brought the good news: and Raguel and Edna his wife blessed the Lord,

And said: We bless thee, O Lord God of Israel, because it hath not happened as we suspected.

For thou hast shewn thy mercy to us, and hast shut out from us the enemy that persecuted us.

And thou hast taken pity upon two only children. Make them, O Lord, bless thee more fully: and to offer up to thee a sacrifice of thy praise, and of their health, that all nations may know, that thou alone art God in all the earth.

And immediately Raguel commanded his servants, to fill up the pit they had made, before it was day.

And he spoke to his wife to make ready a feast, and prepare all kind of provisions that are necessary for such as go a journey.

He caused also two fat kine, and four wethers to be killed, and a banquet to be prepared for all his neighbours, and all his friends.

And Raguel adjured Tobias, to abide with him two weeks.

And of all things which Raguel possessed, he gave one half to Tobias, and made him a writing, that the half that remained should after their decease come also to Tobias.

Chapter 9

Then Tobias called the angel to him, whom he took to be a man, and said to him: Brother Azarias, I pray thee hearken to my words:

If I should give myself to be thy servant I should not make a worthy return for thy care.

However, I beseech thee, to take with thee beasts and servants, and to go to Gabelus to Rages the city of the Medes: and to restore to him his note of hand, and receive of him the money, and desire him to come to my wedding.

For thou knowest that my father numbereth the days for his burial: and if I stay one day more, his soul will be afflicted.

And indeed thou seest how Raguel hath adjured me, whose adjuring I cannot despise.

Then Raphael took four of Raguel's servants, and two camels, and went to Rages the city of the Medes: and finding Gabelus, gave him his note of hand, and received of him all the money.

And he told him concerning Tobias the son of Tobit, all that had been done: and made him come with him to the wedding.

And when he was come into Raguel's house he found Tobias sitting at the table: and he leaped up, and they kissed each other: and Gabelus wept, and blessed God,

And said: The God of Israel bless thee, because thou art the son of a very good and just man, and that feareth God, and doth almsdeeds:

And may a blessing come upon thy wife and upon your parents.

And may you see your children, and your children's children, unto the third and fourth generation: and may your seed be blessed by the God of Israel, who reigneth for ever and ever.

And when all had said, Amen, they went to the feast: but the marriage feast they celebrated also with the fear of the Lord.

Chapter 10

But as Tobias made longer stay upon occasion of the marriage, Tobit his father was solicitous, saying: Why thinkest thou doth my son tarry, or why is he detained there?

Is Gabelus dead, thinkest thou, and no man will pay him the money?

And he began to be exceeding sad, both he and Anna his wife with him: and they began both to weep together: because their son did not return to them on the day appointed.

But his mother wept and was quite disconsolate, and said: Woe, woe is me, my son; why did we send thee to go to a strange country, the light of our eyes, the staff of our old age, the comfort of our life, the hope of our posterity?

We having all things together in thee alone, ought not to have let thee go from us.

And Tobit said to her: Hold thy peace, and be not troubled, our son is safe: that man with whom we sent him is very trusty.

But she could by no means be comforted, but daily running out looked round about, and went into all the ways by which there seemed any hope he might return, that she might if possible see him coming afar off.

But Raguel said to his son in law: Stay here, and I will send a messenger to Tobit thy father, that thou art in health.

And Tobias said to him: I know that my father and mother now count the days, and their spirit is grievously afflicted within them.

And when Raguel had pressed Tobias with many words, and he by no means would hearken to him, he delivered Sara unto him, and half of all his substance in menservants, and womenservants, in cattle, in camels, and in kine, and in much money, and sent him away safe and joyful from him.

Saying: The holy angel of the Lord be with you in your journey, and bring you through safe, and that you may find all things well about your parents, and my eyes see your children before I die.

And the parents taking their daughter kissed her, and let her go:

Admonishing her to honour her father and mother in law, to love her husband, to take care of the family, to govern the house, and to behave herself irreprehensibly.

Chapter 11

And as they were returning they came to Charan, which is in the midway to Niniveh, the eleventh day.

And the angel said: Brother Tobias, thou knowest how thou didst leave thy father.

If it please thee therefore, let us go before, and let the family follow softly after us, together with thy wife, and with the beasts.

And as this their going pleased him, Raphael said to Tobias: Take with thee of the gall of the fish, for it will be necessary. So Tobias took some of that gall and departed.

But Anna sat beside the way daily, on the top of a hill, from whence she might see afar off.

And while she watched his coming from that place, she saw him afar off, and presently perceived it was her son coming: and returning she told her husband, saying: Behold thy son cometh.

And Raphael said to Tobias: As soon as thou shalt come into thy house, forthwith adore the Lord thy God: and giving thanks to him, go to thy father, and kiss him.

And immediately anoint his eyes with this gall of the fish, which thou carriest with thee. For be assured that his eyes shall be presently opened, and thy father shall see the light of heaven, and shall rejoice in the sight of thee.

Then the dog, which had been with them in the way, ran before, and coming as if he had brought the news, shewed his joy by his fawning and wagging his tail.

And his father that was blind, rising up, began to run stumbling with his feet: and giving a servant his hand, went to meet his son.

And receiving him kissed him, as did also his wife, and they began to weep for joy.

And when they had adored God, and given him thanks, they sat down together.

Then Tobias taking of the gall of the fish, anointed his father's eyes.

And he stayed about half an hour: and a white skin began to come out of his eyes, like the skin of an egg.

And Tobias took hold of it, and drew it from his eyes, and immediately he recovered his sight.

And they glorified God, both he and his wife and all that knew them.

And Tobit said: I bless thee, O Lord God of Israel, because thou hast chastised me, and thou hast saved me: and behold I see Tobias my son.

And after seven days Sara his son's wife, and all the family arrived safe, and the cattle, and the camels, and an abundance of money of his wife's: and that money also which he had received of Gabelus:

And he told his parents all the benefits of God, which he had done to him by the man that conducted him.

And Achior and Nabath the kinsmen of Tobias came, rejoicing for Tobias, and congratulating with him for all the good things that God had done for him.

And for seven days they feasted and rejoiced all with great joy.

Chapter 12

Then Tobit called to him his son, and said to him: What can we give to this holy man, that is come with thee?

Tobias answering, said to his father: Father, what wages shall we give him? or what can be worthy of his benefits?

He conducted me and brought me safe again, he received the money of Gabelus, he caused me to have my wife, and he chased from her the evil spirit, he gave joy to her parents, myself he delivered from being devoured by the fish, thee also he hath made to see the light of heaven, and we are filled with all good things through him. What can we give him sufficient for these things?

But I beseech thee, my father, to desire him, that he would vouchsafe to accept one half of all things that have been brought.

So the father and the son, calling him, took him aside: and began to desire him that he would vouchsafe to accept of half of all things that they had brought.

Then he said to them secretly: Bless ye the God of heaven, give glory to him in the sight of all that live, because he hath shewn his mercy to you.

For it is good to hide the secret of a king: but honourable to reveal and confess the works of God.

Prayer is good with fasting and alms more than to lay up treasures of gold:

For alms delivereth from death, and the same is that which purgeth away sins, and maketh to find mercy and life everlasting.

But they that commit sin and iniquity, are enemies to their own soul.

I discover then the truth unto you, and I will not hide the secret from you.

When thou didst pray with tears, and didst bury the dead, and didst leave thy dinner, and hide the dead by day in thy house, and bury them by night, I offered thy prayer to the Lord.

And because thou wast acceptable to God, it was necessary that temptation should prove thee.

And now the Lord hath sent me to heal thee, and to deliver Sara thy son's wife from the devil.

For I am the angel Raphael, one of the seven, who stand before the Lord.

And when they had heard these things, they were troubled, and being seized with fear they fell upon the ground on their face.

And the angel said to them: Peace be to you, fear not.

For when I was with you, I was there by the will of God: bless ye him, and sing praises to him.

I seemed indeed to eat and to drink with you: but I use an invisible meat and drink, which cannot be seen by men.

It is time therefore that I return to him that sent me: but bless ye God, and publish all his wonderful works.

And when he had said these things, he was taken from their sight, and they could see him no more.

Then they lying prostrate for three hours upon their face, blessed God: and rising up, they told all his wonderful works.

Chapter 13

And Tobit the elder opening his mouth, blessed the Lord, and said: Thou art great, O Lord, for ever, and thy kingdom is unto all ages:

For thou scourgest, and thou savest: thou leadest down to hell, and bringest up again: and there is none that can escape thy hand.

Give glory to the Lord, ye children of Israel, and praise him in the sight of the Gentiles:

Because he hath therefore scattered you among the Gentiles, who know not him, that you may declare his wonderful works, and make them know that there is no other almighty God besides him.

He hath chastised us for our iniquities: and he will save us for his own mercy.

See then what he hath done with us, and with fear and trembling give ye glory to him: and extol the eternal King of worlds in your works.

As for me, I will praise him in the land of my captivity: because he hath shewn his majesty toward a sinful nation.

Be converted therefore, ye sinners, and do justice before God, believing that he will shew his mercy to you.

And I and my soul will rejoice in him.

Bless ye the Lord, all his elect, keep days of joy, and give glory to him.

Jerusalem, city of God, the Lord hath chastised thee for the works of thy hands.

Give glory to the Lord for thy good things, and bless the God eternal, that he may rebuild his tabernacle in thee, and may call back all the captives to thee, and thou mayst rejoice for ever and ever.

Thou shalt shine with a glorious light: and all the ends of the earth shall worship thee.

Nations from afar shall come to thee: and shall bring gifts, and shall adore the Lord in thee, and shall esteem thy land as holy.

For they shall call upon the great name in thee.

They shall be cursed that shall despise thee: and they shall be condemned that shall blaspheme thee: and blessed shall they be that shall build thee up.

But thou shalt rejoice in thy children, because they shall all be blessed, and shall be gathered together to the Lord.

Blessed are all they that love thee, and that rejoice in thy peace.

My soul, bless thou the Lord, because the Lord our God hath delivered Jerusalem his city from all her troubles.

Happy shall I be if there shall remain of my seed, to see the glory of Jerusalem.

The gates of Jerusalem shall be built of sapphire, and of emerald, and all the walls thereof round about of precious stones.

All its streets shall be paved with white and clean stones: and Alleluia shall be sung in its streets.

Blessed be the Lord, who hath exalted it, and may he reign over it for ever and ever, Amen.

Chapter 14

And the words of Tobit were ended. And after Tobit was restored to his sight, he lived two and forty years, and saw the children of his grandchildren.

And after he had lived a hundred and two years, he was buried honourably in Niniveh.

For he was six and fifty years old when he lost the sight of his eyes, and sixty when he recovered it again.

And the rest of his life was in joy, and with great increase of the fear of God he departed in peace.

And at the hour of his death he called unto him his son Tobias and his children, seven young men, his grandsons, and said to them:

The destruction of Niniveh is at hand: for the word of the Lord must be fulfilled: and our brethren, that are scattered abroad from the land of Israel, shall return to it.

And all the land thereof that is desert shall be filled with people, and the house of God which is burnt in it, shall again be rebuilt: and all that fear God shall return thither.

And the Gentiles shall leave their idols, and shall come into Jerusalem, and shall dwell in it.

And all the kings of the earth shall rejoice in it, adoring the King of Israel.

Hearken therefore, my children, to your father: serve the Lord in truth, and seek to do the things that please him:

And command your children that they do justice and almsdeeds, and that they be mindful of God, and bless him at all times in truth, and with all their power.

And now, children, hear me, and do not stay here: but as soon as you shall bury your mother by me in one sepulchre, without delay direct your steps to depart hence:

For I see that its iniquity will bring it to destruction.

And it came to pass that after the death of his mother, Tobias departed out of Niniveh with his wife, and children, and children's children, and returned to his father and mother in law.

And he found them in health in a good old age: and he took care of them, and he closed their eyes: and all the inheritance of Raguel's house came to him: and he saw his children's children to the fifth generation.

And after he had lived ninety-nine years in the fear of the Lord, with joy they buried him.

And all his kindred, and all his generation continued in good life, and in holy conversation, so that they were acceptable both to God, and to men, and to all that dwelt in the land.

Egypt: Image of Heaven
Wim Zitman

The ancient Egyptians were the first geographical planners to develop a system in order to establish an 'image of heaven' on earth. According to the astronomer Moore, "the precision [of the Egyptians] was amazing by any standards, and there is no doubt that the Pyramids were astronomically aligned". This book completes Zitman's ten year research into how the Pyramid Field depicts The Constellation of Horus.

311 pages | Paperback | Illustrated

The Templar's Legacy in Montreal, the New Jerusalem
Francine Bernier

Designed in the 17th century as the New Jerusalem of the Christian world, the island of Montreal became the new headquarters of a group of mystics that wanted to live as the flawless Primitive Church of Jesus. But they could not do that in the Old World! They build the Canadian town incorporating knowledge that was suppressed in France.

360 pages | Large paperback | Illustrated

The Stone Puzzle of Rosslyn Chapel
The Truth behind its Templar and Masonic Secrets
Philip Coppens

Rosslyn Chapel has fueled controversy and debate, both recently in several worldbestselling books as well as in past centuries. Revered by Freemasons as a vital part of their history, believed by some to hold evidence of pre-Columbian voyages to America, assumed by others to hold important relics, from the Holy Grail to the Head of Christ, the Scottish chapel is a place full of mystery.

120 pages | Paperback | Illustrated

A~TIME *All there is matters equally*
Kareline van der Burg

A rich illustrated art book, with glossy pictures of painted drums and jewellery and a new calendar, which makes you think about our cosmic nature. A collection of new native art, like goatskinned drums with oils, with feathers and shells. The 52 drums are accompanied by 365 sentences to announce a new mindset to honor Gaia. The book shows jewellery inspired by the Mayan Calendar, revealing the relationship between cosmic cycles and our body. A perfect gift for who loves art and the true spirit of nature. The artist uses her profit to plant trees with children for the future.

190 pages | Hardcover | Illustrated

Nostradamus and the Lost Templar Legacy
by Rudy Cambier

Rudy Cambier's decade-long research and analysis of the verses of Nostradamus' "prophecies" has shown that the language of those verses does not belong in the 16th Century, nor in Nostradamus' region of Provence. The language spoken in the verses belongs to the medieval times of the 14th Century, and the Belgian borders.

204 pages | Large Paperback | Illustrated

Sauniere's Model & the secret of Rennes-le-Château
The priest's final legacy that unveils the location of his terrifying discovery
by André Douzet

In 1916, Berenger Saunière, the enigmatic priest of the French village of Rennes-le-Château, created his ultimate clue: he went to great expense to create a model of a region said to be the Calvary Mount, indicating the "Tomb of Jesus". But the region on the model does not resemble the actual lay-out of Jerusalem. Did Saunière leave a clue as to the true location of his treasure?

116 pages | 6x9 Paperback | Illustrated

The Wanderings of the Grail
The Cathars, the search for the Grail and the discovery of Egyptian relics in the French Pyrenees
by André Douzet

In the 13th century, the Church came down against the Cathars, who had settled in the French Pyrenees. The Cathars practiced a belief in which "perfects" acted as priests that educated their followers in a specific system of believes and who aided the believers in "dying consciously", which was also at heart of ancient Egyptian belief systems. Both the Egyptians and the Cathars felt they had to "cheat" the cycle of reincarnation (the cycle of evil), and "ascend" to the world of light.

95 pages | Paperback

The Canopus Revelation
Stargate of the Gods and the Ark of Osiris
by Philip Coppens

The identification of the constellation Orion with the Egyptian god Osiris has become engrained in human consciousness, yet is one of the biggest misunderstandings dominating the understanding of Egyptian mythology. Rather than the constellation Orion, it is the star Canopus that is linked with Osiris, as identified by ancient writers as well as early 20th century scholars, whose evidence has since been bullied into silence, if not oblivion.

204 pages | Large Paperback | Illustrated

The Secret Vault
The secret societies' manipulation of Saunière and the secret sanctuary of Notre-Dame-de-Marceille
by André Douzet & Philip Coppens
Was Berenger Saunière, the priest at the centre of the enigma of Rennes-le-Château, controlled by a secret society? Yes is the answer, but which one? Freemasonry? The Rosicrucians? None of the above; the group was known as the A.A., said to be the successors of the Compagnie de St Sacrement, a 17th century secret society that was prohibited by the French king Louis XIV.
141 pages | Paperback

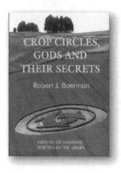

Crop Circles, Gods and their Secrets
History of Mankind Written in the Grain
by Robert J. Boerman
In the more than 30 years that mankind all over the world has been treated with thousands of crop circle formations, nobody has been able to explain this phenomenon. Could it be as sceptics would have us believe, simply human handy work? Could there be assorted jokers world wide busy misleading you and me by night and in all weathers for decades now?
159 pages | Paperback |

Ashes of Faith
A doomesday's cult orchestration of mass murder in Africa
by Robert Bwire
The "Movementforthe Restoration of the Ten Comrnandments of God", a Ugandan millenarian cult proclaimed the end of the world on December 31,1999, The cult claimed that Virgin Mary had delivered this message directly to its three leaders: a half-insane failed politician, a defrocked Catholic priest and a former prostitute. When the world faile d to end, the disillusioned faithful demanded a refund of property and money generously donated to the cult leadership.
176 pages | Paperback

13 Moon Diary of Natural Time
A Way to Live the Ancient Maya Calendar
by Nicole E. Zonderhuis & Sylvia Carrilho
The Mayan Tzolkin Calendar of 260 days marks each day with its own special energy. With this 13-Moon Diary you can see at a glance what day it is, both according to the 'ordinary' 12-month Gregorian calendar as well as in the 13-Moon Calendar. You can find out its meaning and plan your activities accordingly. Or you can check the date afterwards to see if it made sense. You can also learn to calculate your own personal 'Mayan horoscope', and those of your friends.
272 pages | Full Color | Hardcover